Mind Over Matter

Merry Christmas '93
Dad
From
Hugh, Elizabeth,
Louise, Eleanor
& John

Other Books by Ranulph Fiennes

A Talent For Trouble
Ice Fall in Norway
The Headless Valley
Where Soldiers Fear to Tread
Hell on Ice
To the Ends of the Earth
Bothie, the Polar Dog (with Virginia Fiennes)
Living Dangerously (autobiography)
The Feathermen
Atlantis of the Sands

RANULPH FIENNES

Mind Over Matter

*The Epic Crossing
of the Antarctic Continent*

SINCLAIR-STEVENSON

I dedicate this journey and this book
to the bravery of each and every person
with Multiple Sclerosis. May you triumph
through your own journeys and make
the *best* of them however long or painful
they may be. One day, perhaps sooner than
later, a cure *will* be found and then
all your courage will be worthwhile.

First published in Great Britain in 1993
by Sinclair-Stevenson
an imprint of Reed Consumer Books Ltd
Michelin House, 81 Fulham Road, London SW3 6RB
and Auckland, Melbourne, Singapore and Toronto

Reprinted 1993 (eight times)

A CIP catalogue record for this book
is available at the British Library
ISBN 1 85619 375 6

Typeset by CentraCet, Cambridge
Printed and bound in Great Britain
by Clays Ltd, St Ives plc

Contents

Acknowledgements

TEXT PERMISSIONS

The author and publisher thank Bantam Press, a division of Transworld Publishers Ltd, London and Peters, Fraser and Dunlop Ltd, London for extracts from *Crossing Antarctica* by Will Steger and Jon Bowermaster; Stein and Day, USA for extracts from *Mawson's Will* by Lennard Bickel; Jonathan Cape, London for extracts from *The White Desert* by John Giaever and from *In the Footsteps of Scott* by Roger Mear and Robert Swan; Element Books, Dorset for extracts from *Zen and the Art of Climbing Mountains* by Neville Shulman; The *Spectator*, London for extracts from an article by James Buchan; Weidenfeld and Nicolson, London for extracts from *Scott of the Antarctic* by Elspeth Huxley; the Crowood Press, Wiltshire for extracts from *Antarctica: Both Heaven and Hell* by Reinhold Messner; Macmillan Publishing, New York and Cassell, London for extracts from *The Crossing of Antartica* by Edmund Hillary and Sir Vivian Fuchs; Robert Hale, London for extracts from *Amundsen* by Bellamy Partridge; Penguin Books, London for extracts from *The Worst Journey in the World* by Apsley Cherry-Garrard; AP Watt Ltd, London for extracts from *The Last Place on Earth* and *Shackleton* by Roland Huntford; Times Books, New York for extracts from *The Great Antarctic Rescue* by F.A. Worsley and Heinemann, Australia for an extract from *Antarctic Odyssey* by Phillip Law.

PHOTO CREDITS

HFS (Howell, Fiennes, Stroud): 6, 8, 9(backdrop), 9a, 9b, 10, 11, 12, 13, 14, 15, 16, 18, 19, 20, 21c, 21d, 22, 23, 24, 25, 26, 27; Sir Ranulph Fiennes: 2a, 2b, 3, 5, 7b, 9c, 21b; Royal Geographical Society Archives: 7a, 7c, 7d; British Antarctic Survey: 17 (A. Moyes), 28a, 29c (C.J. Gilbert), 29e (J. Coleman), 28b (T. Heilbronn), 28d (E. Jarvis), 28e (I. Collinge), 28g (I. Boyd), 28h (M. Sanders), 28i (D. Williams); Universal Picture Press and Agency Limited: 1, 4; Rex Features: 31; *The Times*: 32; Laurence Howell: 2b; Army Personnel Research Establishment: 30a, 30c; Mike Stroud: 21a, 30b; ECO Productions: 28c, 29a, 29f; Morag Howell: 29b; Françoise Lachon: 28f, 29d, 29g; Spectrum Communications: 29h

List of Maps and Diagrams

I first became involved with Ran Fiennes in 1976 when, as Patron, I took the helm of his ship "M.V. Benjamin Bowring" from Greenwich at the start of the epic Transglobe Expedition, flew the expedition's ski-plane and spoke to his team by radio at both Poles during that unique three year circumpolar journey.

That expedition became the first ever to reach both Poles, to cross the Arctic Ocean, Antarctica and the North West Passage. In the 1980's Ran switched to unsupported travel in the Arctic Ocean and, in 1992, in Antarctica. This book describes the appalling ordeals that he and Doctor Michael Stroud suffered on that last journey. That they were successful bears witness to their physical fitness and to an astonishing mental toughness. Mind over Matter is a thoroughly suitable title.

In 1989 I suggested that Ran raise funds for the Multiple Sclerosis Society through the Expeditions and the results, due to the generosity of the public, have enabled Europe's first M.S. Research Centre to be founded in Cambridge.

This story of the first unsupported crossing of the Antarctic Continent makes fascinating reading. It is a tribute to the vision and endurance of the human spirit, and to the sheer, straightforward courage of two remarkable men.

Charles

Chapter One

'Whatever you can do, or dream you can
. . . begin it.'

Goethe

In the spring of 1990 we struggled over the sea ice some 400 miles north of the Siberian coast.

If our Russian advisers proved correct and the fickle Arctic winds held true to form, a northerly drift would force the pack ice towards the Pole and help us to reach the top of the world before we starved.

The previous week a chunk of frozen flesh had come away from one of my toes, but Mike Stroud, my companion, was a doctor and I trusted his judgement.

'If the wound is not subjected to further trauma and our antibiotics last,' he assured me, 'gangrene will not be a worry.'

In three or four weeks we might make history. To reach the North Pole on foot and unaided by air contact or other assistance had long been the dream of polar specialists from many countries. A climber's equivalent might be the first ascent of Everest without sherpas or oxygen. Amongst polar experts only two journeys ranked as more challenging: the unaided crossings of Antarctica and of the Arctic Ocean.

On the other side of the world a group of three Norwegian ski champions had openly declared their intention to reach the Pole first, and two separate teams of Soviet skiers were somewhere behind us, having set out, like us, from Novaya Zemlya in Siberia. Our radio base, a Soviet Army shack on the

1

island of Sredny, was manned by Lawrence (Flo) and Morag (Mo) Howell with their Russian friend Sergei Malyshev. Only the day before, Mo had managed to make voice contact via our high frequency set and gave us news of our competitors.

'Kagge and his Norwegians are out of the race. One of them has been airlifted to safety with a frostbitten foot. The other two are carrying on but their challenge is compromised.'

By the unwritten but internationally accepted rules of *unsupported* polar travel, *any* air contact en route disqualifies the whole group.

Now we had only the Russians to worry about. There had been a Canadian attempt under Jack McConnell, an old friend of mine, but his team had also withdrawn with frostbite.

'Chukov's men are doing well,' Mo told me through the electronic ripples of auroral interference. 'We estimate they are less than one hundred miles to the south of you.'

'What about Fyodor Konyukhov?' I asked her.

'He is also compromised,' Mo replied. 'A Soviet helicopter picked him up. He was in trouble with breaking ice in a bear-infested zone. They dropped him off further north.' Her voice faded into the electronic clutter.

I knew that Vladimir Chukov was ranked high in the lists of Soviet polar explorers. He had led two unsupported journeys to the Pole in previous years. Both times he had reached the Pole but death and injury of team members had on each occasion necessitated air contact to remove the bodies. Chukov had played by the rules and was now doggedly trying again. He had learned many lessons. He knew the hazardous nature of the drifting Soviet pack ice, far looser and more volatile than the corresponding sea ice on the Canadian side of the Pole. Here, a single error could quickly lead to death, as he had found to his cost. I knew his team's progress would be slow and methodical.

After about 400 miles Mike and I had abandoned our carbon-fibre sledge-boats and continued with basic food, fuel and camp gear carried in Géant rucksacks. Because we were weak and the packs weighed nigh on one hundred pounds each, it was all but impossible to stand up unaided after struggling into the rucksack harnesses.

On half-rations and debilitated, our chances of making the last 2°, 120 miles, to the Pole rested on luck and avoidance of hypothermia.

We packed the tent into a sausage shape and strapped it to my rucksack. Every action was ponderous. Our fingers were blistered; raw in places beneath the plasters. My vision was impaired. For some reason, too much glare perhaps, I seemed to be going slowly blind. I could still make out enough shape and colour to navigate through the chaos of broken ice. Sometimes I skied, sometimes I strapped my skis to the pack and walked. This was less painful for my ulcerated heel but harder work in deep snow.

Mike had no option but to walk. Only seven days from the start one of his steel bindings had broken irreparably. This slowed us down to the speed of a walking expedition, which in turn yielded less mileage output per ration consumed. The fact that Mike had continued this far without skis was a tribute to his remarkable tenacity.

His eyes were deep-sunk, his eyelids hugely puffed out and discoloured. A few days previously, he had come dangerously close to hypothermia. I had erected the tent and, after hot tea, he had recovered. But the signs were ominous.

Mist banks rolled over the wasteland of ice, brown and menacing like the smoke of distant forest fires. They resulted from massive ice-fracturing the previous night. The last thing we wanted, now that we had abandoned the sledge-boats, was open water.

Within the hour narrow cracks began to criss-cross our route. The noise of booming pressure punctured by a staccato crackle, as of automatic rifle fire, sounded to the north, rendered dull and sinister by the blanketing fog.

The sun briefly broke clear, giving perspective to our immediate ice-scape of broken floes and tilted blocks. On a drifted hummock I spotted the spaced prints of an adult bear. The spoor was but recently etched in the snow and I felt that inchoate dread, the prickling of the skin at the nape of the neck, which comes with the fear of imminent danger and personal vulnerability.

I knew I must warn Mike, for polar bears will usually attack the rear member of any group and Mike was defenceless. Only a few days previously we had buried our radio and our revolver as being too heavy to carry in the rucksacks. Some eight years before, a friend and I had been attacked by a bear in the pack ice but on that occasion we were armed with a forty-four magnum pistol. Now I bitterly regretted my decision to abandon our revolver. By doing so I had put us both at risk.

I prayed that we would escape detection by the many bears that roamed the area, and tried to banish from my mind the vivid images of photographs shown to us a month previously by the five inmates of a Siberian radar post near Sredny. A sixth member of this tiny community had gone outside to check the generator and was partly eaten by a bear between the two huts. Three camp huskies frightened the bear away but the Russian soon died, eviscerated by the inch-long claws and carnivore teeth of his attacker.

That week, on the other side of the world, our Norwegian competitors were attacked by a large, male bear which they shot close by their tent.

I tried to bury negative thoughts but the total concentration necessary for successful navigation in broken pack ice was absent that morning.

After an hour of progress over wind-scoured, multi-year floes, we climbed a twenty-foot-high wall of tumbled blocks and immediately found ourselves in an unstable area of newly fractured, young ice.

4

Huge blocks slowly up-ended under million-ton pressure from surrounding floes, and slithered, squealing and grinding on top of one another. I zig-zagged wildly, unable to hold to true North, in a vain attempt to skirt the many pools and canals of newly-open, steaming, black water.

Bubbling mush zones of porridge-like *shuga* increasingly blocked our passage. Frustrated by successive false trails, I decided to jump across an open canal. Mike was some 400 yards behind, following the labyrinthine course of my sledge tracks. The temperature was −37°C and a ten-knot breeze cut knife-like through our cotton clothing whenever we halted to reconnoitre. To survive we had to keep moving. Rest-stops were out of the question.

The canal looked about five feet wide at the point where its banks came closest together but nothing was quite as it seemed. The whole world of sea and ice was in motion. The far, northern bank was coasting to the east at about one knot per hour. Or *perhaps* my own, southern, bank was moving west. There was no way of telling which was reality.

Either way, the canal was slowly opening, its banks shifting apart, for this particular zone was not under pressure from surrounding floes.

I knew I must not hesitate. If these narrows widened by the time Mike arrived, he could try to find another crossing point.

I positioned my skis parallel to the canal and as close to the edge of the bank as possible. I tried to loosen the waist straps of my rucksack but my fingers were too cold to locate the toggle. Crouching to gain maximum spring, I counted to three, then jumped. The ice block under my skis slipped sideways at the crucial moment, my balance was thrown and I plunged sideways into the canal.

Fettered by my skis and rolled face-down by my heavy but marginally buoyant rucksack, I struggled in panic, numbed by the water's temperature.

5

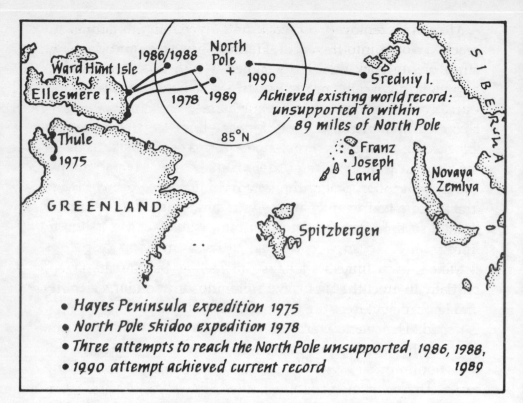

Northern polar journeys by the author, Burton, Shepard, Newman
and, since 1986, Stroud

I managed to force one mitt from the leather wrist-strap of the ski-stick. Then the other. With my hands free, I scrabbled at the four-foot vertical wall of the canal. It was smooth and afforded only a meagre grip. I screamed for Mike and swallowed sea water.

I did not feel cold but was totally aware that I could not escape. My grip began to weaken and the forces of gravity were second by second more difficult to resist.

I felt a sudden blessed lessening of the deadweight forcing me under. Mike had arrived.

'Quickly,' was all I could think to shout. Already my teeth were chattering and my mouth too numb for clear speech.

Mike had removed his pack and, lying on his stomach, reached down into the canal. He managed to grasp a lashing strap of my rucksack. He weighed a fifth less than I and, although physically more powerful, he was weakened by hunger. With no means of leverage and with fingers already lacerated from broken blisters, he hauled me to safety through sheer force of willpower.

Once I was clear of the water, the wind chill factor, many times colder than a deep freeze, drained my body heat away and Mike raced to unlash the tent. My hands were useless, unable to light a match let alone thread poles into the tent lining.

Mike's own fingers had lost all feeling but he managed partially to erect the tent. Within minutes my sodden clothing and boots began to freeze. I squatted inside the tent, muttering furious inanities and tearing at my clothes.

Somehow Mike managed to light the cooker and things began to improve. One by one, and between intervals to re-warm fingers, I squeezed my clothes dry. It would have been best to spend the rest of the day and subsequent 'night' drying out, since we carried no spare clothes. However, our fuel allowance was sufficient only for cooking purposes, not to heat the tent nor to dry clothes: an unsupported polar journey must make do without luxuries. So there was no choice but to carry on and hope that, by the end of the day, my clothes would have dried on my back.

From that day our performance deteriorated. I became all but totally blind and Mike's resistance to the cold faded until he was dangerously hypoglycaemic.

With three days of food rations left between us, no weapon and no radio, I made the decision to give up. By activating our search beacon we alerted Flo and Mo in Siberia and they managed to persuade the Soviets to search for us from a floating ice camp 300 miles from our tent.

7

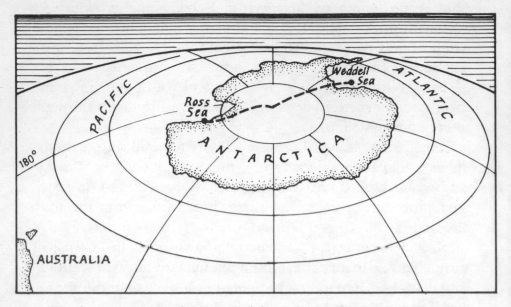

The first unsupported crossing of the Antarctic Continent (1992–93)

When the ex-Afghan gun-ship helicopter located and removed us we were but eighty-nine short miles from our goal. Our journey has remained the world record to this day. But, I had had enough. I vowed I would never again subject my mind or my body to such stresses. Future expeditions would be confined to hot deserts or tropical rain forests. Above all I would eradicate the word *unsupported* from my dictionary of future travels.

Two years later, in the winter of 1992, Mike, Mo and I found ourselves at the opposite end of the world facing a challenge, which I secretly believed to be impossible, but from which I could not turn back.

There was every likelihood that the venture, to cross the Antarctic continent unsupported, would involve far more abuse to our bodies than even the Soviet Arctic journey of

8

1990. Approaching my fiftieth year, I was on the look-out for a less uncomfortable way of earning a living but, unfortunately, I was part of an international rat race which was fast reaching its culmination.

Part of me argued that I must turn my back on further polar travels before my luck ran out. The other self postulated that there remained a finale, the natural conclusion to all the previous work. A fierce competitive urge at length overcame the voice of common sense.

Left to myself, I would never have attempted the journey but, a month after our return from Siberia, I had received a phone call from Charlie Burton. Charlie and I, on Easter Day 1982, had become the first people to reach both Poles by surface travel. In 1980, together with Oliver Shepard, we had completed the longest-yet crossing of Antarctica and Charlie was now suggesting we try a second crossing.

'This time,' he said, 'on foot and without support.'

'Impossible,' was my immediate response.

'Shut your mouth or I'll smash your teeth.' This was Charlie's standard response. 'Come to the Royal Geographical Society tomorrow. Ollie and I will be in the Map Room with all the relevant data. Of course it's possible.' He rang off.

I was working in London at the time as the European representative of Dr Armand Hammer, the ninety-year-old boss of Occidental Petroleum. I slipped out of the office and walked through Hyde Park to Kensington Gore and the Royal Geographical Society's headquarters.

Whether it was Oliver or Charlie who had first come up with the idea was unclear. Either way, they were both sold on the venture despite indisputable evidence that neither man, nor machine, nor pack animal (huskies included) could carry sufficient food and fuel to cross Antarctica from coast to coast.

'No machine devised by man,' I poked Charlie in the stomach by way of emphasis, 'is fuel-efficient enough to make

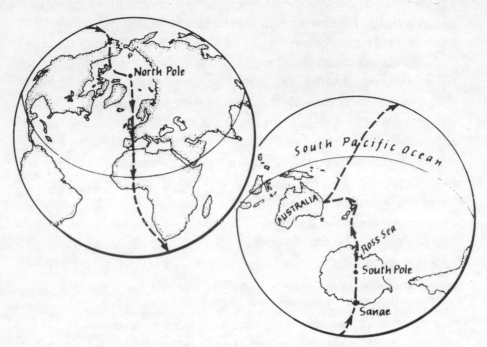

The first polar circumnavigation of earth (1979–82)

such a distance without resupply. The Americans and the Soviets have both tried and failed. As for huskies,' I added, 'Steger's 1990 journey is clear evidence that dogs would be hard pushed to make even 1,000 miles unassisted.'

'We are not talking about dogs,' Ollie interjected.

'I know,' I agreed, 'but, since neither dogs nor machines can make it, humans on foot are out of the question. Amundsen *proved* that dogs outperform people trying to manhaul. If you read Roland Huntford's book on Scott and Amundsen, it is quite clear that Scott's greatest error was in trying to manhaul.'

'Balls,' Charlie shouted. 'Scott was absolutely right in reckoning manpower to be *the* efficient method. Our journey will prove it.'

I looked anxiously about the Map Room. Charlie's raucous

tones must be audible throughout the Royal Geographical Society.

'All right. I'll check your plan over with the experts but, in the unlikely event that it does look possible, what is the form?'

Oliver had everything worked out. 'There are two options. We could start at MacMurdo, since we know that ships and planes go there annually. Ideally, our route would then go straight across the Pole to the British base of Rothera on the far coast. If this proves impossible because the Brits refuse to fly us out, then we go for a return journey from MacMurdo to the Pole.'

'*Very* second best, that,' Charlie thundered.

'For God's sake keep your voice down, Charlie,' I cursed him. 'We will be thrown out.'

'If *we* don't do the journey,' Ollie commented as we packed up the maps, 'somebody else will.'

He knew my Achilles heel.

For centuries sailors had headed south, but the first three claims to have sighted the Antarctic mainland all came within a few days of each other, as recently as February 1819. For a further ninety years humans nibbled nervously at the unknown enormity of the frozen continent. Then, within a month of each other, both Scott and Amundsen reached the South Pole. That race ended with triumph for the Norwegians and death and disaster for the British.

Likewise, at the North Pole, Peary and Cook had made their claims of priority almost simultaneously.

Now, in the early 1990s, history was repeating itself. A rash of polar travellers from different lands were making ready to grab the last of the polar grails.

Exactly the same desire to *be first* holds true with sailors and mountaineers but, in their case, the race is diluted by the very fact that there are still a great number of ocean crossings and unscaled rock faces yet to be 'bagged'. Communist China has only recently made available to Western climbers whole new ranges of virgin mountains.

For polar travellers there are but two Poles, and these were both reached by traditional, supported travel some eighty years ago. All that now remains for the polar fraternity is purist unsupported travel. To cross the Arctic Ocean in this manner would be a very hit and miss affair, since the pack ice conditions vary enormously from year to year. It is natural, therefore, that the eyes of all the international polar groups were, by the early 1990s, focused on an unsupported Antarctic crossing.

I knew most of our likely competitors. In Russia the chief protagonists were Dr Dmitri Shparo (who had organised our own 1990 Anglo-Soviet North Pole attempt) and Colonel Vladimir Chukov, who had narrowly failed in his third unsupported North Pole attempt in 1990.

The Canadian leader was Richard Webber; the Norwegian contenders were Ragnar Thorsketh and Erling Kagge. The main Japanese polar personality, Naomi Uemura, was killed in 1979 (almost certainly in a crevasse) and had no obvious successor. The American polar supremo, who specialised in dog travel, was undoubtedly Will Steger, and the French were headed by Jean-Louis Étienne. The most successful British polar travellers were Sir Vivian Fuchs and Wally Herbert.

National pride in achieving first place has grown, not diminished, since the days of Scott and Peary. The media now quickly broadcast results to worldwide audiences of millions.

What, ask the cynics, is the point of walking to a Pole, scaling any mountain's north face, being first among peers in a sport – be it football, snooker or athletics? There are many answers, but the truest is surely Wally Herbert's: 'And of what value was this journey? It is as well for those who ask such a question that there are others who feel the answer and never need to ask.'

*

12

I pondered Ollie and Charlie's proposal. They had asked me to lead the venture and to ask Ginnie, my wife, to be our base leader and radio operator. Since our circumpolar journey in the 1980s, Ginnie had become a self-taught cattle farmer and found it increasingly difficult to leave our Exmoor home for long periods. Her Aberdeen Angus cows were expected to calve in the English winter: the only period when Antarctica reasonably can be travelled. I knew she would not agree to the proposal, on top of which I hated the thought of leaving her for yet another lonely winter on the moors.

On the other hand, I could not push from my mind the current rumours that rippled through the polar grapevine that a Norwegian team under Erling Kagge had set their sights on crossing the Antarctic continent unassisted. Back in 1990 it had been Kagge who claimed the first unsupported success to the North Pole, choosing to ignore the fact that one of his team had been airlifted out en route. Any form of air contact is, within the rules of unsupported polar travel, the precise parallel of drug abuse by an Olympic competitor.

In 1990 I was quoted in the press as saying that the Norwegians had compromised their attempt (as indeed had Chukov's Russians) by receiving air contact. The Russians admitted this but the Norwegians merely reiterated their own claim and castigated me as a bad sportsman.

The Russians, the British and the Canadians refused to recognise the Norwegian claim and still accept the Fiennes–Stroud 1990 journey as the existing northerly record.

When I was asked to meet Erling Kagge in the public forum of a Royal Geographical Society joint lecture, I had to decline since the date coincided with an expedition I was leading in Arabia. I asked Mike to represent our expedition and later heard from Mo, who attended the lecture, that, when Mike said what he thought of the Norwegian claim, he was openly jeered by members of the Anglo-Norwegian Society.

I had not been able to forget all this. Neither had the

Russians who had greater reason than I for disgust at Kagge's claim. If it *is* acceptable to receive air contact, then Chukov, not Kagge, was first to the Pole unsupported. If air contact is unacceptable then the North Pole has never yet been reached without support. Either way, Kagge's claim was nonsense.

This then was the background to my conflicting reactions to the Antarctic proposal. By the spring of 1991 I had read a great deal about Antarctic expeditions and studied the limitations of various forms of unsupported travel. Dogs were clearly out of the question since an Antarctic crossing would involve over 1,500 miles. The longest unsupported dog journey in history was that of Lindsay, Croft and Godfrey in 1934. They had managed 1,080 miles on the Greenland Icecap. The dog expert Will Steger stated, 'Even Scott and Amundsen set out caches of food and fuel; no one could attempt a return journey to the South Pole without them.'

As far as manhauling went, the situation was similar. Only one team had ever made it as far as the South Pole, the three-man, Anglo-Canadian group led in the field by Roger Mear. They had been airlifted from the Pole after a remarkable seventy-day journey with the heaviest sledges ever hauled, some fifty pounds per load. They were a tough and experienced group, yet they had only managed *half* the challenge that Oliver and Charlie were now considering.

I wrote to the best expedition logistics man that I knew, one Vaughn Purvis whose own manhaul journeys included Spitzbergen and the Arctic pack. He sent me back a carefully calculated summary which concluded that the Antarctic could not be crossed with start-out sledge-loads of less than 400 pounds. We both knew that such weights were not practical; not worth considering.

The least negative response I could think of to all this was Samuel Johnson's doggerel: 'Nothing will ever be attempted if all possible objections must first be overcome.'

*

14

I telephoned Charlie and told him that we might as well get to work and attempt to have everything ready to start in the winter of 1992.

A quick call to Annie Kershaw, boss of Adventure Network, was my first action. She controls the *only* air transport company flying commercially to Antarctica. She quoted me an overall cost of £150,000 to take three people, and the minimal cargo we would need, from Chile to a start-point on the Atlantic coast of Antarctica, somewhere south of Cape Horn.

She made two points of immediate importance. She would charge extra if we insisted on starting out from MacMurdo (on the 'wrong' side of the continent for her Antarctic base of Patriot Hills). Secondly, we must pay £16,000 upfront so that she could pre-position enough drums of aviation fuel to fly us to our coastal start-point.

Initially I favoured Oliver's option of a return journey from MacMurdo to the Pole. Such a route would enable us to position food caches along our *outward* trail, thus reducing the number of days we must haul super-heavy loads. Annie's cost estimates forced me to change my mind and consider a crossing from the South American side of the continent to the Australian (MacMurdo) side.

I stepped up my sponsor-finding visits. Chris Brasher, who had once paced Roger Bannister and Chris Chataway to beat the four-minute mile barrier, was the Chairman of Reebok in Britain. He agreed to pay £16,000 to pre-position our fuel, and to ask his US headquarters for the balance of £134,000.

The Prince of Wales, who had supported my polar journeys for fifteen years, agreed to be Patron and expressed his desire that we should use the journey to raise funds for a Multiple Sclerosis Research Centre in Cambridge. In 1990, on our Siberian journey, we had raised £2,300,000 and the Centre was already in operation. A further major sum would ensure its continued success.

Promises came in from my old Arctic sponsors to provide

15

specially designed sledges, rations, clothing and insurance. All was progressing smoothly when, early in May 1991, Vaughn Purvis, who maintained a sound 'intelligence network' in Scandinavia, warned me that Erling Kagge had announced to the media his intention to cross the Antarctic continent in 1992.

Kagge was, I knew, an exceptionally fine cross-country skier, and speed, with endurance, were the keys to success in Antarctica. Neither Ollie nor Charlie, though totally dependable, was keen on 'pushing themselves to the limits'. I decided to highlight the issue of fitness sooner rather than later.

In mid-May 1991 I went to the London Wine Trade Fair at Olympia where Oliver had organised a sales stand for his employers. By chance, Charlie Burton was in charge of security.

Once I had explained my worries to them both, I suggested that I ask Mike Stroud to join our team.

'He is like a bull terrier,' I told them, 'small in stature but incredibly powerful.'

'That's great,' Charlie remonstrated, 'but where does that leave us oldies? Surely a team moves at the pace of its slowest member?'

It was agreed that some thought would be given to the idea and, not long afterwards, Ollie called me to say they had both decided to change their role in the project.

'We would want to *enjoy* the experience,' Charlie told me later, 'and I know that, once *you* get competitive, any signs of enjoyment are tantamount to mutiny and a clear sign that we should be travelling faster.'

So they took on the role of organisers from London and I approached Mike Stroud by telephone.

The only position that I can tolerate on an expedition is that of team leader. Ollie, Charlie and Mike were totally aware of my peculiarity in this respect, but all three were strong personalities and not 'yes-men'. My policy with everyone on any journey is to follow the democratic route (*when* there is time), of talking about options rather than pronouncing dictatorial and unilateral decisions. If others, whether or not they form a majority, favour an opinion which I believe to be stupid, dangerous, or unlikely to help attain the goal of the expedition, then I overrule them no matter how disaffected this may make them feel. In fact, because most fellow-polar travellers know how to progress over snow and ice, we normally all agree on the best way forward, so contretemps are quite rare.

I knew very little in depth about Mike. This may seem strange since he had, by 1990, already come on four of my Arctic expeditions and we had been through a great deal together. To take *friends* on stressful expeditions has always seemed to me to be foolish, since I can think of no easier way of marring a friendship for ever. An expedition's aim is best achieved by individuals who can look after themselves, need little or no directing or nursing, and are tough in body and mind. I look for professional and dogged people and treat any friendship resulting from an expedition as an unexpected bonus.

Polar expeditions are well known for causing stress and enmity between participants, and quite why Ollie, Mike and I had never come to blows, literally or even verbally, during our Arctic journeys, remains a mystery to me.

'I know you like to lead from the front,' Mike said to me before finally agreeing to joining the Antarctic project, 'but I can't see myself following your trail non-stop for a hundred days. In the Arctic it was different. There were plenty of interesting obstacles but, down south, I think I would go round the twist unless I can navigate from time to time.'

'No problem,' I told him and, a month later, he confirmed that he would join the team. His Dutch-born wife, Thea, had proved sympathetic and his employers, the Army Personnel Research Establishment in Farnborough, agreed on the understanding that he would conduct an extensive physiological research programme throughout the journey. This was bad news since I hate the sight of blood, especially my own, but it seemed a reasonable penalty in order to secure Mike's participation.

Chris Brasher of Reebok called with the unwelcome news that the American and European headquarters of his company were not prepared to share the sponsorship. He gave me the name of the man whose company, the Pentland Group, had sold Reebok to the Americans. Although Pentland were originally a Scottish company, their main office was in Finchley, north London. The Chairman – also the founder's son – Stephen Rubin, agreed to see me for a breakfast meeting at his Finchley home.

A month or two later he agreed that Pentland should become the overall sponsor. 'I do not think we will gain a great deal of publicity from the association,' he did not mince words, 'but my belief is that *all* companies should give at least one per cent of their annual profits to the local community. We have a number of multiple sclerosis sufferers in Finchley and your expedition will benefit them greatly, even if you only get half way.'

This was true. Our sponsoring of multiple sclerosis was partly based on members of the public pledging a penny for every mile we covered. Since Antarctica is over fifty times the size of Great Britain, a lot of pennies were involved.

Because the Antarctic plateau is so high, and so cold, the period when humans can travel there is severely limited. It is both hazardous and uneconomical to keep ships and aeroplanes all the year round on a continent where they can only be safely used from November until March, so the few countries that do operate either form of transport are careful to remove them to warmer climes outside the short southern summer.

Since Pentland's sponsorship covered only the cost of

18

Adventure Network's delivering us to the Atlantic coast and dropping us there, I had to make other plans for escaping from the Pacific coast before the onset of winter.

Three cruise ships take tourists to MacMurdo base in mid-summer each year and one of these was due to depart from Antarctica at 6.30 a.m., and not a minute later than, on 16 February 1993. If we could reach the coast by then the ship's operators, Seaquest, kindly agreed to remove us at no cost and take us to Australia (providing we took passports).

The prospect of walking 1,700 miles between 1 November 1992, the very earliest date Adventure Network could drop us off, and the Seaquest date of 16 February concentrated our minds on pulling at least sixteen miles a day for 108 days with loads likely to exceed 350 pounds each. I knew this was a performance well in excess of any manhauling achievement in history. There was every likelihood that it was not technically feasible.

I put this to Mike who agreed that the figures looked forbidding. Every previous expedition that could do so, including Scott's, Shackleton's and Amundsen's, had used wind-power when possible by taking various designs of sail. Mike was keen that we should do likewise. I was initially against wind assistance but agreed at least to take sails with us and try them out on arrival.

For the sake of being purist over what is or is not *support* one could end up in animal furs with no 'modern' inventions such as skis, ropes, or watches. In the end I agreed to *natural* assistance from wind, or gravity, but nothing else. The problem with windsails turned out to be lack of winds heading in the correct direction and the unwelcome presence of the twelve-pound sails to be lugged for hundreds of windless miles.

As the weeks to departure passed by, my worries about the sledge-loads increased. Certain weight totals were not available until the last month and these included the rations being specially put together by Brian Welsby, who had provided us with Arctic rations for some fifteen years. Mike and he had decided to alter the ration content for Antarctica and even the smallest change had a big effect on weights.

By early October it was becoming apparent that the weight of the new rations would entail sledge-loads of over 400 pounds each. We were entering the realms of the theoretically impossible but it was too late to back out.

More worrying to me than the sheer weight of our sledges was the results of my personal training. In the past I had kept fit by jogging on the moors after work and, on every seventh day, spending an hour on a Nordic Track ski machine in order to put some strength into my naturally weak arms. Mike supplemented his jogging by bicycling to work and we both consumed a great deal of rice and pasta in order to put on weight and increase our glycogen storage levels.

Since the Siberian journey two years before I had found myself less and less motivated to train and increasingly prone to muscle damage. I *was* still training as hard as ever, but the going was tougher. Sprains took longer to disappear and past problems kept resurfacing. Two months before we were due in Antarctica my back went into spasm and jogging was then out of the question.

Dr Bernard Watkin of Wimpole Street is an expert at easing back pains by deep injections of a dextrose/glycerine/phenol solution into the ligaments of the lower back on either side of the spine. After two sessions I felt rejuvenated, but then an attack of haemorrhoids sent me scuttling to Dr Notares, who injects the relevant parts with some form of long-lasting anaesthetic. I had first suffered from this affliction not in polar regions but on SAS training in Brunei. Then one of my ankles became swollen and awkward to run on. I knew no good ankle-doctors so I applied Deep Heat in lavish amounts and hoped for the best.

Not long before departure I reported to the Army Research

20

Establishment where the friendly scientists of Mike's department subjected us both to rigorous tests of strength, endurance, resilience to low temperatures and numerous other performance levels.

Two years earlier Mike had announced that my physical fitness, measured aerobically, was far above that of most twenty-year-olds and highly unusual in a forty-seven-year-old. This time, however, my ratings had dropped considerably. Since I was training just as hard as before, I could not explain my physical deterioration but realised it did not bode well for the coming venture.

Ten days before leaving England we met in the underground London garage where I stored all my old expedition gear, some of it twenty years old. I divided all the new items sent by the sponsors and gave half to Mike. This was our first chance to load the sledges with most of the equipment we would be taking. Miraculously, and by dint of a good deal of force, the loads fitted into or onto the sledges. We tried to pick up a loaded sledge between us but it was impossible. We packed everything into custom-made boxes and a KLM van took the entire cargo to Heathrow Airport.

The testing and packing of all items had taken us just one day. On previous journeys this task had taken weeks, sometimes months, to complete but Mike and I both led busy lives and seldom met up outside the confines of polar journeys.

Pentland held a press conference to announce our departure. This took place at a Thames-side office block, where a couple of rock climbers from a sponsor company attached ropes one hundred feet up the side of the skyscraper. We practised crevasse escape techniques and I felt giddy with fear as strong winds caused the ropes to pendulum eight storeys up.

Mike, an able rock-climber, was in his element and gently teased me as I refused to look down at the photographers below.

21

Later that week he was given a surprise farewell party by his colleagues at the Research Establishment. This included the full 'cake with icing and speeches' treatment and made Mike suddenly aware of exactly what he was about to attempt. As he later told me, he secretly felt 'embarrassed and a bit of a fraud'. The knowledge that our sledge-loads were grossly over the top and that we were unlikely to be able to shift them at all, let alone for 1,700 miles, did nothing to ease his inner thoughts as he responded to the applause and raised glasses of his fellow scientists.

On a gusty morning in late October Ginnie drove me to Heathrow. We said goodbye in the car-park for there would be many people in the terminal. I waved as she drove off and thanked God for her. I had told myself after many previous journeys that I would never again leave her at our bleak Exmoor home for a long and lonely winter. As she left I felt wretchedly guilty. It occurred to me that *I* had never spent a single night alone at our house on the moor.

Chapter Two

'Beyond 40° South is no law.
Beyond 50° South no God.'

19th-Century Whalers' saying

Why do people wish to risk their necks pursuing dangerous, uncomfortable goals? Most of us face daily obstacles but there is a great difference between having to, and wilfully choosing to.

There is an old Indian saying: 'Travellers cross many rivers and climb many mountains. Plainsmen may always live within a single valley but only those seeking the truth will ever reach the summit.' This divides the world between natural pioneers and people content with a humdrum existence. Some of the latter group scoff at the world of adventure, whilst others are happy to be vicariously entertained and to learn the *why* behind the explorer.

As Mike and Mo chatted en route to South America, I idly considered their motives. There is usually a great difference between the explanation that a person chooses to give (especially in autobiographies) and the truth. I had studied the stated motives of many of our predecessors and believed but a few.

Amundsen: (South Pole, 1910)
> Oddly enough it was the sufferings of Sir John Franklin and his men which attracted me most. A strange urge made me wish that I too would one day go through the same thing.

Perhaps it was the idealism of youth, which often takes the form of martyrdom, that got me to see myself as a kind of crusader in Arctic exploration . . . If I were to maintain my reputation as an explorer, I *had* to win a sensational victory one way or another . . . I could not understand why anyone should want to go to a place where somebody else had been . . . or go there for the sake of doing it a different way.

Scott: (South Pole, 1910)

Until now Scott has shown no interest in snow and ice. He himself said he had no predilection for polar exploration. But, as he wrote at the time, he had neither rest nor peace to pursue anything but promotion . . . He was haunted by the naval lieutenant's nightmare of being left on the shelf.

It was clear that Scott's quest for the Pole was an almost Arthurian wish to retrieve a sense of nobility for his race. But also, for himself, there was the desire to exercise his frustrated energies. 'I seem to hold in reserve something that makes for success and yet see no worthy field for it.'

Shackleton: (Antarctica, 1914)

To a question that has been put to me on several occasions; Why seek the Pole? . . . War in the old days made *men*. *We* have not the same stirring times to live in and must look for other outlets for our energy and for the restless spirit that fame alone can satisfy.

At home, as Shackleton knew well, he fretted under domesticity, impatient with his children and wife. It was only in parting, somehow, that his feelings seemed to flower. Yearning for what was out of reach seemed to the Irishman in him a necessary state of mind.

Edmund Hilary about Fuchs: (Antarctica, 1956)

I felt that the underlying urge, whether Fuchs would admit it or not, came more from an honest love of adventure and the pride and prestige that he felt would accrue to his country and himself if he were first to succeed in such a long and hazardous undertaking.

Swan: (South Pole, 1986)
The Pole will unshackle me from the awful fear of failure and the burden of having to win at all costs. I have to feel that life is worthwhile. If or when we pull this [the South Pole] off, I will have done something extraordinary which will give me the opportunity I long for.

I hate living in a stinking tent with other men. I hate being cold and you must be a pervert to like having ice inside your underpants. Someone said it was the cleanest and most isolated way of having a bad time ever devised . . . But it pumps up your ego . . . There is a side of me that wouldn't mind dying out there. In fact I would quite like it in a way.

Co-leader Roger Mear about Swan:
His philosophy is that the Polar journey is essential to his credibility and future . . . His obsession grew. He would let nothing and no one prevent the fulfilment of his dream. His one idea was to march to the South Pole. It seemed that he had no ambition or thought beyond it. His life appeared to end with its conquest and I began to wonder whether he was looking for an heroic death. Success was so important that he no longer contemplated failure.

Étienne: (Antarctica, 1989)
Now we are here, we have to go. We have no choice. We have spent three years with this crossing in our heads and now, sometimes, I feel like I am in prison. A prison of our idea.

Steger: (Antarctica, 1989)
We hope to show that six men from different cultures with little in common other than a passion for cold places can work together towards a common goal and succeed. We know there will be struggles and disagreements . . . but if we can work out a system for travelling, a method for living

25

under some of the cruellest conditions on the planet, our
success might serve as an example for nations and
humankind alike . . . What separates me from most men is
that I rarely see boundaries or limits. If I want to do
something, I do it. As a result there is no profound answer
as to why I love this kind of life or why I want to cross
Antarctica. I simply want to.

Messner: (Antarctica, 1989)

For me travelling in the wilderness is not about the outside
world, but about the world within me . . . I wanted, by my
journey, to demonstrate the wilderness of Antarctica and its
beauty, to point to the problems of its development,
exploitation and division . . . My path is life and raw
experience. I can only learn so much second-hand; nothing
surpasses my expeditions in the wilderness . . . That is one
of the reasons I forced myself again and again to take up a
new expedition, to begin a new journey . . . I knew that, if I
were one day no longer to dream, no longer able to travel, I
would be old and despairing.

I am a person who gets on well in the wilderness. I try to be
a spokesman for it, prompting millions of people to learn, to
esteem, love and defend it.

From the beginning I was against placing our adventure
under the mere cloak of environmental protection. Just as I
didn't like vindicating my doings as a mountaineer with
scientific aims, I found suspect those expeditions which
needed an ecological justification [here Messner is having a
dig at the stated motives of Swan and Steger] . . . Go to the
North Pole for the environment's sake – what a laugh! A
slogan but not sincere.

Naturally I undertook this expedition because I was curious
and was seeking adventure again. Moreover I was a person
with a hunger for recognition, with ambition and the need
for enhancement.

26

Mike Stroud had spent two years of his life, seven years earlier, hoping to walk to the South Pole with Swan and Mear, but, to his dismay, another man was selected, leaving him merely first reserve. Now, whether or not we managed to cross the whole continent, he knew that he stood a chance of at least making it to the Pole.

When asked for *my* motives I openly admitted that expedition leadership was my chosen way of making a living: my passport, for twenty-five years, has stated 'Travel Writer'. Mike found this upsetting and 'commercial'. His own rationale, on the most basic level, was more romantic. He talked of stunning landscapes and equated his adventures with a more intense version of the pleasures he found as a boy from mountaineering, hill-walking and rock-climbing.

'It sounds ridiculous on this scale,' Mike would say, 'but that simple drive is a very important reason for me. However, on top of that, the places themselves are amazing; they may be empty but they are incredibly beautiful and you feel a sort of privilege, on being on what amounts to another planet. This gives you a different and interesting perspective on your life . . .'

I am not introspective and find it awkward having to dig within myself to produce pat replies. Jean-Louis Étienne was asked why he went on polar expeditions and replied, 'Because I like it. You never ask a basketball player why he plays: it is because he enjoys it. It is like asking someone why he likes chocolate.'

Philosophers are happy seeing Antarctica as a vast emptiness that intensifies any human experience within it. A novelist put the lie to that with his remark: 'It's a place for great thoughts and ideals but hardly anyone who goes there has them any more.'

Erling Kagge (South Pole, 1993), a lawyer by profession, is straightforward enough. 'Excitement,' he maintains, 'has disappeared from our lives which are secure, *too* secure. I don't feel guilty about spending $150,000 on living out my urge for adventure.'

As for third-party motives, one of the more interesting rationales, proposed by Roland Huntford, was that of Shackleton's sponsor William Beardmore: when he began to feel that the explorer was becoming over-friendly with his wife, Beardmore sponsored Shackleton in order to get rid of him.

Of Scott's men and their motives, Elspeth Huxley once wrote: 'What persuaded these men to seek out hardships so extreme that most ordinary mortals would give all they possess to avoid them? . . . Fame and fortune . . . also love of country, lust for adventure, devotion to a cause, and more obscure forces like an urge towards martyrdom. Certainly there is a curiosity: desire to know what lies over the next hill . . . on the moon and beyond the stars. All such motives are mixed together and the analyst who tries to sort them out and label them is generally wasting his time.'

The KLM Boeing stopped at São Paulo, Montevideo, Santiago, Puerto Montt and finally Punta Arenas in southern Chile. We were met by Annie Kershaw of Adventure Network. Her truck took us through bleak countryside, littered with low buildings of singular ugliness though enlivened by coats of bright paint. Wild sea channels and coastlines were never far away; Cape Horn was but a short flight to the south. Beyond the Cape and 1,000 miles of the roughest seas on earth lies Antarctica, the reason for Adventure Network's presence in Punta.

In 1985 two Canadian mountaineers were flown to Antarctica by Annie's husband Giles, a pilot with Cathay Pacific and, in his spare time, Britain's most accomplished polar pilot. The two Canadians scaled Mount Vinson, the highest peak on the continent, and later joined with Giles to form Adventure Network (ANI). Their idea was to provide a means for other climbers and adventurers to reach Antarctica by air, previously out of the question except for millionaires or government-funded civil servants.

After facing many obstacles, physical and financial, the pioneer air company was firmly established in Punta with a seasonal base at Patriot Hills, a blue-ice airstrip not far from Mount Vinson. ANI had become the only organisation in the world providing private sector services in Antarctica.

Giles, sadly, was killed in an accident whilst flying a gyrocopter. Annie determined that his work with the company should not have been in vain. She and her fellow directors did well. In 1993, Adventure Network planned to 'deliver' four expeditions, forty-eight Mount Vinson climbers, twenty-six South Pole visitors and ten Emperor Penguin Colony enthusiasts.

Once in Patriot Hills, a fleet of two Twin Otters and a Cessna take clients to their chosen goals, but the trickiest sector is usually the 1,900-mile air journey from Punta to Patriot Hills.

The first DC6 passenger flight of the year was scheduled to depart for Antarctica two days after our arrival in Punta. My original timings, based on the need to catch the Seaquest ship out of Antarctica, *depended* on reaching Patriot Hills by 1 November and our coastal start-point the following day.

The anticipated two-day stop-over in Punta would allow us to rest after the long flight and to complete last-minute checks on the sledge-loads. For the first time *all* our gear, including communications equipment, was in the same place at the same time. One of the heaviest items, the white spirit fuel, could only be obtained in Patriot Hills where it, along with other hazardous items, had been pre-positioned by a cargo-only ANI flight.

The worst was now confirmed. The weight of our sledge-loads, including a rough estimate for fuel, was at least 400 pounds each. I dreaded the possibility that even this ridiculous total would creep upwards. To mention 400 pounds per load to anyone with the slightest knowledge of manhauling was to invite ridicule . . . so we didn't.

For twenty-two years I had made a habit of planning expeditions from a pessimistic viewpoint, especially as regards the likelihood of bad weather, breakdowns both mechanical and human, and Sod's Law in general. This time, only by applying optimism at every level could I project any possibility of success.

The Arabs have a saying: 'Plan ahead. It wasn't raining when Noah built the ark.' Too late now to build any arks. The only hope was for minimal rain.

I was not happy at the prospect of over three months of unmitigated physical toil. John Davis, of Shackleton's ship *Nimrod*, once commented, 'Of all those who have explored Antarctica, few have done so more uncomfortably or with greater hardship than the British.' This was harsh criticism indeed, but meaningful only if targeted at ventures which *could* have been achieved with a lower pain level.

I went over our mathematics again and again to see how we could cross the entire continent with less weight. Every avenue I explored turned out to be a dead end.

By the time we completed our final weight checks on Annie's scales the loads had reached 450 pounds each. Fuel increments and modifications to gear were liable to add thirty pounds more. In army phraseology we were confronting a Mission Impossible. Our inner thoughts, shared only between the three of us, led Morag to write home from Chile, 'Expect me back in a fortnight.'

In our downtown hotel, the Oviedo, we kept busy with needle, cotton and Velcro, making final adjustments to the gear, removing mosquito nets from the tent and finalising radio codes with Morag. Mike and I went for a long walk behind the town. Kara-kara birds screeched from the pine-and-cypress-clad hillsides. In Antarctica, once we were away from the vicinity of the coast, there would be no birds, no animals, not even a germ.

As always when we walked or jogged together there was an unspoken element of competition. I had never quite made up my mind whether this was a key component of whatever success we might have had as a team or whether it was a lethal chemical awaiting a chance tinder spark to ignite.

In this southern Magallanes district of Patagonia, the Chileans have wisely retained large areas of National Park. The rivers are alive with brown trout, the skies with condor and eagle, the lakes with duck, *huala*, *tagua* and waterfowl. Troops of llama-like guanacos roam the open sheep plains, whilst often-impenetrable forests protect puma, fox and skunk.

From the hill-top, braced by winds from the Pole, we gazed over snow-peaked mountains, white-capped seas and, away to the south-east, the great darkness of Tierra del Fuego.

The English word 'chilly' derives from obscure fourteenth-century origins. Chile means *cold* in an old Indian tongue but there is no proof of a language link. The true pioneers of these wild and bitter regions, further south than any land elsewhere, were the Ona, Patagonian and Yagan Indians, but now Punta Arenas is mainly a Chilean navy town (with 138 cat-houses, or brothels, to cope with visiting sailors), and the 200,000-strong population are chiefly of Spanish, Yugoslav, German and Italian ancestry. An American colony works the local oilfields and an almost extinct British presence testifies to the once-dominant activity of sheep-breeding.

Gaunt memorials and a spectacularly baroque cemetery dwell on the often tragic experiences of Spanish pioneers and of innumerable shipwrecks. Little is said of the unfortunate experiences of the early Indians.

Back from our hillside outing any extra fitness I may have gained was offset by the deterioration of my ankle. I found a local doctor who applied ultrasound massage for a few pesetas.

I agreed to pay Annie for any extra cargo, if we were over the weight I had quoted a year previously, in order to obtain an upfront estimate from ANI. Each additional pound would cost US$ 30. Additionally I must pay for the seventeen gallons of cooker fuel we would collect on arrival at Patriot Hills. This would be incredibly costly as is any item purchased in Antarctica. The key to human activity down south is aviation fuel. A forty-five-gallon drum of the stuff costs US$ 120 in Punta, US$ 6,000 by the time it reaches Patriot Hills and US$ 24,000 once it is at the Pole. To transport a single drum to the Pole, Annie's pilots have to burn up nine drums en route.

Annie was written up in the *Spectator* (20 February 1993) as 'Kershaw of the Antarctic'.

The only blonde 32-year-old in Punta, Mrs Kershaw is one of those Scots you meet in end-of-the-road places whose ability seems so out of proportion to their occupations that you get suspicious. But Adventure Network is an unusual company, the strangest I ever saw. General Javier Lopetegui, former Deputy Commander of the Chilean Air Force and associate of Pinochet, wrote in 1986 that Chile need not enforce its sovereign claim to Antarctica (which overlaps that of the UK and Argentina). It need only offer Chile as a springboard for Antarctic tourism to unleash a cascade of economic and political benefits. General Lopetegui became Chairman of ANI's Chilean subsidiary. ANI needed a forward base in Antarctica where so-called 'soft' tourists (Pole-fanciers and penguin-lovers) could be put and which could act as a staging post for the new wave of Antarctic expeditions launched by Fiennes's Transglobe Expedition in 1980–1981. That required a big, wheeled aircraft.

Captain Kershaw and the British glaciologist Charles Swithinbank found what they needed in 1986, a vast sheet of blue ice in the wind-tunnel of a range of low peaks called Patriot Hills . . . of the landing, which is now done in a DC6, there is little to be said except that for some time you are too shaken to know if you are alive or dead . . .

Giles Kershaw was killed in 1990. At the funeral on
Blaiklock Island, a priest read the Roman Catholic service
wearing full canonicals over his parka. The body was carried
up and placed on a high granite shelf. Broke, ill and half-
deranged with grief, Mrs Kershaw returned to Punta Arenas
and, though she had no experience of business, rapidly took
over the management of Adventure Network.

It would be difficult to find a more genuinely saintly person
than Annie, but her business was a harsh one and she had
learned when to give no quarter. As I argued various costings
with her and her fellow director, an ebullient Australian
named Mike McDowell, they spontaneously decided to donate
£1,000 each to our expedition charity, the Multiple Sclerosis
Society. Mike introduced us to the other expedition teams that
would fly with us to Patriot Hills.

A six-strong, all-male Japanese group shook our hands with
much head-nodding and friendly but unintelligible noises.
They would be walking to the Pole from Patriot Hills and
collecting snow and ice samples en route.

A pretty, blonde woman appeared carrying a heavy back-
pack. Sunniva Sorby from California was one of the American
Women's Expedition intending to cross the Antarctic continent
on skis. Like the Japanese, they would be supported by ANI
re-supply flights but, nonetheless, theirs was an awesome
undertaking, for women are not naturally designed to pull
heavy weights. If Sunniva and her three colleagues had been
built like Russian lady shot-putters I might have been less
impressed, but they were all uniformly slim and lightweight.
They were experienced skiers and their leader, Ann Bancroft
from Minnesota, was the first woman to have travelled 'overland' to the North Pole.

Ann was based in Resolute Bay as a member of Will Steger's
1986 husky-powered expedition when I had last met her and
was a friendly and unpretentious person with an infectious
sense of humour. One of her team, Sue Giller, spotted our

wind-sail bags and, discovering that we had no experience of sailing, kindly agreed to give us instruction then and there. The women had all used the sails during a recent Greenland journey.

Our loads were now so heavy that I was on the look-out for any items to eliminate. Sue's remarks about the sails were so positive that I scotched a rising desire to dump my bulky sail-bag before we even left Punta.

With twelve hours to go, Annie's van drove us to the airport to weigh and load our sledge gear and all the equipment for Morag's radio base. The final weight exceeded my 1992 estimate by only forty-two pounds, so the financial penalty, even at US$ 30 per pound, was within my agreement with Pentland.

Loading a sledge into the DC6 fuselage I managed to disturb a muscle in one shoulder which gave me back pains. 'This is unbelievable.' I found myself talking aloud in the empty aeroplane. 'I'm cracking up before we even set out.'

Mike and I made expensive calls back home to tell our wives we would, on the morrow, be out of reach of further telephones until the journey's end.

When the next day came we were in for a shock.

It was 1 November, the date we *should* have started manhauling from the edge of Antarctica. We were already two critical days behind schedule and greatly relieved to be going. A chartered town-bus drove us all to the airport and, after farewells to Annie and the staff, we strapped ourselves into our DC6 seats well-armed with paperbacks and snacks.

After a considerable pause on the tarmac an engineer appeared to announce a fuel leak in one engine necessitating a replacement fuel valve. None being available in Punta, ANI must order one from Miami or Laredo, Texas, and since it was now Sunday morning the item could not be ordered for another twenty-four hours.

A great deal of moaning and gnashing of teeth was audible from the DC6-load of mixed manhaulers (person-haulers),

34

Pole visitors and penguin photographers. All of us knew that, the previous year, bad weather had held up some ANI flights to Patriot Hills by over two weeks. A delay of that sort would certainly kill any chances we might still have.

Back in Punta we learned that a poor weather front (in fact a vicious blizzard) had set in at Patriot Hills. To cope with her frustrated clients Annie sensibly hired a coach to take us all to see a colony of Magellanies penguins some forty miles out of Punta. On arrival at the penguin-keeper's lonely beach hut, our coach bogged itself into waterlogged turf. Leaving the driver to extricate the vehicle, we trooped off behind the keeper, pushed along by a stiff breeze, intermittent hailstones and flurries of light snow.

Wild spume swept off the waves and there were no penguins to be seen, only the occasional ostrich-like rhea and the ever-present kara-karas.

'Penguins?' I asked our Spanish guide.

'Si, si, si,' he agreed with an encouraging grin and plunged on through the penguinless seascape.

My Punta guidebook gave no Spanish phrase for 'Where *are* the penguins?' but a comment on penguin tours in general stated: 'In windy weather the penguins go underground so there is nothing to see.'

Our guide, who answered to Juan, which may even have been his name, knew all about underground penguins and came at length to a ghetto of shallow burrows full of quaintly hissing Magellanies. Two dozen cameras flashed fitfully, their operators forced to wriggle into the soft sand for even half-decent pictures of the hull-down penguins.

Three hours later our coach was defying all attempts by various ANI clients, with or without 'leadership qualities', to supervise debogging operations. I drove away with Juan in a dilapidated Ford to get help and Mike, donning jogging shoes, set off on the track back to Punta.

Juan drove along the beach for three miles to a mining operation which owned a truck that could extricate bogged-down coaches. A long wait ensued whilst the truck was itself repaired and Juan took me to a hidden beach hut owned by two impressive gauchos in worn leather trousers. We shared roll-up cigarillos of remarkable toxicity and watched stocky horses graze on the knife-blade beach grass. When we said 'Adios', I foolishly forgot that gauchos have crushing hand-shakes and so added sore fingers to my growing list of ailments.

I sat for an hour with Juan and his wife drinking tea in the humble keeper's hut, which was their home, owned and paid for by the German School of Punta who were responsible for the penguin colony. After a struggle I managed to comprehend and answer the main query of Juan's wife – why was I going to Antarctica? My explanation, when assimilated, caused Juan to look at me with consternation. Shaking his head, he muttered, 'Usted es demasido viejo para hacer esa clase de trabajo.' Spanish classes in Brighton, more than thirty years before, must have made some impression because I realised that Juan was telling me I was too old, much too old, for such work. I wish now that I had pondered more carefully, and with humility, the penguin-keeper's words.

Back at Punta the three of us walked the windy length of Avenida Libertador O'Higgins (named after the Irish mercen-ary who helped liberate Chile from the mother country), and joined the rest of ANI's 1993 clientele at the bar of the Cabo de Hornos hotel. 'Kagge's arrived,' whispered François Lochon, a famous French war photographer briefly diverted to pen-guins from Sarajevans. 'That is him over there with his Norwegian press gang.'

François, or Froggy as he styled himself to any Briton he met on his world travels, spoke excellent English with the caricaturised accents of Inspector Clouseau of The Pink Panther. His 'press gang' was a group of six Norwegian journalists.

Erling Kagge had arranged to fly them out to Punta, and later to the Pole, in order to cover the solo, unsupported journey that he was now making in preference to the unsupported crossing earlier rumoured.

We joined Erling for dinner in the hotel. I had met him in London four years earlier, but he had now put on weight in readiness for the lean days ahead.

As we walked back to our pension, Morag commented, 'You could have cut the atmosphere in there with a knife.' Mike and I were surprised at this for we had noticed no tensions, nor even sensed ripples of rivalry. After all, Erling was only attempting the Pole whilst we were aiming at twice the distance with twice the weight and a journey of greater duration. Hardly a race.

Mike, who is nothing if not straightforward, had confronted Erling over earlier news reports from Oslo crediting Erling with the words, 'This will be a race against the British.' The Norwegian assured Mike that he had no such notions. Of course there was no race. Yet, soon afterwards, his sycophantic media 'press gang', to whom he referred as his 'staff', were sending back reports which again stressed the race aspect, with overtones of a Scott–Amundsen replay eighty years on. Mike's diary: 'Kagge insists on selling his expedition as a competitive race against ours.'

Mike went jogging to the foothills with Sunniva from the American team. I declined to join them as my ankle and back were still playing up despite daily ultrasound treatment.

On 3 November Annie reported that the DC6 was now ready to fly but Patriot Hills weather reports precluded any take-off.

We read old paperbacks and consumed quantities of king crab, rice, steaks and pasta in most of Punta's restaurants. Mike put on nine pounds that week. Finally, on 8 November, we took off. Even if there were no further problems, our chances of success had been seriously dented by the eight-day delay.

Chapter Three

'If you want a good polar traveller, get a
man without too much muscle, with
good physical tone and let his mind be
on wires – of steel.'

Apsley Cherry-Garrard

We flew south over the South Atlantic for nine hours. Nobody
looked unduly joyful. Too many stories about evil Patriot Hills
ice-landings had made the rounds.

Charles Swithinbank, who had given me expert advice on
polar problems for fifteen years, had lent me his booklet on
Antarctic landing sites. This had become a bible to many pilots
of the region. I glanced through it:

> The choice of an airfield site involves a compromise between
> the aviator's ideal and its distance from his intended
> destination. Pilots who fly transport aircraft into Kai Tak
> Airport (Hong Kong), Narssarsuaq (Greenland), or Valdez
> (Alaska) tolerate obstructions in their approach and climb-
> out paths because there is nowhere else to go. Antarctic
> operations require a similar compromise.
>
> Since wheeled aircraft find it hazardous to land on snow,
> Antarctic landing sites are usually close to mountains that
> have been scoured into sheets of blue ice. Due to this
> connection between wind, topography and blue ice, the
> prevailing wind normally trends *across* the long dimension
> of an airfield leaving a pilot with the unenviable choice of a
> short run facing the side of a mountain or a longer run
> buffeted by vicious side winds.
>
> The smoothest ice and, unfortunately, the most turbulent
> air is commonly found within the first five hundred metres
> from rock features.

At Patriot Hills the strip was a compromise, fairly close to rocks and relatively uneven.

Mike Stroud's diary notes his main concerns during the long flight. He had intimated on more than one occasion that our light-weight dome tent was not tough enough to withstand an Antarctic blizzard. The poles might break, the lining tear, and we would be in immediate danger. After a great many windy camps in Greenland and the Arctic, in the same type of tent, I assured Mike that it would be safe in even the worst of katabatic storms.

He was also worried lest we prove physically unable to pull our sledges when fully laden. He dreaded the ignominy of this or of some early injury leading to a forced withdrawal. He feared that I might prove to be far stronger than him and leave him miles behind, as had often been the case during our Arctic journeys. He thought that the pressure of such a situation might be too taxing for his staying powers, given the unthinkable distances that lay ahead of us.

Lesser concerns included frostbitten hands, the weight and bulk of his scientific gear and the possible failure of our skis to cope with such sledge-loads. He wrote: 'I try to be optimistic about a rapid start and then progress, progress, progress. Unless we move reasonably I think the prospect of our trip will crush us.'

I passed time by opening mail which had arrived as we left Punta. A letter from John Walford, Secretary to the Multiple Sclerosis Society, was encouraging:

> On behalf of our fifty thousand members, I convey the Society's best wishes for your success. Your last expediion has already enabled us to establish in Cambridge the first inter-disciplinary research unit of its kind dedicated to research into M.S. The funds raised by your current Antarctic challenge will mean the pace of work towards finding the cause and control of this most distressing of diseases can be markedly increased.
>
> We know this objective will help spur you on . . .

He was right. The knowledge that each southerly mile would raise thousands of pounds to help M.S. sufferers was a great help. We had found this in the Arctic. The charity link-up was of benefit to us as well as to the Society.

The DC6 broke through cloud cover, a cry went up and sleepy, parka-clad passengers peered downwards. We banked abruptly and descended towards the ice. A glimpse of tiny figures, tents and two Twin Otters. Twice, our Canadian pilot rehearsed the landing with dry runs to test the sixty-knot cross-winds. Then, with a shattering impact that could not have done any part of the DC6 much good, we struck the ice and bounced, rattling over the rippled blue surface.

I do not remember any other landing even half as impressive in thirty years of arriving at remote spots in small aircraft.

Mawson, a contemporary of Scott and Shackleton, was the first to introduce aircraft to Antarctica eighty years ago, a tiny Vickers monoplane which arrived by ship. But the continent will remain untrammelled by mass tourism so long as blue ice runways provide the only touchdown points. Apart from Patriot Hills' visitors, Antarctica's 6,000 or so annual tourists are mostly day-trippers from cruise ships who see nothing but the coastline.

After a few days incarcerated at Patriot Hills, one of Kagge's journalists was to write: 'In Antarctica the senses hibernate. Smell, taste, hearing, touch, they all vanish; only sight opens up those unimaginable vistas of beauty and terror . . . On a clear day, you see so far that you feel like God: a feeling that is transformed after a dozen miles trudging through dry snow or skidding on defective crampons into whining helplessness.'

I found the base leader, a tall Australian (soon to be dismissed by Annie as unsuitable to command). He promised to fly us straight to our start-point without delay. First we must fill up the fuel bottles with white spirit at the camp and tow our sledge gear over to the Twin Otter.

Since we had no crampons, the half-mile distance between the two aircraft proved interesting. Each time a gust of wind, blasting up to sixty knots, struck us, we teetered about and often fell, unable to gain much purchase on the ice. Much of our cargo was moved by camp workers on snowmobiles so there was no chance to try out the sledges with full loads.

Three hours later Mo, Mike and I were flown on with two penguin-watchers in a fuselage crammed with our equipment. The engine noise prevented conversation and various fuel smells made me feel queasy. I tried to check my maps and memorise the route I had selected from the drop-off point, 78° 14' South on the edge of the floating Filchner Ice-Shelf to the actual continental coast some 200 miles to the south. Charles Swithinbank's advice would not be infallible, but he knew Antarctica and its forbidding ways better than any man alive.

His original suggestion had been to traverse Berkner Island from north to south, then follow the 50° West line between the Dufek Massif and the Forrestal Range. This I modified into a plan to head due south from the south-east corner of Berkner Island to the eastern bank of the Support Force Glacier at a point where it skimmed the downside slope of the Argentina Mountains. The point lay close to the confluence of the Recovery and Support Force Glaciers. He warned me that *any* route could run into heavy crevasses and rough ice, but his way would be at least as good as any alternative. He ended his advice note: 'Either way you will have to climb to 3,280 feet even to get level with the Argentinas. What a sweat it will be with gigantic loads. It makes my bones ache.'

Long before we could gain the foothills of the great climb to the Pole, before even reaching the continental start-point of the coastline, there would be many navigational problems to face on the ice-shelf itself.

On the map in the darkened fuselage I could make out two variations to Swithinbank's suggested route. We could try forcing a route up the Support Force Glacier in a straight line

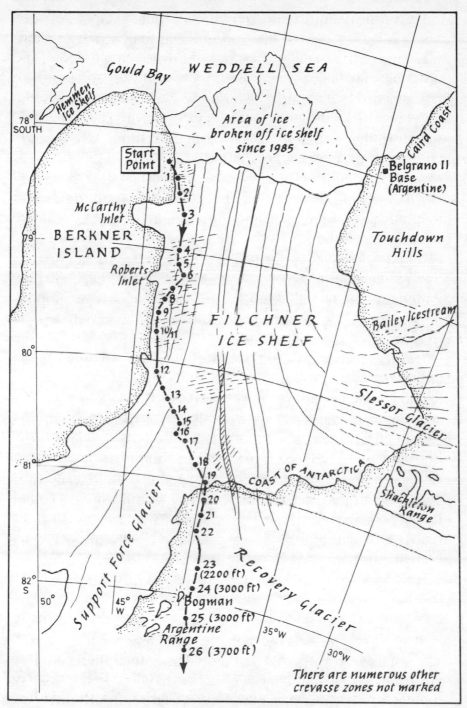

First twenty-six days of the crossing journey

from drop-off point to the Argentinan western edge, thereby risking huge crevasse fields, or we could gain any southerly miles at no risk from crevasses by simply crossing a 3,280 feet high, 170 mile-long feature, Berkner Island. Kagge, I knew, favoured the latter course. For safety reasons I agreed with him, but our loads were too heavy to attempt Berkner. By ascending the glacier itself, however hazardous, we would avoid up to 3,280 feet of extra climbing.

Major flow lines of glaciers and heavily crevassed zones were marked on the chart but I knew there would be many other crevasses, unmarked and therefore unavoidable, whichever route I selected.

The pilot, a Canadian named Warren Randle, beckoned me forward. Leaning between him and his co-pilot I was initially blinded by the overall glare of the ice-shelf. As my pupils adjusted I saw the passage beneath us of serrated blue scars, huge crevasses in parallel lines.

'Berkner Island,' Warren shouted over his shoulder and banked the Twin Otter to the west.

Following his pointing finger I could just make out that the snow-fields to the left appeared slightly darker than those beneath. 'Dark' was a relative term since all the world was white and painful to look upon without sun-glasses.

I knew that the Weddell Sea lay immediately ahead, the flowing ice of the Filchner Ice-Shelf below and the 3,280 feet high Berkner Island to our left or west flank. I knew all this because the map told me it was so, but visually the sea, the ice-shelf, and the island were uniform in their whiteness, except where complex crevassing caused fissures and therefore shadows.

No map of an ice-shelf can hope to remain accurate for long since the ice is in perpetual motion. Charles had produced my map from a mosaic of images obtained by Landsat 5 satellite orbits in 1986. Landsat coloured mapping images record ter-

44

rain in visible light and otherwise invisible near-infra-red wavelengths which geologists and glaciologists find revealing. Only five months later the Giant Chasm, the ice front region to our immediate east had split away from the shelf and an 'iceberg' of over 5,000 square miles floated out to sea. Since some forty-six square miles of new ice flow down annually from the inland plateau to augment the ice-shelf, such huge splits as the Giant Chasm have not necessarily diminished the feature since William Filchner first discovered it in 1912.

Berkner Island divides the Filchner from the far larger Ronne Ice-Shelf to the west. The two shelves together cover an area as big as France and vary in thickness from 660 feet at the seaward edge, where we were about to land, and 2,000 feet at the point where it flows over the continental coastline 200 miles to our south.

I like to imagine Antarctica as a large wedding cake covered by glutinous icing that is slowly flowing outwards and downwards. The accumulation of ice over millennia has created an icecap over a mile deep and covering great mountain ranges. Ninety per cent of the world's ice and seventy per cent of all fresh water is held captive in this 15,000,000-year-old ice-cage.

During the winter months the Antarctic ice-mass increases by an additional 11,000,000 square miles of frozen sea ice. The warmer waters of the Pacific, Indian and Atlantic oceans meet the polar waters at the Antarctic Convergence, where billions of plankton and algae are released by melting pack ice. The resulting nutrients feed krill, which is the fodder of some sixty-five million penguins, thirty-five million seals, billions of other sea creatures and the true monarchs of the polar seas, the whales.

Nature can be wild and cruel in these climes. Most of the eight or so manned bases of the continent are built along the coastline. Even short journeys by the scientists outside the immediate safety of their bases have ended in death by blizzard or crevasse. Sea ice hazards have also claimed many

45

lives, including three experienced Britons within sight of their scientific base at Horseshoe. The coastal ice is unpredictable even by experts and, on the occasion in question, the base leader at Horseshoe had watched the three men travelling across the local bay at two o'clock in the afternoon. That same night he was woken by a premonition of disaster. He walked to the beach and saw to his horror that the entire bay was now open sea. He returned to his hut stunned. For many days he led dangerous searches for his missing men. No one ever ascertained what had happened to the lost scientists but anyone who has travelled on polar sea ice knows the risk. Bad weather causes you to camp out on the sea ice just when you need to make all speed for the safety of land. Strong winds then fracture the ice into floes which head out to sea. Death follows, by starvation or drowning; a frightening way to go. Killer whales lurk about the floes and will batter through quite thick ice to grasp their prey in their jagged rows of teeth.

The killer is not beyond attacking small boats. Frank Worsley, captain of Shackleton's ship *Endurance*, wrote of the killers: 'These brutes grow to a length of twenty-five feet and have a mouth with a four-foot stretch and teeth "according". It has been recorded that one, after being harpooned and cut up, contained twelve seals and ten porpoises. They will attack a blue whale which may weigh a hundred tons. While two killers seize the great whale by the lower jaw and, bearing down, force the mouth open, two others plunge in and tear out the tongue, weighing perhaps two tons. The killer pack devour this delicacy, leaving their unfortunate victim to a slow death.'

Although the presence of pack ice can act like oil to calm the polar seas, the Southern Ocean can be as hostile to man as the ice continent which it surrounds.

The Antarctic Pilot states: 'Navigation in this area is rendered difficult by sea-ice, violent weather changes, dangerous shoals, large seas and swells, instability of compass, inadequate charts, absence of nagivation aids, whiteouts and kelp entanglement.'

Worsley knew the Weddell Sea, of which our Filchner Ice-Shelf formed a southern part, better than most men. He wrote:

> The great unceasing westerly swell of the Southern Ocean rolls almost unchecked around this end of the world in the Roaring Forties and the Stormy Fifties. The highest, broadest swells in the world, rising forty or fifty feet and more from hollow to crest, they rage in disorder during gales. At times their crests sweep up until their front forms an almost perpendicular wall of green, rushing water that smashes on a ship's deck, flattening steel bulwarks and crushing deckhouses like eggshells. These blue water hills in a heavy gale move as fast as twenty-five miles an hour. The impact of hundreds of tons of solid water at this speed is difficult to imagine.

In 1979, prior to landing for my previous Antarctic crossing, our ship had rolled forty-seven degrees, in either direction, during a sudden storm. (Two other expedition ships, Bill Tilman's *En Avant* and the German *Gottland II*, were sunk that season. Neither Tilman nor his crew were ever found.) Our ship was the same *Kista Dan* that in 1954 had helped prepare for the first crossing of Antarctica under the leadership of Vivian Fuchs. One of his team wrote of their voyage in the *Kista Dan*, 'In six hours the wind rose from Force Eight (thirty seven knots) through Force Twelve (eighty knots) to Force Fourteen (at which point no attempt is made to estimate wind speeds). The captain lost control of the ship and she broached to, lying on her port side, drifting helplessly, pounded by every breaking wave and rolling from ten degrees to starboard to seventy degrees to port. An extreme roll dipped the ship's port side so far that the saloon portholes (high up on the ship) looked down into green water.'

*

Our Twin Otter briefly roared over the ice-front of the Weddell Sea, a vertical cliff forming the seaward face of the Filchner Ice-Shelf. After several cautious rehearsals, Warren found a relatively smooth stretch of snow at the point where Berkner Island meets both the ice-shelf and the sea. We were down at 78° 19.8' south, 43° 47' west.

Morag helped us unload and wished us well. For the next few months she would attempt to keep radio contact with us and with our UK base, which was manned by her husband Flo at their home in Aberdeen. When Flo returned from work each evening he would switch on his sets and tune in the antennae which he had erected in a seven-acre field outside the kitchen window. This, at least, was our plan.

In fact Morag, intent on a brief foray to visit a penguin colony, was dropped off and abandoned for ten days at an isolated base manned by an all-male group of twelve Argentinian soldiers.

We watched the little aircraft depart until the engine noise was a distant drone and the great silence of Antarctica closed about us.

Months of unspoken apprehension were coming to a head. The key question was whether or not *full* loads, including the one hundred days of fuel taken on at Patriot Hills, could be moved by the two of us.

There were other worries. All of my sponsors' budget had already been paid to ANI. In the event of a rescue operation, which my highly specific insurance policy did not cover, all costs would be charged to me, personally, and could run into hundreds of thousands of dollars. I could expect no help from Mike or any other team member. My favourite philosopher, King Solomon, would have advocated, 'Best not to think about it.'

I knew Steger's supported 1990 crossings had cost US$ 11,000,000 and Messner's US$ 600,000. Because we *intended* to have no support flights, the project should not

48

exceed the sponsors' overall US\$ 225,000 budget, but the best-laid plans are inclined to founder in Antarctica even more than elsewhere.

We each placed a stack of our equipment in the snow to the side of our empty sledge. I shook my head at Mike.

'It will be a miracle if it all fits in, never mind if we can tow the end results.'

He nodded. We began to load up with the heavier items first.

I glanced with distaste at the bag of HF radio gear which Morag had prepared for me. Previous polar journeys, with and without communications gear, had taught me that when weight is critical it is best to ditch the radio. I agreed with the saying, 'Half the world's problems are caused by poor communications, the other half by good communications.'

When Mike first accepted my offer to join our Antarctic team, he made it clear he would only participate if we took a radio. His family was, rightly, all-important to him and he felt he could only approach his wife Thea, at the outset, if he knew that we would at least try to keep two-way communications. One of his children might become ill or have an accident and he must retain the option of knowing about it, so that, if he so decided, he could cut short the expedition.

I was so keen to have Mike on board that I capitulated on this point even though it meant lugging some twenty pounds about that were not key to our survival.

Although few people realise it, wireless was in regular use during Scott and Amundsen's era. Amundsen stated: 'I have decided not to carry a wireless for this reason . . . Imagine we suddenly get a dispatch that some of our dear ones are seriously ill . . . what would be the result? Nobody can tell but the worst might happen.'

I packed the radio. There were no spare parts. Bumping about and operating at wildly fluctuating temperatures, there was every likelihood that it would stop working, at which point I could eject it with a clear conscience. Until then I would make the best of its presence and hope to receive third-hand news from home if the ether allowed.

Next came thirty-six one-litre alloy fuel bottles. By allowing enough naphtha (white spirit) to melt and boil snow to rehydrate our rations for one hundred days, we needed seventy pounds of fuel per sledge.

In case of separation we each carried a small cooker which screwed directly into the alloy bottles, doing away with the need for a separate cooker tank as on the old primus stove of my previous journeys. The primus, first invented in 1892 by Franz Lindquist, a Swede, worked by vaporising paraffin under pressure applied by a small air pump. It could boil water in three minutes, against the ten minutes required by the old wick and spirit lamps. The primus, by reducing fuel consumption, vastly increased the distance potential of polar travellers.

Scott's death has been largely attributed to the failure of his fuel containers, which leaked, and we were soon to face a similar and potentially lethal problem: At Patriot Hills Mike, who organised all our rations and cooking arrangements, was keen not to fill the bottles to the brim since there would then be no tiny air gaps with which to form the initial vaporising pressure. We filled the bottles in extremely awkward conditions and blowing snow, so it was difficult to avoid either under- or over-pouring from the gallon container cans. I made a practice of over-filling, knowing that it would later be easy to pour a little out but impossible to pour a little in: a sort of 'wise virgin' scheme which was not to go down well with poor Mike whenever he tried pressurising a new and over-full bottle.

Equally important both to our chances of success and to Mike's physiological research were the rations themselves. Each bag was packed to provide two men with twenty-four hours of food at a daily intake of 5,200 caloies. They had evolved over a period of sixteen years of polar journeys beginning with my first North Pole attempt in 1976.

I find figures both confusing and boring and hope not to clutter this book with them, but calories were critical to our survival: lack of them was to all but kill us over the months ahead.

Modern Antarctic authorities have a simple philosophy when feeding their field parties for summer travel: 'Extreme cold tends to make people hungry and hard work uses energy. A dog-sledger may need 5,000 calories, a snowmobile traveller 3,350 calories and an inside station worker 2,750 calories.'

The average daily intake of both Scott's and Amundsen's team was 4,500 calories per man. This proved enough for the Norwegians who skied unencumbered and with husky power. To counter the grotesquely hard labour of the British manhaulers, the amount was insufficient and they slowly starved to death. The first man to weaken and die was the biggest and heaviest on Scott's team: the man they 'least expected to fail'.

I considered our team's vital statistics. I was eleven years older than Mike and approaching my fiftieth year. I was taller by five inches and heavier by three stone (forty-two pounds). But, in terms of sheer strength, especially the vital lower limb power base, Mike was clinically tested as considerably stronger.

At home, Ginnie gives me twice her own food portions although she works harder – she on the farm and me at my desk. She also feeds her large water-dogs four times what she feeds her Jack Russell terrier although he is by far the most active of our dogs. Over the months ahead I would be consuming *exactly* the same calorific intake as Mike. I feared that, like the heavily-built Evans on Scott's team, my performance would deteriorate first and more markedly than Mike's. I determined from the outset, therefore, to avoid my normal course of forging ahead at maximum output.

With every last item loaded, I found it impossible to zip up

51

the canvas shroud designed to cover the cargo and render it snow-proof. I solved this by lashing the spare ski and double sleeping bag on top, once all the other items were crammed within the zipped-up coffin.

As each piece of equipment was loaded we ticked it off in our notebooks, alongside its weight, down to the nearest ounce. The total was 485 pounds each: a figure well beyond our worst nightmares.

Only by studying previous Antarctic journeys could we estimate our own chances with these dismal loads.

Amundsen avoided manhauling like the plague. Each of his huskies could manage ninety pounds. The maximum load known to have been pulled by dogs for up to 300 polar miles is 150 pounds each. Amundsen used the manhaul harness to symbolise the penalty of failure, reasoning that the sight of it, to his Norwegians, resembled an instrument of torture to be avoided for as long as they could keep their dogs going.

In 1903 Scott, Shackleton and Wilson hauled loads of 175 pounds each. Eight years later, on the 'worst journey in the world', Wilson, Bowers and Cherry-Garrard started out with 'enormous weights for such travelling – *two hundred and fifty-three pounds* a man'.

In 1913, on their last tragic South Pole journey, Scott's men pulled *200 pounds* each up to the polar plateau. The strongest man, Bowers, was also the smallest. He said: 'The starting was worse than the pulling as it required from ten to fifteen desperate jerks on the harness to move the sledge at all . . . I have never pulled so hard or so nearly crushed my inside into my backbone by the everlasting jerking with all my strength on the canvas band round my unfortunate tummy.'

In 1985 Roger Mear, writing of his attempt at the first unsupported journey to the South Pole: 'How much could a man pull? . . . If I had known our sledgeloads would weigh *three hundred and fifty-three pounds*, I would have considered the journey impossible.' Mear based his plans on the experience

52

of the Tyrolean Dr Robert Peroni who had led a three-man, 838 mile crossing of the Greenland Icecap. Peroni had told Mear, 'Even a spare button is too much.' At the outset each sledgeload was 321 *pounds* but this 'was too heavy to move'.

All these expeditions involved powerful men with strong wills and we could hardly say to ourselves: 'We are different. We can do better.' Especially unnerving was the evidence of our only manhauling predecessors, Messner and Fuchs, in 1990.

Reinhold Messner, revered internationally as the greatest mountaineer in history, is a man with exceptional physical stamina and an iron will. His colleague, Arved Fuchs, is Germany's top polar explorer. I had serious doubts that Mike and I could outperform such a team. Of his journey Messner wrote: 'With sledge loads of *two hundred and sixty-four pounds*, the longest stretch would be murderously strenuous. Perhaps even impossible . . . *two hundred and sixty-four pounds* is a load for a horse not a human being.'

I could not ignore such warnings. Mike and I faced a journey of 1,700 miles, much of it above 10,000 feet altitude with start loads of *485 pounds* each. Not far short of 1,000 pounds between us. If we failed to manage these loads the fault would be entirely mine. I should have anticipated the unarguable force of the mathematics. As leader I could blame nobody else. In silent desperation I glared at my sledge. If only we could jettison *something*.

There was no answer to hand. Each and every item had already been subject to numerous 'need-to-take' discussions. Each of our toothbrushes had been cut down to mere bristles. Every scrap of excess packaging paper was removed from the rations. No spare clothing was allowed. Even repair materials were minimal and equipment I usually considered *de rigueur*, such as instep crampons for ice gradients, had been eliminated.

Mike kept his medical and science packs as light as he could and, just before leaving Punta, he removed a supply of chocolate bars which would have upped our daily intake from 5,200 to 5,500 calories.

There was no excuse for delay; nothing to be gained by considering any further the unpalatable facts. Goethe wrote: 'Whatever you can do or dream you can . . . begin it. Boldness has genius, power and magic in it.' A spot of magic would be more than welcome.

We adjusted the manhaul harnesses about our stomachs and shoulders. I leant against the traces with my full 210-pound bodyweight. The near half-ton sledge paid *no* attention.

I looked back and spotted an eight-inch ice rut across the front of the runners. I tugged again with my left shoulder only, and the sledge, avoiding the rut, *moved forward*. I will never forget that instant. Never. I *could* pull the sledge. The fear that the full load would prove immovable had been growing into an ogre. That was now dispelled.

After a hundred yards I stopped. Mike was labouring hard but he too could move his load. The expedition was under way nine days behind its own very tight schedule.

Mike is one of the two most dogged and determined people I have met. He was a climber of mountains long before he visited the polar regions. In his book *Zen and the Art of Climbing Mountains*, Neville Shulman wrote: 'Mountaineers are very special people. From the moment they decide to climb a mountain, everything else becomes of lesser consequence. Only what and where they are *now* means anything to them. All that matters is how they will inter-react with the mountain.'

That night, in his diary, Mike wrote: 'A snow petrel flew overhead as we started – which must be a good omen.'

A thousand jumbled thoughts helped to dull the appalling realisation that this was but the first day of a hundred, the first one hundred yards of several million.

My mood swung through a gamut of emotions as though it

54

1 The author, at fifteen stone, one week before leaving London for Antarctica

2a Charlie Burton (with rucksack) and Oliver Shepard, who crossed Antarctica with the author in 1980 and organised the 1993 Antarctic unsupported crossing

2b Morag (Mo) Howell and Laurence (Flo) Howell, probably the most efficient and experienced polar communicators in the world. Mo was the Antarctic Base Leader and Flo manned the UK radio base

3 Doctor Mike Stroud, the author's companion
over five major polar expeditions.
His smiling face belies a mean streak
with injection needles

4 Crevasse practise in London

5 The Arctic ocean 400 miles north of the Siberian Coast. The 1990
North Pole unsupported attempt. Crossing a canal of newly-forming ice
by lashing the sledges together with skis

6a The A.N.I. ski-plane drops the team on the Atlantic ice-front of Antarctica with just under 1000lbs to manhaul between them

6b The author and Dr Mike Stroud set out. Mike's sledge (left) was split in two within the week. Note crevasse shining on the skyline ahead

6c A fair parallel to the expedition's task would be to tow three stocky six-foot tall men in a plastic bath over 1200 miles of sand dunes

6d Two fleas at the edge of a vast white sheet

7a A member of Scott's team poses for a sponsor-photo for Heinz

7b The team do likewise for a dehydrated food sponsor some eighty years later

7c Shackleton's men manhaul a ship's boat in the manner traditional to the eighteenth- and nineteenth-century British explorers of the north polar regions

7d Scott's men deflating a balloon used for aerial ice reconnaissance. Early Antarctic explorers, including on occasions Scott, Mawson, Shackleton and Amundsen, used radios, tracked and wheeled motorized vehicles and monoplanes wherever suitable

8 The author man-hauling beside Berkner Island on a rare clear day

9a (top) The time is local noon and the author is treading on his shadow as a means of navigating due south

9b (bottom left) Dr Mike Stroud at the upper rim of the crevasse from which he was lucky to escape alive

9c (bottom right) *Sastrugi*: a word from Russian meaning icy features built from snow. These iron-hard ridges were a great problem both on the 1993 manhaul journey and, even more so, on the 1980 Transglobe Expedition. Here, on that earlier expedition, Oliver Shepard's sledge is jammed on a three-foot-high sastruga

10a The author in full cold-weather outfit, the same Lancashire 100 percent cotton available to polar explorers in 1901

10b The author and Dr Mike Stroud pause for eighty minutes at the South Pole

11 Dr Mike Stroud in the
upper reaches of the Mill Glacier

12a Chess on the cook-box with urine-sample vials

12b Manufacturing ski-skin clamps and rivets out of alloy strips cut from used fuel bottles

13a Making rope crampons in readiness for the blue ice descent

13b Mending mitts with wool cut from socks

14 Blue ice on the Beardmore Glacier.
As slippery as an ice rink

15a The first view of the Trans-Antarctic Mountains

15b A camp at the edge of a crevasse field

16 The gap between the author
and Dr Mike Stroud . . . the
cause of much friction on every
Antarctic manhaul expedition

were a weather vane in a storm, or a paranoic Russian high on vodka.

When Amundsen first set out, his lead skier wrote: 'I hope it won't be a fiasco . . . If I emerge from this journey unscathed, I must see that I get out of polar exploration.' Swan, the day he set out for the Pole in 1985, wrote: 'I leave in fine company on a great journey. I hardly know what to expect, but I leave with a lion's heart that will roar with everything he has when he sees the Pole, the South Pole, think of that. I want it now.'

The thought of pulling my sledge for an entire mile, never mind to the South Pole and beyond, was appalling. Looking into the white glare to the south-west I could not actually see the point where the flank of the island became one with the ice-shelf, but I knew it to be about a mile from our landing point.

The map or, strictly speaking, chart (since the sea was beneath us) showed a rash of blue lines, the crevasse symbol, running south along the foot of Berkner Island for some eighty miles.

Should we fix a safety line between us before reaching the first crevasse? I knew this was our agreed drill but the sheer weight of the sledge had already biased me against *any* action beyond the sheer task of progress. Even though we were descending a gentle incline, the sledge was totally inert. The very instant I stopped pulling, it stopped moving. There was not the least glissade. I conjured up a parallel. If I were to lash together three average-sized adults, each weighing 160 pounds, dump them in a fibreglass bathtub with no legs, and then drag them through sand dunes for 1,700 miles, the difficulties involved would be similar.

My sledge-load soon grew to represent something animate and hostile. I knew the pattern well. First my inner anger would be directed at the weather, the equipment and the ice. Later at my companion. The same would hold good for Mike.

55

I determined *never* to allow myself to think unnecessarily far ahead. Sufficient unto each day is the mileage thereof . . . providing daily progress tallies with the schedule.

I did not speak to Mike. There was no point and, already out of breath, I found the manhaul harness extremely uncomfortable, especially at the shoulders and hips.

At least there was no wind. The weather was perfect. I sweated freely at −10°C. This was an estimate, for thermometers had long since been eliminated as non-vital weight.

After two hours I felt certain we had reached the ice-shelf. About a mile to our immediate north was the ice-front, a chaotic jumble of giant fragments where shelf met true sea ice. In every other direction there was nothing but mirage shimmer and the great white glare of Antarctica.

After five and a half hours it was time to halt, for we had been awake for twenty-four hours since leaving Punta Arenas. For navigation purposes, we must keep to a carefully timed daily schedule. I intended to use my watch and body shadow to establish direction all the way to the Pole, and that meant keeping the sun due north at local midday.

We each slept in only one of our double-layer bags but woke halfway through the night feeling cold. The term *night* was symbolic since there were twenty-four hours of daylight. I felt tired but elated. I had no desire to query the fact that we were both hauling loads well beyond the accepted maximum. In five and a half hours we had managed nearly four miles. They had been flat and easy-going with a compact, smooth surface. And we were still full of fine Punta food.

There were, I reasoned, only another 1,696 miles to cover and since we had rations for a hundred days, there was yet time to find a way of increasing the daily average to sixteen miles. There must be *no* rest days or we would fail.

Beneath our tent the entire ice-shelf rose and fell with the tide. In the middle of the continent, the ice sheet is more than a mile deep and moves outwards at a rate of up to several

56

thousand yards a year. On reaching the coast it pushes on over the sea's surface, sometimes for hundreds of miles, until eventually breaking off as icebergs that can be bigger than Yorkshire.

Everything about this place is too big to contemplate comfortably. A snow petrel swooped low outside the tent, turning on sharp swishing wings. They too must be overawed by the endless whiteness. Perhaps they welcomed the sight of our small yellow tent. Tomorrow, I knew, we would meet the first crevasses. I lay on my back for my hips were already bruised from the harness.

Ahead there would be more bruises on what Scott called 'the long trail, the lone trail, the outward trail, the darkward trail'.

Chapter Four

'Every durable bond between human
beings is founded in or heightened by
some element of competition.'

R. L. Stevenson

I nursed the hope that Fate would allow us progress without
injury or delay for at least a month before we met major
obstacles. If only we could tuck a decent mileage under our
belts *before* our morale was sorely tested . . .

On 10 November I decided to take the straighter route south
through the crevasse zone in order to save a few miles. We
woke to a brisk north-westerly wind. Since south winds from
the Pole are the norm, we had not been expecting so early a
chance to use our sails.

Shackleton, Scott, Amundsen and Messner all used sails of
various designs. Ours were shaped like parachutes and could
be attached to the skier, or the sledge, or both. Taking careful
note of the instructions given us by the American woman at
Punta, we experimented and, to our great delight, found
ourselves towed along at some four miles per hour, struggling
to keep upright and, unsuccessfully, to steer a southerly
course.

Within a very short time it became obvious that we were
being blown too far east and were heading for trouble. We
packed away the sails and in poor visibility struggled to gain
ground to the south. At this stage we were over a thousand
miles from the South Magnetic Pole so the magnetic variation
was a mere ten degrees off the true bearing.

By the feel of the wind and with frequent glances at my chest compass, I could be certain to keep a steady course. One corner of the southern skies was a deeper shade of grey and provided an adequate aim-off point by which to memorise the previous compass check.

After three hours, exhausted, we stopped to drink soup from one of two Thermos flasks.

'It must be broken,' Mike exclaimed in dismay. As he poured, the contents slurped out in glutinous lumps of congealed butter fat. Somehow the soup he had prepared the previous evening had gone cold. Since the Thermos was of steel, we assumed there must be an invisible puncture which had destroyed the vacuum. This was a major disappointment, especially at such an early stage. Now we had but a single working flask to replenish our energy and heat level during the long days of manhauling.

For five hours we slogged through the gloom. Snow petrels twice flew around for several minutes, their plaintive cries at one with the wilderness.

The hard surfaces of the immediate sea front had given way to softer snow and I began to find the going harder. Shooting pains in my shoulder blades were the result of manhauling with our standard bandolier harnesses.

The double stitching on every joint of the harnesses was designed for work with heavy sledge-loads. Unfortunately the maximum which the manufacturers had in mind was approximately half the stress-load which we were pulling. The result, in only two days of work, was torn stitching and twisted shoulder-bands. Not noticing the torn traces, I continued to drag my sledge with my harness slightly out of alignment. The resulting twist to my torso must have pulled at some muscle which now caused the sharp pains in my shoulders.

To counter this, I loosened off the shoulder-traces and tightened up my waistband. Within minutes both my hips and the skin at my waist began to complain. By the end of the day my midriff was raw on both sides where the waistband was pulled inwards at each forward strain.

Each and every step of progress was possible only due to a forceful *tug* on the 480-pound load. The pressure points involved, apart from our shoulders and waists, were chiefly our feet, boots and skis.

The skis often slid backward, despite the brand-new seal-skin strips that were fixed to their undersides by fastenings at either end and with a devilishly clever Austrian glue, which remained sticky even after the skins had been taken on and off several times.

We would have pulled in vain but for the thousands of invidivual sealskin hairs which pressed down into the snow and gave us grip.

As my new skins stretched, so they became loose and sideways pressure soon wore away the adhesive. My skis kept slipping and my halts to tighten up the end fastenings of the skis had to be more frequent. Mike did not complain or, if he did, it was under his breath. Perhaps he was having the same skins problem, or maybe he was treating the delays as a welcome respite.

Most of the day we said nothing to each other. If someone did shout, the normal response was, 'What?' Any movement caused noise: the crinkle of a cotton or woollen balaclava over the ears, the loud beat of your heart and the grind or shriek of ski-sticks thrusting you forwards. It was best to avoid the irritation caused by trying to converse.

Our course had settled down and ran about a mile out to the east of, and parallel with, Berkner Island. Remembering my promise to Mike, I alternated the navigation with him at hourly intervals. I found this increasingly annoying since I had spent well over twenty years leading expeditions from the front and mistrusted anyone else's navigating abilities. In the wildly fragmented Arctic pack ice, navigation is based on experience and sound knowledge of a myriad different colours, drift patterns, shapes and shadows. Anybody can steer more or less to the north but the ability to find a course for a heavy sledge, avoiding the worst obstacles, both short- and long-term, comes only with a great deal of practice.

In Antarctica navigation is far more simple. A basic working knowledge of the compass and the longitudinal behaviour of the sun is sufficient to keep a reasonable course to the Pole. Simple mathematics and attention to the magnetic variation are needed to set a sound course *from* the Pole but otherwise the inland plateau presents no problems in direction-finding.

Nonetheless, I had to force my irritation down each time my hour ended and I halted to let Mike take over. This inner struggle was a great help in the ongoing problem of trying to face the slow passage of time. Time was our enemy. Every minute was long and tedious. At all costs, we had to avoid pondering the ever-increasing bodily pains, which would lead to self-pity and, at this early stage, God alone knew what that would result in. But, instead of antipathy towards Mike (since he happened to be the only other human available at whom to aim my feelings), I was able to indulge in apprehension and fill my mind with thoughts about crevasses, how best to avoid them, what to do if and when either or both of us fell into them, what it would feel like to plunge unroped into the maw of a 200-foot-deep ice-hole, how to retrieve Mike from even a small fifty-foot fissure? All these and many other allied thoughts helped the long hours and the slow miles to pass by without our dwelling on the sheer size of the task and the knowledge that an increasing amount of discomfort was likely to accrue as our bodies slowly broke down.

I had read a great deal about crevasses and, in 1980, had plunged many feet into a deep, narrow crack close by Mount Erebus. Charles Swithinbank sees crevasses not as lethal mantraps but as fascinating examples of ice movement. On a journey of exploration in the 1950s, his fellow geologist Fred Roots wrote:

> The interior of a large crevasse has a simple, sinister beauty that cannot fail to impress all who are privileged to see it. The 'bottomless' appearance of some of them is hard to explain. Most of the large crevasses, if 'clean', probably have a depth of about one hundred and twenty-five feet; it is doubtful if any on the open ice are more than one hundred and eighty feet deep. Many of the larger ones are so choked with collapsed bridges that they have an unstable 'false floor' at about fifty or sixty feet.
>
> The main emotion most people experience when peering into a crevasse is a feeling of intense depth; a feeling engendered no doubt mainly by the stark clearness and smoothness of the walls, upon which a very occasional small ledge, splintered flake or snow-powdered cluster of rime crystals only seems to emphasize the verticality and implacable impregnability of the whole; and by the colour – a pure glacial blue that becomes more and more intense before it deepens into indigo and sometimes into blackness.

Most polar travellers are not scientifically enamoured of crevasses and describe them with less affection. Cherry-Garrard wrote: 'The Lord only knows how deep these vast chasms go down. They seem to extend into blue-black nothingness thousands of feet below.'

According to Amundsen, 'These crevasses are impressive when one lies at the edge and stares down in them. A bottomless chasm goes from light blue into the thickest darkness. The ugliest formations we have found here are huge holes that could take our ship the *Fram* and a lot more besides. These holes are covered by a thin wind crust. If one gets into such a delightful spot, one is irrevocably lost.'

The author of *Mawson's Will*, describing the tragic journey in 1912 of Mawson, Mertz and Ninnis, captured the moment of a crevasse fall:

Ninnis knew exactly what to do. To cut short his time on the
snow bridge he would move to the left and go directly
across. He could re-direct the dogs better on the ground
rather than from the sledge, with his one good hand tugging
at the traces.

   He jumped from the rear of the sledge. His toes hit the
surface like a heavily weighted dart. His body plunged
through the disintegrating snow and the sledge plummeted,
tumbled with him. He heard the frightened wail of his lead
dog, Basilisk, as the impetus of the sledge dragged all the
dogs into the depths. Ninnis opened his mouth to scream
his terror. The fine snow choked his eyes, ears and throat
and he did not hear his own smothered death cry. Down in
cold darkness, one hundred and fifty feet down, his falling
body smashed into a projecting ledge of iron clad ice. With
the shattered remains of his sledge, with the doomed dogs,
Belgrave Ninnis plunged deeper and deeper into the abyss.

I remembered a journalist, as we left England, telling me, 'Of
course, it isn't the same nowadays as it was eighty years ago.
Now you have all the trappings of the technical age. The sense
of adventure and the dangers are gone.' I tried to think what
technical items I carried on my sledge which might stop me
decending into a crevasse or help me out once I was down
one.

   The aftermath of a fall can also be fatal for the survivors who
will, like Mawson and Mertz, often find that key items or
rations have disappeared along with their late colleague.
Mawson used a wireless on some of his journeys but that
would be of little use if carried on the lost sledge. The same
held true of our own situation.

   Mawson's Will goes on to describe the aftermath of Ninnis's
fall.

Mawson stopped his dogs and looked over his shoulder.
The landscape was empty. Afraid, he ran hurriedly back
along the track . . . there was the hope that Ninnis and his

dogs were wedged and hanging in their harness. The gaping hole in the frozen snow bridge killed that hope.

From near the edge of the dangerously cracked rim Mawson peered into an icy pit and an awful feeling of catastrophe gripped him. He heard the wail of a dog coming out of the depths, a mingling cry of pain and fear.

Mertz joined Mawson and they lay on the edge to call and call into the depths. The hard sheer walls fell away into the deep darknes of the glacial depths.

For three grief-stricken hours they circled the broken snow before they faced the savage fact: this was their companion's grave.

I concentrated on the snow to my immediate front. Whenever my goggles fogged over, I stopped to scrape them clear of rime, for visibility was the key to survival.

We were on a flat stretch, with not the least sign of an undulation, when I found myself suddenly shooting downwards. I flung both arms out, ski-sticks flailing. My descent stopped short at my armpits. I felt my legs involuntarily treading air, swimming on the void. Gingerly I tried to turn my neck to look backwards at the sledge. My greatest fear at that moment was that it too would break through the thin trap-door and, like Ninnis, I would cartwheel downwards to snap my spine or crack open my skull on some sharp icy ledge below.

The last time I had crossed active crevasses en route to the Pole, in the Hinge Zone of Norwegian Antarctica, I had come within inches of an unroped fall into oblivion. In that same region, a year later, twelve South Africans lost two heavy snow machines, and a young scientist fell ninety feet and broke his neck whilst patrolling ahead with a crevasse prod. Further round the coast that year two British scientists on skidoos were killed in a fissure close to their base. That base was stuffed to the gunwales with radios and all the gadgets of the twentieth century. Twin Otter ski-planes were on call to the inmates.

Crevasses are today, just as in the time of Scott and Mawson, the chief threat to Antarctic travellers, and the danger has not lessened one iota over the intervening years. This does not stop ignorant media reporters (who have never travelled through crevasse fields), nor old buffs (who have, but regard their own heyday in the 1930s, 1940s or 1950s as being the end of the heroic era of no gadgetry), from denouncing polar travellers of today as cosseted joyriders who have but to press a red knob to receive instant rescue from all predicaments.

Up to my armpits in deep, soft snow, with my lower torso dangling over nothingness, I only wished that the 'red knob' fallacy had some basis in reality. Too much movement in trying to extricate my body could in an instant collapse the whole snow bridge. My attempt to look back at my sledge failed, for the hood of my parka and my cotton balaclava prevented sufficient lateral movement of my neck. Furthermore I had breathed into the balaclava as I fell, which had the immediate effect of misting up my goggles. The mist had quickly frozen across the inside of the lens. To all intents and purposes I was blind since I had no hand free to tear off the goggles.

The alloy trace leading back from my harness to the sledge had snapped in half close behind me – which, in a perverse way, helped me by allowing sufficient movement to wriggle up, inch by inch, until my hips were out of the hole. The rest was easy.

Sweating with relief, I crawled to one side of the crater and hauled the sledge well away from its vicinity before I again dared to stand up, make a botch-up repair to the trace and carry on.

Mike, navigating at the time, had disappeared into the mist but his track was still visible. It was best to fall into crevasses when you happened to be navigating. That way you were in front and could expect help from behind in minutes, not

66

hours. Neither of us expected the other to keep checking backwards. There was enough to do and to fear, to prevent yourself running into trouble, or losing direction. Each man looked after himself. By the end of the day valuable miles were saved by that policy. Only when blowing snow or total white-out made tracks quickly invisible did we adhere to the Army buddy-buddy system of constant visual check-ups on each other's well-being.

There is a great difference between mere bad visibility and total white-out. As yet we had not run into the latter condition, which was just as well for the immediate area was as treacherous and rotten as a crusted Iranian salt bog.

Comments from Mike's diary at the time included: 'gaping holes left and right, a few yards away in the gloom' . . . 'nerve-racking' . . . 'The bridges are soft and difficult.'

Many of the crevasses were over a hundred feet wide with sagging bridges. The weakest point was not, as might be expected, in the centre but along the fault-line, where the bridge was joined to the crevasse wall's lip. In the most dangerous cases the whole bridge had already descended a few feet down into the maw before catching on some unseen temporary 'stopper'. New snow had then partially filled the resulting gap.

Hauling the sledges *down* onto such teetering bridges presented no great physical task since gravity was on our side. If the bridge held, under our initial weight, we pulled onwards over the centre span. At this point the going became singularly off-putting because, in order to manhaul our monster loads *up* the far side of the disintegrating bridge, maximum downwards pressure with skis and sticks must be applied at its weakest point. There were moments of sickening apprehension as our straining ski sticks plunged through the crust, or part of a sledge lurched backwards, its prow or stern having broken through.

I never grew inured to the crevasse hazard and continued to

sweat and silently curse as each new death trap loomed ahead or to my immediate flank.

Suddenly, I looked up. Mike must have shouted. Then, there followed an immediate sound of rushing air and snow thunder from the bridge beneath him, as it collapsed. I was about 500 yards away and could now see nothing but his head, a dark blob against the snow, apparently quite bodiless, and then the alloy manhaul poles and the sledge itself.

A crevasse of only six feet in width but with sheer, clean sides had opened up beneath both Mike and his sledge. Mike's hips were athwart the far lip and his arms reaching out for a grip. But his alloy traces prevented him from moving in any direction because the sledge was poised for half its length over the chasm. If Mike moved at all, he was liable to precipitate disaster.

I tore myself clear of my harness and grabbed the back of Mike's sledge. My first priority was to stop the sledge moving even fractionally forwards. Once it began to slide into the hole I would not be able to stop it and Mike would certainly be jerked off his precarious perch by its downward-plunging bulk.

Although my instinct was to pull the sledge towards me and away from the crevasse, commonsense luckily prevailed as I remembered a similar situation in the Arctic with Mike poised over a narrow water canal.

'I'll try to push,' I shouted, 'and you try to crawl as far forwards as your traces allow. Hopefully you will be on firm ground before the sledge drops.'

Once Mike was clear, after an inch-by-inch process that must have been incredibly frightening for him, he unclipped his harness. Now, if the sledge did go down, it would not drag him too. We each took up a firm position on either side of the crevasse and together applied sudden force to his sledge. I pushed and he pulled. The resulting forward momentum narrowly defeated gravity as, his face red with the strain,

Mike flung himself backwards and dragged the 480-pound deadweight over the far lip of the fissure.

That night the ice beneath and around us pushed on towards the sea as it had for millennia.

Sometimes a giant boulder, house-high, is torn from an inland nunatak and transported on ice for hundreds of miles to the nearest coast; then out over vast ice-shelves until at length it floats to sea on an iceberg. Sometimes the ice beneath the boulder will melt *above* the sea's surface but, for many weeks, continue to float about the southern ocean with only its rocky burden visible to awestruck passing sailors.

How long, I wondered, since the ice that bore our tent that night had left the lofty polar plateau? Perhaps when dinosaurs roamed Earth or when apes became men? Certainly eons before humans began to rule the world. How little it really mattered who was President of the United States, or even if Mike cooked dehydrated 'chicken' that night instead of dehydrated 'spaghetti bolognese'.

My philosophising seduced me into a sense of well-being based on the total irrelevance of what might happen to me or any other individual human being. This excellent attitude sadly disappeared the moment a series of staccato cracks, and threatening rumbles, emanated from the same shifting ice somewhere close by the tent.

Mike wrote: 'Towards the end of the day I felt desperately tired and arrived at the tent ten minutes after Ran, sick with fatigue. I felt quite dazed and cold . . . Ran also felt it was one of his "hardest days ever".'

A katabatic wind from the interior roared down the Support Force Glacier and over the Filchner Ice-Shelf during the night. We slept through the storm until, at 'dawn', we unzipped the entry flap and a blinding sheet of powder snow entered the tent.

I thought to myself: 'This is a lousy way of making a living. I am too old. I should never have come. It is too far and the loads will kill us. God knows what will happen when the climbing starts, when we begin to starve and the cold weather comes.' Such thoughts were to become repetitive, especially on waking in the mornings. I *had* to shake them off.

For four hours, blowing snow precluded any movement. Within fifty feet of our tent we knew of at least one major crevasse and we needed visibility to escape to safer ground.

Every half-hour one of us squinted through the flap until, at midday, conditions improved due to the sun's position rather than any lessening of the wind. From some three yards away it was now posible to detect a major open crevasse by the faint difference between light blue and blue-white when seen through sun goggles.

Since we had started out four hours late we needed to finish the day that much later. A chance to make up the miles came in the evening when the wind boxed the compass and settled briefly as a northerly and gusting sea breeze.

Unpacking the wind sails, we clipped them to our harnesses and, for the first time, *sailed south*. The experience was wonderful but sadly short-lived for, although we were both experienced skiers – if such a qualification can ever apply to an Englishman – the combination of violent gusts and the brutal weight of the sledges made balance all but impossible.

After a hectic ten minutes of being dragged over ice ridges, crossing ski-tips and being struck in the back by the sledge, I had managed a six hundred-feet dash without a fall. Silently jubilant at the thought that I was becoming an adept, I suddenly spotted a blueish shadow some forty feet ahead.

I smashed my gloved fist onto the Velcro strip which served as a sail-collapsing release. Nothing happened and a violent gust pulled me forward. Twenty feet ahead, I could now see an ice-bulge five feet high, beyond which the far lip of a crevasse was just visible.

70

I threw myself down and screamed a warning at Mike who was close behind me. My sail collapsed ahead of me and disappeared into the crevasse. I saw Mike approach at speed and screamed again. He could see very little and, having watched me fall many times in the past half-hour, decided to cut between me and the ice-bulge if he could. He spotted the danger too late and a further gust tore at his sail.

I watched him skim over the bulge as though on the ramp of a ski-jump. For an instant he was flying through thin air with his sledge, an aerial torpedo, just behind and fastened to his body harness by its two alloy tow-bars.

Then he dropped out of sight and a sickening series of dull thuds was followed by silence.

Covered by snow, I struggled to unfasten my harness, skis, sticks and goggles. Appalling thoughts crowded my mind: chiefly how I would explain Mike's death to his wife and mother.

I called, but there was no reply. If Mike had fallen less than sixty feet, the length of our rope, I might manage to pull him out. Luckily I was carrying the rope at the time. Due to the weight problem, we only carried one rope between us.

I realised that, even if Mike had somehow survived the impact of the fall, the deadweight of his captive sledge dropping onto him from above could cause crushing injuries.

A muffled cry cut short my worries. 'I'm okay' was all I heard, but it was enough.

Unroped and with caution, I crawled to the top of the ice-bulge and saw Mike's head some twenty feet below. He had landed on a ledge below which the fissure fell away to hidden depths. Somehow his sledge, striking the far crevasse wall with great force, had missed Mike by a whisker, but the alloy traces were buckled like matchwood and the sledge itself was obviously damaged.

With great care Mike removed his harness and climbed

upwards to a ramp of blown snow that ran from his ledge to within six feet of the crevasse lip.

I threw him one end of the rope and, item by item, hauled up his sledge contents, the sledge and finally Mike himself. Miraculously, he was uninjured. He attributed his luck to the uplifting gust that had dragged his sledge into an aerial trajectory which had prevented it landing on him.

Damage to the sledge did not seem too serious. The prow was buckled and various long splits had opened up in the fibreglass body, but none big enough to affect the critical aerodynamics of its underbelly and runners.

Before continuing we drank tea from our one good vacuum flask. The day was long for the ice-shelf had begun to rise slowly inland and many ripples of recently formed drifts slowed our progress to a crawl.

When we stopped to camp at midnight our relief at Mike's lucky escape was dampened by the discovery that the bottle which we had initially screwed to the cooker-head in Patriot Hills seemed to have damaged the hardened plastic thread which normally mated easily with the female alloy thread of all our standard bottles, giving a tight seal against possible leakage. The cooker would not function if pressure, pumped into the bottle, forced fuel or vaporised fuel to leak out at the faulty seal. An explosion or fire could follow if any attempt were made to light the cooker in this state.

Since all our food must be soaked to rehydrate and make it edible, fuel was needed to melt snow and boil water. Without a cooker the expedition would come to an abrupt halt and, without a tight seal every time we mated a new bottle to the cooker-head, we were bereft of any heat source for cooking. No matter how simple the route ahead might turn out to be, we would stand *no* chance without a cooker in this hostile land.

Distinctly worried, I reached into the spare cooker bag which travelled on my sledge and handed the spare cooker-head to Mike.

72

There was silence in the tent as he tried out this second and last cooker. Would it mate with any of the bottles? Was this the end of the expedition? Was there any innovative repair we could apply? After half an hour of futile attempts which further burred the plastic cooker threads, there was no doubt left in our minds.

Since the second cooker also failed to mate with any given bottle it was obviously not a simple matter of chance damage to the original cooker's threads. For some unknown reason the 1992 issue of fuel bottles, although from the same manufacturers and designed for the same cookers that we had used on four previous journeys, would *not* fit our cookers.

I squirmed mentally as the full realisation of our predicament sank in. We would not last long without a means of melting snow. The only answer, unless we could find a way around the problem, was evacuation. I could imagine the reaction of our sponsors on hearing the sole reason for our withdrawal a few miles from the coast.

I should, of course, have tested *every* bottle thread back in London as soon as I took delivery of them. I had wrongly assumed that what had worked well in the past would again be correct so I had failed to double-check: a potentially fatal mistake.

'Maybe the special winter washers would form a seal,' I suggested, 'I packed three of them.'

These were special silicone rings which remained malleable at −60°c. We did not expect such temperatures but, since they were as light as feathers, I had brought a few for safety.

They were too soft. The vapour still escaped. 'There are other standard washers in the cooker spares,' Mike mused, 'perhaps, if I use two instead of one, the threads might mate better.'

It was not the ideal answer but, with great care and patience, it worked. Whether the vulnerable cooker thread would burr

73

further under pressures for which it was not designed, only time would tell.

Only when certain there was no vapour leak did Mike apply a match. Welcome heat seeped into the tent but, from now on, however far south we might manage to struggle, our fate would depend on the strength of a few millimetres of plastic threading.

For three days foul weather closed in on the ice-shelf. Exposed skin was frost-nipped. Crotch-rot developed on the inside of our thighs and I suffered a resurgence of haemorrhoids despite the deep injections in London. My back and shoulders continued to complain through the long hours.

Harnesses, skis and skins needed frequent repairs but the repair materials were not limitless. Like everything else, they had been cut down to the bare minimum.

Sixty-knot winds and blowing snow created sloughs, soft and deep, through which we forced the sledges at snail's pace. I regretted my decision to follow the straight line up the ice-shelf. I should have chosen the slightly longer but safer Berkner Island route.

Attempts to close again with the island were pointless for the next three or four days, due to an embayment called McCarthy Inlet which lay somewhere to our immediate west and ate into the island like the mark of some giant's bite.

On Friday 13 November, I began to aim west of south but a rash of great holes kept us out on the shelf.

Mike: 'The crevasses seem to be everywhere' . . . 'Today I fell through. It was a vertical-sided chasm. My ski was pressed against one side. My arm and shoulder on the other. I could see no bottom at all, just blue-grey going to black.'

From time to time we were sufficiently scared by near-escapes to fix safety ropes to our waists, but this was a last resort since the rear person is forever treading on the rope, which jerks the navigator off-balance and provides yet another

74

general embuggeration factor at a time when tolerance levels are low.

My crotch-rot reached the stage where both scrotum and inner thighs were raw and uncomfortable despite the daily application of Canesten powder. My cotton boxer shorts (which I wore under a pair of thin wick-away long johns and some Army baggy cotton trousers) were continually rucking up and exacerbating the raw patches.

I buried the pants, my only pair, and the crotch-rot did in due course begin to get better. But the remaining two protective layers of underclothing were not enough even at sea level and, with the sharp winds off Berkner, my private parts were nipped and swelled up. When I mentioned this to Mike, it turned out that he was having the same problem only worse, with a blistered end. He was circumcised and therefore, in effect, had one less layer of insulation. I made a note of this factor in terms of selecting future candidates for polar expeditions.

Fifteen miles above us, as was first discovered by the British Antarctic Survey nine years before, a hole in the ozone layer opened up at this time of the year (at its worst in November) and allowed dangerous levels of ultraviolet rays to descend unfiltered to Antarctica and southerly lands like Australasia and Patagonia.

Every year the hole grows bigger and more animals, including humans, suffer the resulting cancers, blindness and weakened immune systems. In Australia and New Zealand malignant melanomas have taken over from other cancers and heart disease as man's chief killers. In Patagonia, where sheep outnumber humans, whole flocks are going blind.

Since we were travelling directly under the ozone hole's epicentre at the worst time of the year, it made sense to cover our skin. But we needed to breathe without fogging our goggles, so the sun shone day after day on our lips and noses.

Perhaps Mike protected himself the better with sun-cream

75

or merely manhauled in a more hunched position, shading his face. Whatever the reason, my lips deteriorated more rapidly from burns and my nose swelled into a bulbous blister.

When we scooped our evening meal from the communal cook-pot, my spoon would invariably contain dribbles of the blood which welled out of the deep cracks in my blistered lips.

The scabs always grew together ovenight and, when I woke, the act of tearing my lips apart (in order to speak and drink) invariably opened up all the raw places. Breakfast consisted of porridge oats in a gravy of blood. Mike gave me three different lip balms but none of them seemed to help the deep ultra-violet burns.

The muscles of our lower limbs, stomachs and those parts of our backs involved with the haulage hurt less by the end of the first week's work. They were accustoming themselves to their endlessly repeated tasks and, since at this stage we were still well muscled, we both began to haul with less frequent halts along the way. Nonetheless the bad weather, the deep drifts and above all the sheer weight of the loads sat heavily on our thoughts.

Mike wrote: 'I must admit it was only pride that stopped me from saying, "Let's make it a short day." That and the thought that short days can only lead to failure.'

Our minds churned over against the inescapable fact that our loads were too heavy and we were progressing too slowly. Despite no rest days, no halts for bad weather and a mere ten minutes rest daily for Thermos stops, our eight or nine hours per day were still averaging under ten miles.

At this rate our crossing would take 120 days. Yet our rations would only last a hundred days, unless we cut down our food early on. Mike was firmly against this. Nutrition was after all *his* expertise and, having long ago asked him to take charge of all matters relating to food, I wished to follow his advice on this key point. He estimated that, if we had brought food worth 5,500 calories per man per day (we actually had

5,200 calories), we would lose thirty pounds in body weight over 100 days: a serious loss but not catastrophic.

'The more we eat, the more weight we lose off the sledges,' Mike was adamant. 'Our bodies must have all the nutrition they can get if we are to make it even as far as the Pole. Better to cut down to half-rations at the end, not at the beginning.'

I let the matter rest and turned to other possible items to eliminate. After the evening meal I made up my mind.

'Mike, I'm chucking my duvet. I have hardly worn it all week. We work so hard we will keep warm even when winter comes.'

He nodded. We both knew it was a big decision. The weather was now warm – in polar, not European, terms – and we were still close to sea-level with some effect from the comparative warmth of the Southern Ocean.

Maybe we would have second thoughts later. But there would be no later if we could not get a move on *now*. Next morning we buried the two down-filled jackets along with the empty ration packs. From now on our only clothing would be the light, mainly cotton garments that were just enough to protect us in the current coastal conditions.

In retrospect I would sorely regret the decision, but it is easy to be wise with hindsight.

Chapter Five

'We master our minutes, or become
slaves to them; we use them, or they use
us.'

William A. Ward

We entered a zone of great instability.

Any chance of seeing the hidden holes was lessened by frequent misting up of my goggles due to breathing problems. My normal mouth cover arrangements had rubbed against the daily-renewed scabs on my lip so I had modified my face-mask. This worked well for the lip sores but channelled my breath under parts of the mask and goggles. Both my cheeks and eyelids were heavily pouched with body liquids, especially in the mornings. This further impaired my vision. Mike was not certain what caused our faces to puff up in this manner. There was nothing we could do to prevent it.

The prevailing winds came from the south-east and blistered my left ear and nostril despite the protection of two cotton face masks. I had sewn patches of Gortex windproof material onto the outer mask in the relevant places and now congratulated myself on reducing the number of daily discomforts.

I nursed complex thoughts about Mike's equivalent list of increasing ailments. On the one hand I dreaded any reason for the least delay and was well aware that a debilitating injury to Mike could hinder or even halt the expedition. But an unpleasant voice kept surfacing during those endless hours and telling me how good it would be to stop the undeniable nastiness of this journey. If Mike broke a leg or merely twisted an ankle we would have to stop and, the voice continued, the 'blame' would be his.

Mike nurtured exactly the same thought processes, with the additional idea that a severe injury to his own body would create the need to call off all our sufferings. Without the taint of 'giving in'. That night he wrote: 'My feet are very soggy and sore; the blisters a horrible sight.'

Throughout the morning of the eighth day we moved with our umbilical safety-line in place, for the mists cut down visibility and the crevasses were both large and frequent. By good luck our zig-zag route through this half-hidden mine-field took us slowly in the desired direction, closer to the imagined safety of Berkner Island.

Somewhere to the south-east of Roberts Inlet the wind changed to a north-westerly breeze and, despite the earlier unfortunate results, we again clipped the sails to our harnesses. The fog cleared suddenly and, for fifteen happy minutes, I forgot the toil and my various hurts. Now we could see the outline of the island to the west, much closer than I had thought, possibly only a mile away had we been able to travel in straight lines.

The wind currents curled about the contours of Berkner Island, making it difficult it for us to stay close together. Intense concentration was needed to dodge weak-looking crevasse bridges and to avoid being tripped by sastrugi. Since the breeze was weak and fitful we moved at a snail's pace – but even that was an improvement on manhauling.

A thunderous roar sounded through my face-mask. I glanced right and saw that Mike was not in trouble. I must have imagined the noise. But a minute later my heart missed a beat as the rumble of some great unseen disturbance took several seconds to die away.

I collapsed the sail and came to a halt, listening intently. Within the space of two minutes I found myself flinching to the thunder of three further explosions. I felt deep vibrations as though the source of each sound was right beneath my feet. I wanted to warn Mike but he would never hear me and anyway there was, as far as I could see, no specific danger to avoid. I suspected avalanches somewhere in the vicinity, because of the noise, yet I could see no features liable to avalanche. It was much like hearing sonic booms with no evidence of aircraft.

Mike must have heard or sensed something for I saw that he had now also halted and packed away his sail. I moved across and was close behind him when a cloud of snow dust rose immediately to his front and, simultaneously, the thunderclap of another 'avalanche' reverberated through the ice-shelf.

The real source of the phenomenon was now frighteningly clear. This whole region of the ice-shelf had entered a hyper-active phase, causing hitherto 'safe' snow bridges to collapse into the great crevasses that laced the entire feature. It was by terrible bad luck that we were in such a place at such a time.

No amount of experience or ice-lore could keep us out of trouble. The gaping hole some ten paces ahead of Mike was forty-five feet wide by 120 feet in length and lay directly across his intended path. In another minute he and his sledge would have disappeared along with several tons of plunging snow bridge.

All around us renewed rumbles announced further cratering. The sensation was memorably frightening. We must escape at once to a safer area. But, where *was* safer? Only the looming bulk of Berkner Island offered certain stability. We roped up with nervous fingers, fearing that at any moment the snow beneath us would open up and drop us hundreds of feet.

The surface shook and reverberated again and again. Puffs of snow dust rose into the air. The feeling was similar to closing on enemy troops when under mortar fire. As each new crump exploded at random, the fear increased that the next would have your name on it.

Mike's comment that evening was brief: 'Frightening stuff and not compatible with my promise to Thea that I will survive.'

The nylon rope between us was sixty feet in length. We moved as fast as the sledges and the wings of fear allowed. Time stood still.

I came to an abrupt halt as a wave of cold air rushed past, accompanied by the loudest and closest of the explosions. I ducked, for the all-engulfing sound seemed to pass both overhead *and* underfoot.

Immediately *between* Mike and me an immense crater appeared. One moment the ice-shelf ahead was solid and white. The next a maw like the mouth of the Underworld, steaming gently with snow vapour, lay across our ski track and wide enough to swallow a double-decker bus. The roaring echoes of imploding snow cascading into the bowels of the ice-shelf returned in successive waves, like shore-ripples from an undersea volcano.

Although a cold wind scoured the ice-sheet, I sweated with fear. The next hour was a nightmare of apprehension; *nowhere* was safe. Only pure luck enabled us to escape from this volatile zone.

Late that night we came at last to the ice-foot of Berkner Island and camped, with a luxurious feeling of safety, on the narrow causeway which, wrongly or rightly, we felt to be clear of crevassing.

A week into our journey we had already pulled seventy-three southerly miles. Another 1,627 miles to go. To *think* in terms of travelling all the way to the Pole, never mind beyond it, was foolish, so I divided my map of the continent into geographical sections and determined under no circumstances to contemplate a single mile beyond the current 'section'.

82

My first leg ended at an unnamed inlet where it seemed sensible to leave the comparative shelter of the island and head south-east on a magnetic bearing for the exact point on the coastline of Antarctica which Charles Swithinbank had originally recommended. We should abandon Berkner Island at 80° south in some four days' time, to begin the ice-shelf crossing. With the self-imposed blinkers of this 'sectioning of the whole' method, I hoped to be able to cope mentally with the appalling distances ahead.

On the ninth day the ice-shelf beside the island showed signs of climbing towards the interior. There were no spot heights on my local chart, and my small-scale map of Antarctica showed only that we were about to enter the largest crevasse field on the Filchner Ice-Shelf, a disturbed area of some fifty square miles which appeared to collide, on its western boundary, with the very edge of Berkner Island.

Mike agreed that we *seemed* to be climbing but maintained that the undulating series of rising steppes, which I could *see* through the wafting mists, were in reality only an illusion caused by the heavy loads and mirage effects.

Fortunately, the deep drifts of the ice-shelf did not extend to the island's wind-scoured flanks so the going was easier than at any time since the firm coastal strip. Temperatures of around −15°C were not low enough to coarsen the surface and Mike, when navigating, set a pace that seemed to me as the day went by increasingly and unnecessarily fast.

I resolved not to comment and at first found no difficulty in keeping hard on his heels. My shoulder blades and lower back screamed at me but the old competitive urge came back. Why let this guy steam ahead? For almost twenty years now I had pulled sledges, in all conditions, faster than any colleague of any age, and for the past six years I had out-pulled Mike, day after day, in even the worst of Arctic conditions.

I talked persuasively to myself in this vein but all the time Mike's small but powerful legs pulled on piston-like and I began to realise it was self-defeating for me to keep up such a pace. Quite why I should be experiencing this problem for the first time was unclear. Perhaps I was having an off-day. Perhaps Mike was not in fact going particularly fast at all, indeed, with such great loads, the term 'fast' was ridiculous.

Then, at the end of the seventh hour, as I took over for the final hour's stint up front, Mike smiled and said, 'This is wonderful. The surface is great. I cannot remember ever having pulled better.'

I said nothing and, out of misplaced pride, hauled hard, despite non-stop complaints from my back, until the last minute. As I halted by my chosen tent site, I glanced back expecting and hoping to find a reasonable gap behind me. I needed to prove to myself that I could still leave Mike way behind as in the past. But he had remained close behind me. That night he was quietly elated, even his blisters forgotten.

I slept badly. I felt I should restrain Mike, remind him that the very key to long hard journeys on foot must be to conserve energy from the first day.

Amundsen, the greatest polar traveller of the century, was the keenest believer in pacing yourself. Huntford summed this up in his biography of the Norwegian:

> The Eskimo did not hurry. His whole being rebelled at over-taxing his strength. There is a proper pace for working and it must be respected. To an outsider it may appear as an incomprehensible inertia but to those who understand the climate it is common sense.
>
> Amundsen thus learned a cardinal rule of polar travel: not to exceed what the body and spirit of man (or dog) could comfortably bear. Conservation of energy also leaves resources which can be drawn upon in an emergency.

More recently Will Steger, crossing Antarctica with dogs in 1990, wrote:

> Establishing a steady rhythm is essential. I thought a lot
> about pacing prompted by thoughts of Reinhold Messner
> who will soon attempt to ski and manhaul across Antarctica.
> While he is perhaps the world's best climber, I am curious
> how he will adjust to having to pace himself over what will
> be a one-hundred-plus-day march. Because this kind of
> travel demands a steady rhythm, he faces the possibility of
> burning himself out. I wonder if he knows his own limits.

These were my very thoughts about Mike. He was as strong a man as any I had travelled with. In particular his lower limbs were unusually powerful. In leg-strength tests monitored by Research Establishment scientists, two months before, Mike had proved far superior to me in general aerobic fitness and in leg power.

Only two years previously, just prior to our Siberian journey, the reverse had been true. Despite training more consistently and for longer hours during the interim years I had for some reason achieved far lower results in 1992. Two years before, the scientists had described my physiological measurements as those of 'a top-flight athlete'.

At thirty-nine Mike was in his prime. In Siberia, when he was thirty-six and I was forty-seven, I had no difficulty keeping well ahead as in previous years. So, at that stage, his eleven-year advantage made no difference. Something must have happened since. I began to suspect the inescapable effects of the ageing process.

Just as my eyes first turned short-sighted at forty-seven, I believe that, at that same age, my body began to deteriorate markedly. I could no longer happily run a daily marathon (which is what we were now doing in terms of energy expenditure), week after week, without rest and with ever-dwindling calorific replacement.

Morbid pondering of these hard facts during the endless hours of struggle over the ice-shelf led me to accept two principles. Firstly, I had made a serious mistake in attempting

85

a journey of such physical hardship at my age. Secondly, since there was no point in 'crying over spilled milk' I must make every effort from now on to conserve my energy by adapting a 'polar plod', which would use up minimal energy and preserve what body strength I had for the many hundreds of hours and miles which lay ahead.

At first I resolved to say nothing of this to Mike in the hope that he would realise his own need for long-term energy conservation. And the less said between individuals under extreme stress the better. Especially when the matter is likely to prove contentious.

By the evening Mike's energetic pace was naturally taking its toll. He wrote: 'Each day is a battle not to make some excuse to stop early.'

My own diary notes were not effusive:

'Bad visibility all day but a faint outline of crevasse shadows halfway up the island's flanks gives us enough direction. Agony from shoulder blades and hips. Bottom lip now like raw blubber. Crotch bad and lower back twinges. M. cooked excellent spaghetti. His willy is frostbitten and blistered.'

I dreaded every tenth day particularly, for Mike became Doctor Stroud or, his nickname from earlier days, Doctor Shroud. For reasons best known to himself, his most active 'protein'-sampling days were in multiples of ten. The only camp-stops that I did *not* greet with total end-of-the-day relief were these blood-sucking days when he would unpack his nasty bag of hypodermics and phials.

The urine samples which he took daily were no problem except when associated with intakes of special 'heavy' water (which cost £400 per gulp). In cold weather, the heavy-water twenty-four-hour urine collections were to lead to further frostbitten privates, but they were never as bad as the blood-sucking.

Since before I can remember I have fainted at the sight of

my own or anybody else's blood. The scientists at Mike's Research Establishment made jokes about my fainting each time I visited but, in England, I had no strong objection to losing a few pints of blood. Out on the ice things were different or, if in fact they were not, I certainly *thought* they were, on the grounds that I needed *every* drip of blood for energy.

To date I had kept to myself my inner grumbles and cursing at Doctor Shroud's blood removing habits. His dedication to his research was undeniable and he did try to keep the procedure as painless as possible. Unfortunately, the locating and piercing of veins in a cramped, cold tent was less easy than in a surgery, and the results tended to be a touch amateurish.

I normally lay down in readiness for fainting and Mike would then place my forearm over the cook-box. On many an occasion, with my hand pressed against my forehead and my eyes clenched shut, I listened to him curse as the blood refused to flow up the needle and he had to insert it elsewhere.

He then had to help me stab *his* selected vein and try to draw *steadily* on the hypodermic's plunger. To do this without looking was impossible. I know this because I tried it and Mike's arm ended up like a pin-cushion.

When the various glass phials were eventually filled with dark blood and correctly labelled, they were secured to the roof of the tent along with items of damp clothing. It was all too easy to reach for a sock and detach the blood phials which would then drop into the simmering stew on the cook-box below. Once the anti-coagulant in the blood had separated and the red cells settled, Mike would suck out a few millimetres of white cells (plasma) with a syringe and discard the rest.

Mike's saliva tests were no problem although, because some were conducted on the move, it could be awkward trying to project spittle from a dry mouth with bloody lips, and an iced-up face mask, into a tiny plastic phial. Much of the saliva was destined for a specialist researcher in Archangel.

By far the worst of the Shroud tests was the muscle biopsy carried out by two doctors who would appear at the Research Establishment in sombre suits and carrying their instruments of torture in black attaché cases. I had once described them as the 'Nottingham KGB' to a journalist, who then quoted me. I feared revenge and, during their visit immediately before we left for Antarctica, they did manage to perfect a technique which caused exquisite pain. Lest it be felt that I am exaggerating, I should stress that Mike found the experience equally unpleasant and *two* of his hardened staff nurses fainted whilst watching the biopsies being performed on us.

A double needle is used to suck out a portion of muscle from deep within the thigh. The outer needle looks similar to a biro and, on first glimpsing it, I pleaded with the assistant to anaesthetise me or at least give me painkillers. But no, that would not be possible as the state of the muscle might be affected.

The thought that the whole nauseous operation was to be repeated on our return from Antarctica was not something I relished.

Mike admitted that his department was finding it difficult to recruit enough Army volunteers for muscle biopsies, but they were hoping to offer £50 rewards to victims in the near future. He assured me that I would *not* be eligible.

Doctor David Drewry, Director of the British Antarctic Survey, had given his official support to our research work as had Doctor John Heap, Director of the Scott Polar Research Institute, who had commented to the press, 'It is virtually impossible to get people in laboratory conditions to go to the limit. If you ask the average person with an average metabolic rate to spend one hundred days on a treadmill with limited food, they simply won't do it.'

Our daily diet was 57% fat, which was vastly in excess of normal recommended levels. Scientists at the University of Surrey were studying the effects of such a diet as part of wider research into the role of dietary fats in diabetes and heart diseases. By monitoring the deterioration of our bodies they hoped to gain clues as to how exercise can influence the way people metabolise fat.

On the twelfth day I took a bearing away from Berkner Island and heading for the actual coastline of Antarctica at a point fourteen miles west of the Recovery Glacier.

Once again I forced myself not to think of anywhere beyond this landing-point, the true start-point for our continental crossing attempt. This journey over the eighty-six-mile width of the Support Force Glacier would probably take from eight to ten days, assuming I had planned the crossing sufficiently far south to avoid the Filchner's worst crevasse zones.

For two days the surface remained excellent and the temptation to pull at maximum output while the going was good was hard to resist. Mike did not resist. He went hard and fast whenever up front, and foolishly I matched his pace rather than allow a gap to grow between us.

I was increasingly disturbed by finding, at each day's end, that I was tired and light-headed. This had never happened before and I felt deeply concerned.

In every direction the ice-shelf stretched to the horizon as an infinite carpet of whiteness, and as we walked it was entirely uninspiring and no use at all in warding off the endlessly revolving worries that fed on one another. I thought of previous polar travellers, of *their* age at the time of their longest journeys:

Admiral Peary, first claimant to reach the North Pole, was fifty-two years old, but he used dogs to pull his sledge. Sir Vivian Fuchs, leader of the first crossing of Antarctica, was fifty but he travelled in a vehicle cab.

Professor David, aged fifty, completed a manhaul journey of unprecedented length in 1908, but his leader, Mawson, wrote of his performance: 'The Prof. is certainly a fine example of a man for his age but he is a great drag. He does not pull as much as a younger man.'

Captain Scott was forty-four when, in 1912, he led the expedition that killed him and all of his team. Unlike Professor David he was less than forty-seven, the age I believe at which most fit men will pass their peak.

Will Steger, Jean-Louis Étienne and Reinhold Messner were all forty-five during their 1990 supported crossings of Antarctica. Shackleton, by the time he was even Mike's age, thirty-nine, was saying, 'I feel much older and a bit weary but perhaps the Antarctic will make me young again.'

Shackleton's initial specification for choosing polar colleagues was: 'A man between the age of twenty-nine and thirty-five would be most suitable.' By the time he was himself thirty-five he would say to companions, 'It's the old dog for the road, every time.' One of his favourite manhauling dirges, from Tennyson's 'Ulysses' ran: 'Tho we are not now that strength which in the old days moved earth and heaven, that which we are, we are . . . made weak by time and fate.'

Mike told me whilst lancing my foot: 'To be attempting this journey while you're approaching fifty is quite extraordinary.' This served to make me think my body might be on the verge of breaking up, of suddenly yielding to reality. I remembered the words of Doctor Phillip Law, head of Australia's Antarctic Services, when selecting men for Antarctica: 'Our standards of fitness are very high. It is unusual for a man past forty years to possess the necessary physical drive and energy we require.'

Like Shackleton I seemed to be growing utterly preoccupied by the ageing process. I attempted to shake off the obsession but this was no place to break free of the nightmares loose in your skull. All I could see ahead was the greatest void on earth. Be it grey with fog, or blinding from the glare, it yielded nothing at all upon which to fix my gaze and concentrate, nothing to take my mind off the festering broth of my thoughts. Each of them tumbled about as in a washing machine with no stop-switch; the slightest niggle soon achieved obsession rating and bodily sores screamed their presence through every long and toilsome day. I swore silently when Mike changed gear and I was forced by pride to abandon the rhythm of my polar plod.

I had always believed that my bigger, heavier frame was a bonus. This did not hold true of Charlie Burton, with whom I had manhauled many miles in the Arctic, for he was larger and heavier, yet much slower. But it was, nonetheless, a myth that I had happily nursed through the years.

Now I saw things differently. I *was* bigger and heavier but not as *strong* as Mike. How should that affect our relative progress? Again I thought back to previous journeys both recent and long past.

Bowers, who died with Scott, was unusually small with powerful legs. His strength lasted longer even than Scott's, although for much of their fateful journey only he had travelled without skis. Their companion Evans died first. In the words of Scott's biographer Huntford, 'Biggest and heaviest of the party, Evans nonetheless had to make do with the same rations as the others. He was therefore starving more, deficiencies were accelerated and his condition grew proportionately worse. Everyone was thinning but Evans most of all.'

Lennard Bickel wrote of Douglas Mawson: 'He was bigger than both his companions with a larger skin area; heat loss was greater and heat was body energy generated by food – and they meticulously all had the same amount of food.'

In 1990 Messner, far smaller than his partner Fuchs, sped miles ahead and complained bitterly as hour after hour he would wait for his larger companion, Germany's top polar traveller, to catch up.

Likewise, five years earlier, on their manhaul journey to the South Pole, that strongest and beefiest of individuals, Robert

Swan, was constantly out-performed by the diminutive Roger Mear.

I could think of no single example that, through precedent, might help my morale.

Self-pity is not an attractive trait and I do not remember indulging in it on previous occasions. At this stage I said nothing to Mike, but there were many hundreds of miles ahead of us and the worst of it by far was yet to come, including the 11,000-foot climb described by Charles Swithinbank as bone-crushing toil.

Chapter Six

'The climb that never ends is like a
penance out of purgatory. Frustration,
fury, self-pity follow in its wake. This
intensified the conflict and stress that
Shackleton and his companions were
now undergoing. Manhauling was the
crux.'

Roland Huntford

The days of whiteness floated by. To move eleven miles a day
was my objective. No amount of discomfort must impede this
short-term aim or the overall goal would fade from our grasp.

However slow my polar plod, we could achieve the daily
aim if we kept up our daily hours of march, but to halt and
camp *early* for any reason would be fatal.

Many training advisers and Special Forces instructors advise
allowing for rest days or at least rest periods on long (over ten-
day) forced marches. Without periods of recuperation, they
argue, even the fittest and toughest will 'fall by the wayside'.
I agreed to some extent with the sense of this reasoning but
the simple mathematics of the Herculean task in which Mike
and I had each wilfully involved ourselves simply did not
allow for *any* rest beyond the eight hours set aside for sleep.
For that reason I had to try to stop either of us giving in to the
urge to halt early or remain tent-bound in blizzards or white-
outs.

The temptation was enormous and, as our condition inexor-
ably deteriorated, so the desire to give up, or at least to have a
brief rest, became all-pervasive. I could and did conduct an
on-going struggle within myself and I am sure Mike experienced the same.

Real potential for trouble would exist if and when one of us began to cave in but the other resisted. This had never been an issue during our Arctic travels but then far lesser factors of time, distance and weight were involved.

The first clouds began to gather between us as we crept across the ice-shelf and before we even reached the Atlantic coast of Antarctica.

A blizzard swept the ice-shelf and we woke to find the tent poles straining to the awesome blast of a katabatic windstorm. Blown snow, gusting to sixty or seventy knots, produced total white-out. In an area where there were known to be no crevasses, travel might well have been possible if not sensible but, on this heavily fissured glacier, I was prepared to accept Mike's obvious reluctance to travel as commonsense. We agreed to keep checking visibility conditions and to remain tent-bound until there was some improvement. This was to be the only time we accepted defeat by the weather and I have wondered ever since whether we could have, in fact, made some mileage if only we had taken the bit between our teeth.

The wind roar made us lean closer in order to hear each other speak. I remembered Mike's urging me, back in London, to switch from this circular geodetic tent to a more aerodynamic tunnel design with less danger of broken poles – and worse.

I had great confidence in our little home but I found myself thinking nonetheless of other people's tales of Antarctic katabatic storms. A British Antarctic Survey group had died of exposure when their pyramid design tent had been torn away; and an ex-BAS friend, Geoff Somers, had commented during his 1990 dog-crossing of Antarctica, 'These are frightening days. I'm never sure if my tent will still be in place in one or two seconds' time. Occasionally the thought petrifies me but it's like being a passenger in an airplane – you have no control.'

And as I considered the changing weather, I thought of Scott's men, in 1903, sheltered on the *Discovery* from a blizzard: 'If a man ventured as far as the deck he gasped for breath and

94

half-suffocated with ears, eyes and nose stuffed with snow. Had he gone mere yards from the ship, he could scarcely have survived. A bitch who gave birth to a litter of puppies in the afterdeck was found with her tongue torn out; it had frozen to the feeding tin.'

Ten years later, on Mawson's expedition, 'It demanded physical steel, iron nerve, to step out from shelter into a ninety-mile (eighty-knot) gale, blowing cold at around twenty degrees below freezing. Sometimes men stood at forty-five degrees, leaning into the steady gale, to cut the ice for melting . . . Throughout May the wind normally blew around ninety-five miles per hour and men attending the wind recorders suffered frostbite . . . On May 25 Mawson examined the instruments and recorded that there had been blasts above two hundred miles an hour.'

We had no recorder so we could only estimate wind speeds as up to fifty or seventy knots.

The day was spent dozing fitfully, and frustration built up inside me until I felt fit to explode. We agreed to eat only some oxtail soup and porridge oats left over from the previous week. That way we would not 'waste' any rations.

When, after eight hours, the storm still raged, I suggested to Mike that we paint a draughts-board onto the lid of our square wooden cooker-box and use Mike's urine sample phials for draughts. Mike designed an excellent board with his sample-marker, felt pen and a ski stick for a ruler. When we moved on to chess, he used full urine-samples for kings, queens and bishops. Red-topped (Stroud) urine-phials differentiated happily from blue-top (Fiennes) phials. As Mike commented, this colour coding was apt, since I was a great supporter of Margaret Thatcher whereas he, to put it mildly, was not. Since I had never properly played chess before, Mike agreed to teach me. I found he was a very good instructor and, for the first time and despite many previous abortive attempts, I began to understand the rules.

When the cooker's fuel bottle ran dry, Mike carefully threaded a new one to the cooker-head, using two makeshift 'O' ring washers as before. The vapour seal appeared to hold the pressure when he gave the plunger a few pumps, so he lit the cooker and began to heat a pot of melted snow water.

Without warning, vapour began to escape through the seals and caught fire. Flames ran over the tent floor and under our sleeping bags.

Flashbacks of previous Arctic tent fires when Geoff Newman and I had narrowly escaped immolation sent me instantly to the door-zipper, diving out into the snow and screaming at Mike to throw the lethal cooker outside. He did so and quickly smothered the flaming tent floor with one of our jackets.

An hour later we had cleaned up the mess, sewn up a few holes in burnt bags, and, after considerable problems, Mike managed to reposition the two vital 'O' rings so that the pressure could not escape. He warned me that, each and every time we needed to change over fuel bottles, we risked a fire and, far worse, the threat of both our cookers' plastic threading no longer mating with any of the bottles. In those conditions we were lucky to have contained the fire. There was no spare tent.

One way of trying to keep warm when sleeping on ice every night is to keep at least half an inch of closed-cell bed matting under the sleeping bag. This we did by unrolling *two* thin karrimats each, one on top of the other, under our bags.

In an effort further to cut down weight, we each agreed to bury one mat and one layer of our double-sleeping bag. This reduced each of our loads by nine pounds but, in the light of our subsequent suffering, was probably a mistake. Both items, many days later, could have served as protective clothing.

In the mornings, on waking, I learnt to lie still and force out the immediate dread that inevitably came with the realisation of where I was and what the day held in store. The physical priority on waking was *not* to open my mouth. This was easy to remember after two early mistakes when I tore my lip scabs off first thing.

The best method was to reach out for my tube of lip salve, some excellent army stuff of Mike's, and smear it onto the lumpy scabs. Then gently to work the tip of my tongue against my lips from inside until they slowly parted with minimal damage to the scabbing that had welded in the night.

Doctor Phillip Law, describing his life's work in Antarctica and relationships in polar bases, wrote, 'Personal habits of others can be intolerable, even the way someone eats, talks or laughs. The weaknesses or mistakes of others also become unbearable and the unfortunate individual is blamed and hated for them.'

Mike and I were well aware of this and tried to watch ourselves for annoying traits. If either of us started to develop such a wart, the other quickly pointed it out. We did not allow resentment to fester if we could help it.

I used my penknife scissors to cut off my eyebrows, moustache and beard soon after we left Berkner Island. This was anti-social. Mike, who was cooking, found bits of hair in the stew and the porridge. After one oblique comment from Mike, I took the hint and conducted future barber operations into a bag on my lap.

The job of repairing our ski-skin lashing points, key to our continued progress, involved much sawing and cutting of the alloy from empty fuel bottles. Since I had to fashion new plates, washers and studs exactly to the size of the broken or lost items, there was a good deal of metal filing to be done. This I also treated with great care lest alloy powder ended up in the soup.

The immediate environs of the ice-shelf were almost certainly a bad weather trap and the sooner we gained distance from the sea the less white-outs we were likely to encounter. There were no local statistics to hand to prove this but we agreed to *attempt* travel the following morning even if conditions were unchanged. I suggested we might even try a twelve-hour day to make up for some of the lost distance. We eventually did manage this despite a bitter wind throughout the day. By the time we camped, Mike's hands, feet and nose were all nipped, and he told me my lips were 'in a dreadful state'.

Whenever the wind boxed to the north we tried to sail but invariably found we were taken too far west and gave up.

On the thirteenth day my crotch was particularly sore, great raw patches chafing with each step. All day we struggled to maintain a bearing of 150° magnetic in order to reach the coast at 39° west, as advised by Charles Swithinbank. Since visibility was poor, we advanced by using the slightest of visual aids as marker, a mere hint of some ghostly shadow glimpsed through the floating gloom had to suffice to maintain even the roughest bearing.

Mike wrote: 'I spent a lot of time in my imagination but the day was still long. However, Ran looks worse than me: he seems bowed by his load.' And: 'My foot is painful. My left shoulder too. I find the days really long and difficult. I often wonder whether this can ever be worth it. Day after day, week after week of nothing. And with it a deep missing of the children and real sadness that Thea is on her own looking after them. I will not do it to her again.' Mike's term for getting lost in his thoughts was 'mind-travelling', a vital form of defence against the negative thoughts which otherwise crowd in.

Cherry-Garrard, on nightmarish Antarctic treks, repeated endless mantras to himself such as: 'Stick it out . . . stick it out . . . stick it out.' A favourite of mine is: '*Always* a little further, Pilgrim, I will go.' Any apt doggerel will do and helps to stave off thoughts of continuing pain or the vast distance ahead, on the principle of self-hypnosis.

Sometimes I would check my watch and find to my disgust that an excellent run of absorbing thoughts had after all only

98

eliminated a few minutes of reality. At other times, to my delight, I would hear a shout from Mike that I should stop, having exceeded my hour up-front whilst lost in some success-ful daydream. All day my only guides to reality were my watch and, if it was visible, the sun.

The mountaineer Chris Bonington wrote: 'During any climb we all have to fight those demons lurking on the mountain itself and those inside our minds. When you are climbing, struggling to reach your goal for that day, everything else must be put aside or your determination might flag, which can be disastrous on a mountain.'

This determined concentration to drive out mental demons, whether by mantras, or Mike's 'mind-travelling', or other such means of controlling the brain, can be difficult for even the strongest of characters.

I once watched the French polar traveller, Jean-Louis Étienne, pull himself through a severe mental struggle at the start of a solo Arctic journey which few other men would have managed. Yet, four years after that, and during the Antarctic dog-crossing which he co-led, his partner Will Steger wrote: 'Jean-Louis sounded extremely defeated and the rest of us were stunned by his negativism. Normally the most optimistic of us, he was at the most defeated I had ever seen him. He was allowing the conditions to beat him down.'

Steger went on to expound his own philosophy. 'Over the years I've learned to keep such pessimism at bay. When I get into a dangerous situation, my mind and my spirit go into a kind of peaceful "over-drive". I don't allow anger or frustration to absorb me. Travel in these conditions is seventy per cent mental.'

Such easy answers become less easy to apply to the mind when the brain is receiving constant pain messages from various parts of the body, which demand that the body stop NOW, not several hundred miles later.

*

We passed the unseen marker of 80° of latitude. 90° seemed a long way away. What helped our individual morale was to notice a fall-off in each other's performance – which often meant the development of some new source of pain – unless, of course, the injury reached the stage where it threatened our daily performance as a unit.

Mike, on the fifteenth day: 'A very long day. Tiring and painful due to blisters. Ran's lips are still awful and he has neck trouble. He is generally in good nick although, for about the first time ever, he actually could not keep up with me during one session. He took this new experience in good grace.'

That night the tent door-zipper broke which, in a land of blizzards and blowing snow which bored its way through the tiniest aperture, was a serious threat. With Mike's help and a good deal of luck, I managed to repair the damaged plastic zipper, using Dentafloss and a curved needle.

Every night we were meant to send our exact position to Morag for onward transmission to the Multiple Sclerosis headquarters. There were two ways of doing this; to switch on a COSPA-Sarsat beacon which sent a coded bleep to RCC Plymouth, a naval listening station, or to obtain and pass on back bearings off three polar-routed satellites. The three dimensional cross-point of these back bearings gave us an accurate position and a reasonable altitude. On my previous crossing of Antarctica, only twelve years earlier, I had to use a heavy theodolite and aneroid barometer to obtain this data.

Mike muttered unhappily. The AA batteries which powered the little Magellan GPS 'satellite-fixer' had gone dead long before we had expected. We possessed minimal spare batteries.

'What about your science gizmos?' I asked Mike. 'Are none of them battery-powered?'

Luckily he located some weighing scales, no bigger than a flattened cricket ball, which he had brought to record our dwindling body weight every tenth day. Mike had proved adept at the precarious art of standing on tiptoe on the little scales. Only if you were able to maintain pressure from the ball of your foot on the exact epicentre of the scales for an entire second would an annoying Japanese jingle issue forth confirming that your weight had been logged. I, to Mike's disgust, was usually incapable of standing hunched up in the tiny tent for long enough before overbalancing. Part of the trouble was the lack of any firm surface underneath the scales. Mike's only hope was that we might find a piece of flat wood at the South Pole. In the meanwhile he was happy to share the scales' batteries with the Magellan.

If the Magellan failed to work for any one of a hundred good reasons, there were few local features to use to identify our position. One could be the point at which we crossed from ice-shelf to the inland ice-sheet if it turned out to be a visible feature. On those days free of mist we could look back and see the faint outline of Berkner Island but, up ahead, there was nothing to indicate a change of scenery.

From time to time the wind boxed and we tried to sail. Invariably we were taken too far west and had to desist. By now we were pulling between nine and ten hours daily and any extra yard away from a direct southerly bearing was anathema to us. To compensate for westerly sail-travel, I kept resetting the compass.

On sunny days we seldom used magnetic bearings, preferring the easier method of sun-and-watch direction finding. But long periods of mist on the ice-shelf kept the compass in frequent use.

I had a tendency to zig-zag along the misty corridor heading south, whereas Mike would veer slowly to the east. The thicker the mist, the more pronounced my zig-zag and Mike's curves. Each of us was on occasion irritated by the other's meanderings.

As the days struggled by and the stress mounted, we faced

increasing tensions between us. We could not ease the pain, the fear, above all the sheer burden of the sledge-loads, by kicking our sledges. We took it out on each other, at first silently, as had been our wont in the Arctic, but then with controlled outbursts 'in public'.

The first open forum was calm enough and consisted of a fairly even discussion about relative pace. We both acknowledged that the pace difference was small, at most three minutes in the hour, so our ability to attain the daily ten-mile yardstick was not affected. Nonetheless it did adversely affect the morale of the man with the slower pace on any given day whilst boosting the morale of the other. We agreed that the obvious answer was to balance the weight of our sledge-loads accordingly.

After only five miles of progress on the seventeenth day Mike's foot blisters became painful and he told me he thought it would be sensible to stop. I said nothing in the interests of diplomacy and we camped four hours early; to my mind a dangerous precedent.

In 1990, during the first and only unsupported manhaul to the South Pole, Robert Swan had asked the field leader Roger Mear that they cut an hour off the day so that he might complete some maintenance to his skis without depleting the precious time for sleep. Mear's response was that any curtailment of hauling hours was 'a precedent we cannot afford'.

Scott's team, with half our weight to haul, travelled for nine and a half hours most days, slept for eight hours, but were still 'so dead tired we could sleep half into the next day'. Scott allowed no curtailment of hours. Nor did Steger but, unlike us, they did have many rest days which usually, and sensibly, coincided with bad weather. Messner and Fuchs rested on every tenth day. Steger wrote: 'The constant wind against our bodies wears us down. I'm desperately looking forward to our next day off which isn't for another two weeks.'

The very fact that there were to be *no* days off on our schedule, and no shortening of hours of travel, was a further mental burden that turned the screws on our fragile relationship. If two saintly monks were to manhaul heavy loads, whilst increasingly deprived of food and subjected to mounting discomforts, *they* might maintain at least an outward show of mutual tolerance. If so, they would be the exception to the rule.

Even though the practice of our gentlemanly ancestors was to acknowledge no soured relations, when writing about their endeavours, there were those who ignored this etiquette. Of Scott's 1911 expedition, Cherry-Garrard wrote: 'We have forgotten how the loss of a biscuit crumb left a sense of injury which lasted for a week; how the greatest friends were so much on one another's nerves that they did not speak for days for fear of quarrelling;' and in Roland Huntford's words, 'Survival in extreme conditions depends on judgement and intuition. Conflict, suppressed or not, disturbs both and is an invitation to disaster. When Shackleton accidentally burned a hole in the tent floor while cooking, Scott erupted with wrath. The two men were wholly incompatible; the strains of the journey made feelings boil over and any triviality was enough to detonate an explosion.'

Scott's colleague, Lieutenant Evans, commenting on other members of the team, said, 'Their normal social relations had been suspended and replaced by a primitive unmannerliness which demonstrated how queer these people become under the influence of prolonged and trying association with each other.'

Even Amundsen, generally held to be the greatest of all polar leaders, fell out with his second-in-command Johansen. In the words of Huntford, a great admirer of Amundsen, 'Johansen flared up and bitterly rebuked Amundsen for his behaviour in becoming separated from his followers. "I don't call it an expedition," declared Johansen. "It's panic."

Then he launched into a tirade against Amundsen's whole leadership.'

Huntford accurately summed up the overall problem: 'The particular risk of polar exploration is the strain of being cooped up for long in isolation. Friction is inevitable. The maddening proximity of a too-familiar face may be a torture in itself. The clash of personality has always been a danger more sinister than climate or terrain.'

More recently, on the Mear/Swan 1985 expedition, Mear wrote, 'We sat in our sleeping bags under the thin fabric of the tent, a microcosm of human pettiness . . . As the cooking ended, the whole dammed-up business, the irritations and resentments, came flooding out. Gareth (Wood) said he hated my presence. He found me arrogant, unbearably moody, rude, ill-mannered, selfish, inconsiderate and totally unsympathetic. Robert (Swan) was merely contradictory and manipulative.'

Matters between Mike and me reached a head of steam on the evening of the eighteenth day. My diary records: 'Excellent surface today. Best yet. The temptation to pull with maximum exertion is great but should be resisted. We must think and pull long-term. We managed eleven miles in nine and a half hours. Loads now four hundred and five pounds each.'

Mike's diary shows his mounting anger. 'Ran found it hard to keep up again and I had to slow down and go frustratingly slow behind him. I was also very unhappy with him because last night he had agreed to tell Morag that Erling Kagge would know our positions since I insisted on that point. Then, this morning, he came up with some patronising crap about "deciding it was against our sponsor's interest" as it might help Kagge pace himself to beat us to the Pole. Personally I think Ran is just too competitive and can't help but see Kagge as the enemy whilst I have changed my mind and think he should have all the help he can get. Anyway, with this "decision" of Ran's I began to be irritated by many things, particularly his being slow, meandering wildly as he leads, his

104

multiple adjustment stops and his stupid way of wearing his harness all loose and moaning about it.'

Mike's diary entry was much in the fashion of time-honoured comments by his predecessors. Shackleton's colleague, Wild, wrote, 'Neither of them have been pulling a damn. If we only had Joyce and Marston here instead of those two grub-scoffing, useless beggars we would have done it easily . . .' and, of his compatriot Marshall, 'he does not pull the weight of his food, the big, hulking, lazy hog'.

Mear wrote of Swan, a far larger, heavier man: 'Robert was surprisingly slow today, many minutes behind at stops. He assures me he is simply holding back. It's not just that, I'm sure, the bravado has diminished, the "huh!" as he pulls from a dead start, and the five minute spurt at the end of the day, have all gone.'

Few individuals can match speeds evenly. Even the two most powerful of men, Messner and Fuchs, had trouble. Messner, of his Antarctic manhaul, wrote: 'We started every stage together but the gap between us was soon measured in kilometres. We were unable to go at a common speed. When Arved was four kilometres behind, I could scarcely see him . . . He was cross about my speed and hated me on and off for my hurrying ahead. I noticed his anger but could not help him . . . We argued more and more and the speed which resulted was for us both a compromise. I finally dictated my anger on tape. I had to get rid of it. I am of the opinion that Arved is physically too weak to make such a hard trip. He can't do more than six hours daily with this weight of sledge.'

On the nineteenth day, unaware of Mike's mounting anger, I was having my own problems caused by a resurgence of shoulder pains. A week earlier I had stuck plasters over the raw sores on my waist and altered my harness so that much of the sledge weight was taken off my shoulders. Now there were new sores along the edges of the plasters, so I was forced to readjust the harness, with inevitable results.

I spent the day fighting the urge not to call a halt. There was no mist, so navigation by body-shadow was easy. Due to shoulder troubles I was not as fussy as I should have been over the directness of my southerly bearing.

Mike stayed a few yards behind me and had obviously worked himself up to a fine state by the sixth hour. At the change-over he was uncharacteristically aggressive and, in turn, I no longer hid my own thoughts as to our pace difference. I told him clearly that I needed to maintain a sensible pace, however flat the terrain on any one day, and I suggested that he was doing himself no long-term good by succumbing to 'surge-urges'.

My diary that night: 'His new-found speed has gone to his head and he finds himself unable to curb his frustration when to him I appear to go slow . . . He must learn to mature or he will spoil a hitherto good working relationship. From now on I will speak my mind too as regards pace.'

Although we had travelled so many polar miles together in harmony over the past six years, I had never forgotten my ancient prejudices based on the adage: 'small Yorkshire spectacles'. In a nutshell I had spent many years on many expeditions following the general rule that a great deal of trouble can be avoided by *never* selecting Yorkshiremen for my teams, because they are dour and nurse grievances, small men because they need to work hard to make themselves seen and heard, and spectacled men because, when their spectacles break, they may become pains in the neck.

Mike was not a spectacled Yorkshireman but he was undeniably short. Before I met him he had spent over a year in Antarctica hoping to become the third man to go with Roger Mear and Robert Swan to the Pole. I had read Mear's book about that journey and would never have even contemplated Mike for one of my journeys had I not met him *prior* to reading the book.

An American naval psychologist based at MacMurdo had

been asked to assess the characters of the expedition team including Mike. Her report, as published in the appendix to *Footsteps of Scott*, ran:

> All five individuals did not function well as a group. Michael Stroud had extremes in his character greater than most of the expedition members. He sees himself as expedient, dominant, forthright and undisciplined. Secondly, and almost equally, he sees himself as enthusiastic, tender-minded, imaginative and experimenting.
>
> Individuals like Mike see themselves as assertive to aggressive, authoritative, competitive and stubborn. People like him disregard rules and feel few obligations. They do not feel group pressure to conform.
>
> In a group his type may slow up group performance and upset group morale by undue fussiness. Being inner-directed and self-motivated, while also imaginatively creative, this sometimes can lead to unrealistic situations accompanied by expressive outburst.

The book had made me aware of a side to Mike that I had not witnessed in the Arctic. 'Mike,' wrote Mear, 'was also angry with me for once again he felt that his ideas had been treated with contempt. I felt isolated, and threatened by Mike in whom I sensed a rising hostility. It seemed to me that he had begun to contradict every decision I made. It is impossible, in this environment, to be guided by reason in all one's decisions and yet, because I have lost faith in Mike's judgement, I am forced to treat all my decisions as infallible.'

In our tent, two hours after his outburst, there was no tension and no sulking. As in the best of marriages, we could speak our minds and hot words could fly without fear of them continuing to smoulder.

He noted that we were not consuming all the daily butter and porridge and he felt that the left-overs which were on his sledge could be buried. I had no objection but still, when we moved on from that camp, Mike was under the impression my load was twenty pounds lighter than his, whilst I was equally convinced that the difference was a mere fifteen pounds. Either way there was a radical change in our relative performances the very next day and, since we were both still carrying not far short of 400 pounds, any slight weight change was not the reason for such a performance shift – rather, it was because the Antarctic coast had passed under our feet some time that morning. At first any uphill gradient was imperceptible but, by the afternoon, each and every heave on the traces required concentrated mental and physical effort.

For quite a while I was fascinated by a shape floating on the glare-blurred horizon to our front, as of something different, and visible a good half-hour before we came upon it. 'Sastrugi,' Mike breathed, for our change-over coincided with our arrival beside a two-foot-high, six-foot-long wall of ice. There was no obvious reason for its presence but memories came rushing back of the great sastrugi fields I had crossed with Charlie and Oliver in 1980. God forbid that Mike and I should meet such obstacles. I sent up a silent but fervent prayer.

There was no way we could shift our current loads through even ten miles of giant sastrugi. In 1980 we crossed some sixty miles of unexplored snowfields on the high plateau where prevailing winds had cut the ice-sheet into a ploughed field. Each furrow was of ice averaging three feet in height, like athletes' hurdles, but set a mere five feet apart. In many places we had progressed only by cutting a path with tree axes.

Because our sledges on that occasion were pulled by two-stroke engine snowmobiles we had eventually won through, but only with great difficulty and delay. That region was well to the east of our present route but Dr Vivian Fuchs, during the first crossing of the continent, had taken his heavy vehicles over sixty miles of sastrugi with ridges up to four feet high and *his* route was not so very far to the east of our own.

'Sastrugi' comes from a Russian word that describes icy

features built from snow. Antarctic winter winds cut these features into the snow-fields, sometimes as sharply defined ridges, often as rounded hummocks, or weirdly convoluted phantasmagoria fit for a Dantesque nightmare.

Fuchs had found fields with 'giant sastrugi four feet high and shaped like torpedoes on pedestals which form an impassable barrier'. On the far side of the continent, Edmund Hillary's group logged 'huge sastrugi five to six feet high'.

You do not *force* a way through such ridges, for the wind has cut them from snow into smooth and slippery ebony, as hard as concrete.

Our first lone sastruga was joined by other solitary outrunners until a great rash of iron-hard furrows lay directly across our route.

My determination to conserve energy could cope with the competitive urge to race Mike (if shackled tortoises can race), but crumbled before my instinctive reaction to *attack* ice obstacles. I knew of no other way to advance when the ice gets nasty. You must attack head-on and with every ounce of gristle at your disposal. There can be *no* holding back. Tightening my harness and stick-straps, I focused on each successive wall of ice and threw energy conservation to the winds.

My various blisters and chafing sores were not helped by this onslaught but there was now an identifiable enemy, not just the endless flat glare of the ice-shelf where the persistent struggle was all in the mind.

Now there was no difficulty following Mike. Indeed, I found it necessary to take pauses every few minutes as he slipped and fell. His legs were stronger but mine were longer. To a great extent this advantage was cut down by the skis – extensions to our legs – which were approximately the same length. When I navigated, Mike could not keep up. I would pull for fifteen or twenty minutes, then wait, so that we were never out of sight.

In addition to the sastrugi, we experienced our first major

slope. I began to appreciate Swithinbank's 'bone-crunching toil'. The work was breathtaking. Even the briefest of halts, with sledge pointing downhill or astride a sastruga, was a bad mistake for, once the load began to slide backwards, skis followed suit and then an undignified tangle of falling body, flailing sticks and more bruises on the sharp-edged ridges.

Towards the end of the day, after eleven hours of uphill hauling, we came to an especially rugged zone of serrated ice and Mike lagged well behind, despite my many pauses for him to catch up.

At the end of the final hour I had the tent up in time for his arrival and knew at once that he was livid. Now that we were openly expressing our concerns Mike let rip. I had surged ahead despite the evil terrain and, worse, I had gone *straight* at the sastrugi instead of taking a sensible, though less direct, route between the worst ice-walls.

It was agreed that we would even out the weights again by Mike's rations being used on consecutive days. So within forty-eight hours we were back to similar weights. Mike continued to believe he was fifteen pounds the heavier and I did not waste breath on arguing the point.

For some reason the often hostile feelings that I nursed towards Mike, whilst on the move, almost invariably evaporated once we were back in the tent. This appeared to apply also to Mike – which saved the journey for both of us from becoming a non-stop nightmare.

We would both wake two or three times a night with an urge for the pee bottle. This was a graduated two-litre container that Mike used to measure our urine output and from which to take nightly samples. Since it was annoying to keep waking and having to struggle out of the sleeping bag, I once tried to use the pee bottle *inside* my bag, having ascertained that Mike was fast asleep. The experiment was a disaster.

110

Unfortunately, the pee bottle was white and prone to get mislaid every time we camped. Its loss would have been a disaster since we would then have had to use an alloy fuel bottle. The rims of the bottles were wide enough in diameter but they were, of course, metal, which could have caused serious embarrassment: I well remembered a dark winter night at a remote Arctic camp when my wife had gone to the outside lavatory, a hut with a bucket and loose plastic seat. The seat had slipped and, since the temperature was well into the minus forties, Ginnie had found her backside frozen to the bucket rim. She rushed back to our hut with a long cold burn down one cheek. I placed her close by the oil heater, clucking with sympathy, but, unfortunately, pushed her too close to the red-hot steel frame. She then received a nasty hot burn on the other cheek. I was not popular.

At about the time we began the climb from the ice-shelf, Doctor Stroud gave me the pee bottle with a severe warning that under no circumstances was I to let a single drop escape during the following twenty-four hours. After three hours of manhauling I was about to add to the bottle's contents when I found the neck blocked with a bung of frozen urine. I screwed the lid as tight as possible and wrapped the bottle in my sleeping bag, after first breaking the bung with my knife and warming the contents with a refill. At the end of the day I discovered the bottle had leaked into my sleeping bag. I noted in my diary that greater love hath no man for the cause of science than that he let pee bottles spill all over his sleeping bag.

Far from being sympathetic Doctor Shroud took blood that same evening and bade me strip down to my underwear so that he could apply skin callipers and tape measure to record my fat loss.

Because he had stacked the measuring tape with the unbelievably sticky ski-skins adhesive, and because the latter had leaked, he discovered, after applying the measure around my waist, that it would only come away by unpeeling it, leaving scales of red glue all over my midriff. He then applied the tape to my neck with the same results.

Every new day was now noted in our diaries as 'the hardest yet'. Not so much because of our accelerating deterioration but because, at that stage, we had not yet realised how quickly we were becoming debilitated and shedding vital pounds in body fat. The conditions that were now of greatest concern were the sastrugi and the ever-steeper gradient.

'Will altitude affect us?' I asked Mike

'No.' He was emphatic. 'At 11,000 feet there should be no more problem than in a high alpine resort. Nothing to affect our performance.'

This surprised me, for both Messner and Steger had experienced debilitating effects from altitude. Nonetheless Mike seemed certain and I had always trusted his medical and mountaineering know-how.

In early December the gradient began to increase in severity. There were times when our skis slipped backwards at every step and the only way upwards was to tack at 45° to the slope, adding a deal of extra distance to the whole. On these interminable, grinding ascents there was little to be done but grit your teeth and force any images of *future* or distance *ahead* out of your thoughts.

Mike wrote: 'Day 26. The fact that the terrain offered no easy sections and we were utterly done in at the end made it the worst yet. If we have any more like it, I'm sure body and soul will crack.'

My diary that day records: 'Vast hills of whiteness always going UP. The Pole is four hundred and sixty miles away. My mind requires strict controlling. Roll on the Thought Police. Must *not* consider enormity of distance and climbs ahead. Mike looks very thin and haggard.'

We passed through a region of rolling grey hills to the east

112

that flanked our bearing and pushed us slightly to the west. This made me a touch uneasy for there was a chance of unmapped mountains and associated chasms if we prematurely trespassed east of the 40° longitude on which I was basing our present route. However, there was no option but to veer east, since the grey hills to our left were far too slippery and steep to ascend or even traverse. I kept close to the foot of this feature, hoping to find a south-leading pass through their midst.

Suddenly a great patchwork of blue ice 'lakes' and 'ponds' straddled our path, everywhere blotched with islets of coarse but unmelted snow.

Once we were on the blue ice there was no ski traction at all. The *only* propulsion method available was our ski-stick points on those rare occasions when we managed to gain purchase without their slipping on the shiny glass surface. More often than not my sledge would lodge itself on a coarse snow patch whilst I was skidding about and falling on the next stretch of ice, much like a spider trying to climb out of a sink. At some point that day the outer side of my right foot, some two inches back from the small toe, was bruised against the inside of the ski-boot.

I hoped to escape from the region of blue-ice before we camped, since the ice was evidence of a katabatic wind channel scouring the foot of these grey hills; not an ideal place to linger, nor one with any flat snow surface into which to drive our alloy tent pegs against a blizzard.

It was not a comfortable night but we were lucky for there was no wind and, after two further slippery hours the next morning, the blue ice gave way to three glorious miles of grey ice over which the sledges rumbled with ease yet the skis gained good traction. This was the stuff dreams are made of. My hauling mantra altered accordingly to Lewis Carroll's : 'O frabjous day! Callooh! Callay!' Such levity was short-lived for the grey ice veered too far south-west and I was forced to take a southerly line where the foothills, in the east, seemed lower than before.

There were a number of obvious faults and crevasse lines but all were well bridged and, in spite of a foot-by-foot struggle to progress up the steepest gradients, we reached the brow of the foothills and a renewed vista of boundless, white wastes, ever climbing to nowhere.

By this time we had climbed above 2,000 feet and, when periods of no wind coincided with a cloudless sky, the sun beat down 'through the ozone hole' and we grew so hot that we stripped to our vests. Sweat dribbled into our eyes. Our unwashed hair and bodies itched and emitted a powerful stench. The sweat-salt stung my crotch sores and the renewed assault from ultra-violet burns further damaged my lips, from which blood and pus leaked into the chin cover of my face-mask.

Our goggles needed constant wiping and, whilst so engaged, I saw a mountain top to the south-west. The charted region of Charles Swithinbank's map ran out close to 82° of latitude, and the last feature marked was an unnamed outpost of the Argentina Range.

For three days this lonely peak moved slowly by to our west, only visible when we emerged from the trough of each successive steppe. Since the rock peak had no name, I dubbed it the Bogman, a nickname I had long given to Mike (Stroud being the epicentre of the boglands in Arthurian England).

The joys of sun and warmth quickly ceded to a twenty-five-knot easterly wind. Mike had circulation troubles in one hand and, due to severe sastrugi patches, found it hard work to keep up.

After twenty-five days we both looked and felt worn out. Overall, if we could somehow keep going, there was still a slim chance of success. We might even reach the Seaquest ship by its departure date, given a long list of favourable ifs and buts.

On just one of the Bogman days we dragged the 400-pound

114

loads up the southern face of a basin-like hollow, some ten miles in radius, and gained 800 feet before camping.

Somewhere, a hundred miles or more to our west and beyond the Argentina, Erling Kagge was hauling his 200-pound sledge towards the Pole. My immediate feelings were of envy. Our own loads would still be in excess of 200 pounds when we reached the Pole. For Kagge, the Pole would mean good food, journey's end and an ANI airlift. For us the Pole would pose a great temptation to yield to our ever-increasing desire to give up. There was no other reason to stop or even pause there. The greatest privations and hazards lay beyond the Pole. Mike said he would like to see inside the polar dome and ask the US doctor there to help with part of our research tests. I was strongly against this and told Mike so.

I found myself treating Kagge as a competitor even though ours could only be described as a race between hare and tortoise with the tortoise aiming to travel twice as far. In the back of my mind the thought kept recurring: 'You never know, he may be injured or his sledge may crack up. Perhaps we could reach the Pole before him.'

Morally, such thoughts were inexcusable. Practically, as with my hours of silent hostility towards Mike when on the move, they were worth their weight in gold by way of occupational therapy.

On 4 December, inching our way up a hillside littered with ice-furrows, we spotted deep scar lines many miles to the south and athwart our compass bearing. They were welcome, as was almost anything different, since they provided a source of wonderment as well as a tangible goal.

There was nothing marked on my map of the area but then, to the best of our knowledge, only satellites had previously viewed this region and they would not have spotted each and every upheaval in the ice surface.

The scars proved to be giant trenches, snow-filled crevasses, some ninety feet wide and two to three miles long. Filled with wind-scoured grey ice and running a mere 20° off due south, they were a welcome distraction.

That night I checked my map, a US Global Navigation and Planning Chart, with care for the symbol of *Area of Disturbed Ice*. A comment – 'Deep crevasses reported 1963' – was noted in a wide area across our route but some 200 miles closer to the Pole. Nothing else was shown for hundreds of miles save the endlessly climbing contour lines.

The ice-sheet at this point was pouring down from the high inland plateau with greater velocity than further north. Not so fast that it became an *ice stream* but enough to provide a gradient angled to the sun. During his 1957 journey over the ice-sheet to our immediate east, Vivian Fuchs had travelled close to rock features and met up with an obstacle that we were spared. Wide streams of melt-water running into lakes and rivers fed by waterfalls which poured off rock-faces testified to the amount of solar heat absorbed by the rock when the sun was high in the sky. 'As the day advanced,' Fuchs wrote, 'and the sun sank, it seemed that an invisible hand slowly shut off the supply of water, reducing the spouts and torrents to mere trickles.'

I unpacked two of six extra chocolate bars I had secretly packed and gave one to Mike to celebrate our arrival at the eighty-second line of latitude. Now there were only 480 miles to the Pole. Mike increased the sense of well-being at our party by brewing up *two* cups of tea each. The event was slightly marred for me by the salty taste of blood caused by opening my mouth wide enough to accept a chunk of the king-size one hundred grammes Mars Bar. This opened many of my lip scabs and encouraged me to design a special lip-protector that very evening.

As I modified the elasticated end of one cut-off leg of my long underpants, Mike talked of a Wendy house he was planning to build for his young children, Callan and Tarn. He had profitably whittled away quite a few hours of manhauling whilst planning every detailed step in the making of the little house. He was a caring father and on those occasions Morag managed to radio through a message from his family he always perked up visibly.

Two days later his mood swung to one of deep dejection, which cannot have been helped by the antibiotics he was taking in an effort to combat a swollen abscess on his Achilles tendon. This was pressured by the rim of his ski-boot and was now exacerbated by the worst conditions of the journey so far.

Rolling dunes and sharp-ridged walls of sastrugi confronted us hour after hour. Balanced upon one wall we would attempt to bridge the next trench with an outstretched ski, only to be jerked backwards by the sledge running foul and jamming. At other times, lunging forward to shift the apparently recalcitrant sledge, it came easily and, unbalanced, one would fall forwards, cross skis, and tumble down into the trench, cursing with frustration.

The worse this became, the greater my efforts to battle onwards. Mike's diary reflected his reaction. 'Got stuck repeatedly and cursed Ran continuously.' He was every bit as upset by my shooting ahead as I was when the situation was reversed.

Perhaps because of the antibiotics, Mike was stricken by stomach trouble in the night. 'Rough,' he wrote. 'Got diarrhoea three times overnight. With one disaster I missed the empty ration bag and got shit on my sleeping bag cover. I then spilled a load of water from the cook pot as I tried to clear up – Thank God Ran was asleep.'

I did notice an unusual aroma the next morning but we set out on time and I was surprised and dismayed when, after only forty minutes, Mike halted and told me he felt weak as a kitten and must stop. I tried to appear sympathetic and to cover my impatience as I unpacked the tent.

After hot tea and Lomotil tablets Mike slept for four hours and I buried my frustration by forming the plot for a novel to be written on our return. This was something I had intended to do if ever we were delayed because I had stupidly become a 'name' at Lloyd's of London three years before, and was annually having to pay out very large sums of money that we did not possess. Since I had no plans and no contract for a book about Antarctica, a successful novel was my big hope of staying solvent. I contemplated the IRA blowing up the Prime Minister inside the Channel Tunnel but then discarded the idea under the presumption that at least a dozen authors were already hard at work on such an obvious plot.

Mike woke and we drank more tea. I refrained from pressurising him but was delighted when he said he would try to go on. There was still time to get in five hours of hauling, but at seven in the evening he again halted and told me he felt drained of energy. I seethed inwardly. How dare Mike comment earlier on my polar plod when, by *twice* cutting full days short due to mere blisters and diarrhoea, he had wasted the equivalent of many weeks of polar plods.

As Mike rehydrated the 'spaghetti bolognese' powder for our meal, I fought back and forth in my mind whether or not I should come out with my thoughts on his early stops.

Whatever our pace, and no matter whether he or I was on any given day slower than the other, we had invariably managed to complete our vital ten-mile minimum. Only when his problems had caused early halts had we dropped miles which would be hard ever to regain.

Mike further riled me with the sudden news that his watch had stopped with a dead battery. He acknowledged that, two months before we left London, I had asked if he would send me his watch for a free check-up at Rolex. He had been too busy to post off the watch.

We depended for our navigation, on sunny days, entirely on our watches. To keep fastening or unfastening my watch

118

every hour, when we changed over to navigate, was unthinkable. It seems simple enough on the face of it but, with two pairs of mitts and cold fingers, it would be asking for frostbite, and we both knew this.

Without our being able to look at a watch, the time *within* each hour could seem endless. I knew that Mike, a zealous time-keeper like most doctors, was especially keen on regulating the moments for change-overs to suit our ever-changing state of energy level. There was only one answer. I gave Mike my watch.

'When *my* hour ends,' I suggested, 'just shout at me to stop. It should act as a brake to stop me getting too far ahead in sastrugi zones since I will not want to be out of hearing distance.'

From then on I was to be watch-less all day and every day of the journey.

Before I had made up my mind to deliver some peroration after our meal, Mike announced that his abscess was so swollen that he had decided to operate. I watched with intense admiration as he gave himself two deep injections of Xylocaine anaesthetic and then plunged a scalpel blade deep into the swelling with diagonally crossed incisions. Pus poured out of the wounds and the swelling visibly decreased. Mike then bandaged up his heel and packed away his medical kit. I am not sure whether or not he felt faint but I certainly did. I said nothing about the early halts or the stricken Rolex.

Chapter Seven

'Can two people walk together except
they be agreed?'

Amos

Most of the plasters over our blisters and crotch-rot were not changed daily. They became semi-permanent fixtures because plasters, like everything else, were in short supply. This state of affairs sometimes caused sores to deteriorate and after thirty days my right foot began to hurt when travelling.

I removed the bandage one evening and noticed that a two-inch area was soggy and swollen. Mike incised the area with a half-inch slit and relieved the pain immediately. I rubbed hae-morrhoid cream, of which Mike had a plentiful supply, into the foot slit (and also onto my raw lips), before re-plastering the foot. By now there were nine separate bandaged areas on my feet. Mike had applied Granuflex pressure-sore pads to his blisters and swore by the results which seemed to have miracu-lously cured some of his worst sores. I tried one but found it too bulky for my relatively tight-fitting plastic boots.

I usually woke at around 7.30 a.m., lit the cooker and melted a pot of snow. On one occasion I pumped the cooker too many times soon after Mike had changed over fuel bottles. The result was a vapour escape that I failed to notice. I placed the snow-pot on the cooker and applied my lighter. On ignition, flames at once spread over the floor and a serious fire was only narrowly averted.

*

Over the next three days we climbed to 5,000 feet above sea level with constant Force Eight winds in our faces. At one stage the wind veered through 90° and we tried to sail. This was an instant disaster. Forty-knot squalls simply filled the sails, giving us no chance to brace ourselves before being hurtled into the next ice ridge with painful force. The sails were quickly rebagged, an activity that made us both dangerously cold. That afternoon was too bitter even to stop for a four-minute Thermos break. Unless we kept up maximum effort with *no* pauses until the very moment of erecting the tent, we knew we would be in serious trouble.

For two days my stomach felt loose but the cold wind strengthened my resolution not to take my pants down en route. Our long-practised custom, diarrhoea excepted, was to defecate just before striking camp, using the lee of the tent, or a sledge, as an imperfect windbreak. When outside conditions were especially foul (or when my haemorrhoids were playing up) we would use an empty ration bag strategically positioned inside the tent. This was, of course, a smelly affair and kept to a minimum.

The three days of strong south-easterlies left a fresh carpet of coarse blown sand into which the sledge runners sank and through which they moved only grudgingly. Mike wrote: 'At one point I felt so low I wanted to pitch the tent and play chess. Not much fun but too cold to stop.' I wrote: 'Sledges slow, unmanoeuvrable and hell.'

Through the blizzard Mike spotted a black object to the south-west. At first we both thought it was a tent, Kagge perhaps, but we knew from Morag that he was too far away so this had to be a rock feature either small and close, or large and faraway. In any case I could not positively identify it on my map and cared little about it or anything else beyond surviving the fearful conditions of the day.

On arrival in camp our balaclavas were badly caked with ice all about our mouths. One morning Mike knocked from my chin a seven-inch stalactite formed from frozen nose dribble and saliva which stuck out like a unicorn's horn.

In the tent my face-mask was firmly embedded in my beard and, despite trying to remove it with care, a chunk of skin and beard came away, attached to the chin pad, leaving a raw and bleeding patch the size of a silver dollar. This was annoying since I had tried hard to avoid just such a recurrence of chin troubles.

In a few days my chin became swollen. I tried to avoid the balaclava tearing off bits each evening, by cutting away the beard hairs with my penknife scissors, but the damaged area grew more poisoned and Mike gave me antibiotics from his dwindling supply.

Arriving some distance ahead of Mike one evening I began to erect the tent by fixing a safety line to my sledge before trying to slot the ten-foot-long alloy poles into the sleeving.

The fourth and last pole was almost positioned when an especially violent blast tore the tent from my mitts and buckled one of the poles. Since I only carried a single eighteen-inch spare pole section for the entire journey I left the bent pole in place and prayed we would be spared a 'big katabatic' in the days ahead.

I thought of Ginnie back on Exmoor. She had lit a church candle and intended to keep it burning day and night until I returned. It was four feet long but so many hundreds of miles stretched ahead of us I could not help but think the candle would run out long before I came home.

After the three-day winds the mists returned with a vengeance. Our weather was almost certainly emanating from the Recovery Glacier, somewhere to our east, with powerful winds rushing down at this time of year to replace warmer air rising from the ice-shelf below. In places we came across inclines scoured so hard and so smooth by these winds that we could not ascend them. The sledges merely pulled us back downhill.

One such grey ice re-entrant caught us by surprise in the mist, for we could see no perspective, neither 'ups' nor 'downs', and we suddenly found the sledges sliding *forwards* without having to be dragged. A beautiful experience, but one that only lasted the five-minute duration of the unseen and sadly unique downhill-to-the-Pole hillock.

This was the prelude to a major climb, also polished to a shining grey, which loomed, west-east across our route.

As we struggled ineffectually to zig-zag up the face of this slippery wall a freak north-easterly wind came from nowhere.

'Sails?' screamed Mike.

I gave him a thumbs-up sign. For twenty minutes, with a number of heavy falls, we progressed up or at least across the frozen hill face. The wind veered east and became unusable, but by then the slope was manageable.

As we paused to pack the sails, I noticed a small black item behind Mike's sledge. It turned out to be a spare battery – Mike looked grim, as well he might, for he had packed the battery deep inside his load and there was no way it could have escaped but through a hole in the hull.

We rolled his sledge onto one side and then the other, revealing a ragged split across its entire width. The sledge was now sundered and held together only by the two narrow longitudinal runners. Many of the half-inch screws which held the runners to the base of the hull were loose but, fortunately, responded to tightening by the screwdriver on Mike's knife.

We erected the tent as a new gale blew up and, having unloaded all contents, pulled the front end of the stricken sledge inside. Away from the wind, we were now able to detach the custom-made alloy strong points from the front end of the sledge which was now both smaller and more damaged than the rear section.

In England I had stressed that the sledges must be designed so they could be pulled from either end. Somehow the manufacturers had forgotten to fix strong points at both ends, nor had they drilled suitably spaced holes so that we could effect an easy change-over. Luckily, in Punta, Mike had spotted this omission and, borrowing a drill (not an option on our pen-knives), we had prepared suitable holes 'against a rainy day'.

Mike restacked his more solid gear, mainly the food and fuel, into what was now the front end, about two-thirds of the sledge, and stowed only bulky light equipment, such as his sleeping bag, in the broken rear section.

We then retreated to the tent, shivering, to stir up our circulation with soup from the Thermos. This we discovered, through its unusual taste, had fermented due to the difficulty of cleaning it out on a daily basis. Our recurring diarrhoea troubles might be partially caused by well-brewed Thermos bacteria.

'The whole sledge could fall apart any day,' Mike ruminated.

'You could always tow half of it,' I added unhelpfully. 'Moby MacLean once designed an edible sledge, made from toughened pemmican, which he aimed to consume from back to front.'

'And what happened?'

'It never got off the drawing board. Polar buffs whom he approached cut the idea to ribbons.'

'Exactly,' said Mike, wholly unimpressed at the idea of towing half a sledge anywhere.

I carried Mike's bed mat for him but everything else fitted well enough and the undamaged runners seemed unaffected.

'Oh well,' I picked up my mitts from the tent floor, 'if we are to catch up the remaining four hours, we had better be going.'

'Is it worth it?' Mike commented. 'Just for four hours! Now we've camped we might as well stay put.'

Rather hurriedly I assured him that there was every point and, without stopping to argue the issue, pushed out of the door flap. We completed our ten miles that day but sustained further face and finger nip, for the wind switched to a full south-easterly which penetrated our inadequate gear.

Allowing for a slight improvement to our current rate of progress as the sledge-loads slowly lessened, but taking no account of altitude or bodily deterioration, I estimated that we were now half-way to the Pole time-wise. Thirty-four days behind us and thirty-four to go.

We discussed the wisdom of trying to save small amounts of food whenever feasible. Mike was against this on the principle that we already seemed to be losing both weight and strength. We could, he felt, ill afford to eat less than our full rations. At the end of each daily meal we were left ravenously hungry. We took it in turns to scrape every last scrap from the cook pot. Our spoons were exactly the same size and we dipped them into the stew alternately, keeping all the while an eagle eye on one another's portions.

Mike finally agreed to put aside very small portions of some items like porridge oats. He had already collected what we called a 'squirel cache' of saved tea bags and milk sachets.

The following day brought our first true white-out along with uneven sastrugi and heavy crust snowdrifts, through which the sledges ploughed only with the most determined haulage.

The direction of the wind and the low temperatures created particularly bad misting of our goggles. I stopped time and again to scrape rime off the lens. Demisting fluid, fine for an alpine resort or even mild summer Antartic conditions, was useless on such a day.

For twenty years, largely in the Arctic, I had navigated in the worst of glare-ice, month after month, without eye protection. But in Siberia this stupidity, born of the frustration of misted goggles, had caught up with me and the best London ophthalmic surgeon had warned me I would risk blindness if I ever again subjected my retinas to further overdoses of blue and ultra-violet light. Frightened, I no longer gave in to the

126

temptation to tear off misted goggles, but I fully sympathised when Mike did so.

To travel through a white-out is to move blindly through a world without shadow. All surface definition goes and there are no horizons. The white snow blends with the white sky to form *white night*. The thick cloud ceiling of common stratus and the snow floor both reflect and refract the glare so that there is zero perception of depth to human vision.

I had in the 1970s tried to design a machine which could, on the principle of the needle in a photographer's light meter, read the strength of sunlight. If the meter was pointed *towards* the sun through a thick mist the needle should peak.

After two years of experiments, a British Aerospace student, named Zoomski, eventually produced a meter based on infra-red sourcing, which was accurate to within fifteen degrees, enough for my needs in the North-West Passage, where magnetic compasses are useless due to the proximity of the north magnetic Pole.

Under true white-out conditions it is quite possible for people to walk off cliffs and for aircraft to 'land' by mistake. Some individuals are physically sickened by white-out travel and, that morning, Mike complained of feeling 'disturbed and totally disorientated', when he removed his jacket hood to prevent his goggles misting. As a result he kept his hood up, his goggles became unwearable and, in an especially bad sastrugi field, he removed them for a period of two hours or so.

Towards noon the clouds shifted and a slight horizon was visible. This enabled us to hold our bearing by simply crossing successive sastrugi trenches at an angle of seventy degrees.

When we camped, after a memorably nasty ten hours lurching over unseen obstacles, crossing ski-tips and crashing into invisible trenches, I found both my cheeks burning and inflamed by UV rays. A mole on one cheek was especially tender. I had exposed my cheeks to help demist my goggles

127

but it had been a mistake. The cheeks were later to blister because the burn conditions had been so bad. Mike's eyes, even though he wore goggles for all but two hours throughout the day, were also damaged. Soon after we camped he developed snow blindness symptoms. Only the mildest of attacks, but enough to have him lying back in considerable pain.

There is an accurate description of the feeling of sun-blindness by Scott's biographer, Elspeth Huxley. 'He was in agony from snow blindness which even cocaine could not alleviate. The victim of this horrible complaint felt as if his eyeballs were being tattooed by red hot needles or bombarded by gritty sand.'

We had no cocaine but carried a bottle of amethocaine eye drops and these provided Mike with exquisite relief for about an hour, after which he would wake in renewed pain and apply further drops.

That day Kagge overtook us at around 84° of latitude and at 5,500 feet, close to half-way in both distance and altitude to the Pole.

Kagge travelled alone. Why? I did not know the answer. No one but Kagge himself could give his reasons. He could say he preferred to commune with nature or that to travel solo was a greater challenge. He could point to the fact that, like most polar travellers, he needed to be 'first' in order to achieve sponsorship. Since the British had already claimed the first unsupported journey to the South Pole (Mear, Swan and Wood in 1986) and since he was unable by 1993 to prepare logistics for an attempt at the first unsupported crossing of the whole continent, there was only one possible 'first' left to him and that was a 'solo unsupported to the Pole'.

The difference between this and the 1986 British achievement was very small. He was after all doing almost to the mile, although with a lighter load, what the three individuals in 1986 had already done.

128

Nonetheless, in his Norwegian homeland, polar travel was held in the highest regard, in the way football is in other European countries. This was largely due to the epic journey of Nansen who, like Kagge, was tall and blond and treated by his countrymen as a hero.

One of Nansen's friends wrote in the Norwegian press: 'Norway lies closer to the Polar Regions than any other country . . . We could provide an élite corps of tough and experienced men, used to travel in snow and ice. We ought to have the advantage over Englishmen and the other nationalities.'

By enabling Oslo journalists to announce a polar race against a British team, Kagge was on to a winner. I admired his personal strength and determination, for solo travel through crevassed regions is doubly hazardous.

I wished Kagge well and I understood his rationale for hyping his journey as a race against us. Nonetheless I was irked by it, for I would have enjoyed a race and was frustrated at being the heavy dragoon, laughed at by the light cavalry.

When he learnt that Reinhold Messner would also be attempting to cross Antartica in 1990, Steger wrote, 'What I have heard about him has not been positive, especially that he views our both being in Antartica this season as a competition to be "first" to cross the continent . . . I'm curious about him. Face it, few men even attempt such travel or lead the lives we both do. I would like to think that for those who have chosen this life there could be some fraternity. Unfortunately, by past experience, I know that may be too great an expectation.'

I had often considered solo travel but never for long. Half the fun of an expedition is the planning of it and, as with old soldiers, the shared memories afterwards. Practically speaking too, since expeditions are my livelihood, I needed photographs for books and lectures. With no companions, there could be no memories to share and a very limited supply of pictures. However, on the plus side, the solo traveller suffers less frustrations caused through discontent, rivalry and, as with Mike and I, differences of pace.

Since our overall speed and rate of progress for the first forty days were slightly better than for any previous Antarctic manhauling journey on record, our pace should not theoretically have caused dissension. But we were both suffering increasing strain and our bodies, under the stress of slow starvation combined with enormous energy expenditure, were altering chemically.

Subsequent analysis of our blood samples was to show that our whole enzyme system, everything that controlled our absorption of fat, was changing and we were getting levels of gut hormones twice as high as were previously known to science. We were adapting to our high-fat rations in a way hitherto unrecognised. Furthermore, we were losing muscle and weight from our hearts as well as our body mass.

During this period of the steep climb to the Pole and beyond we were losing muscle fast. Mike later said, after our results were analysed, 'Ran was at times using nearly 10,000 calories a day. This is more than has been documented *ever* for any length of time.'

It is hardly surprising then that our normally placid working relationship was beginning to crack at the seams.

Mike openly admitted that it did him a world of good mentally to push hard so that 'the pressure is off me'. By pressing the pace when navigating he could gain a headway, at most, of four minutes in one and a half hours. That way, whilst waiting for me to catch up and take over with the compass, he could win four precious minutes of rest. In nine to ten hours of non-stop hauling these few minutes were of great value to him mentally, even though from a physical viewpoint they were undoubtedly damaging. His leg muscles alone suffered far greater loss of strength, as was subsequently evidenced by analysis, than my much weaker legs which I carefully pampered through most of the journey.

Whenever the terrain was crowded with obstacles or the weather was bitingly cold I was forced to pull at maximum efficiency and would then move faster than Mike. When the surface was flat and the temperatures kind, I reverted to the polar plod and made every effort to persuade Mike to slow down for his own physical good and my mental state of well-being.

Whichever of us was resting from navigation could benefit greatly by 'dogging' the navigator. This was the term we used for following closely. It was far easier to self-induce an almost hypnotic trance and to let your skis fall into a timed rhythm, when the other sledge was *just* ahead of you.

By the fifth week Mike's surges were telling on him. Entries in his diary at this time included 'I felt a bit hypoglycaemic in the last hour', and 'I feel totally bushed in the last hour, sick and lightheaded'. One evening he wrote, 'Felt terrible. thought I had reactive hypoglycaemia.' He told me that he could 'feel the weight falling off'.

This last comment was borne out when he again tried to record our weight on his miniature scales. This time he sensibly placed them on our cooking box, which provided a fairly hard bearing surface, and successfully obtained good readings. The results were not encouraging.

Despite consuming 5,200 calories a day we had already, only a third of the way into the journey, lost twenty pounds in my case and fifteen pounds in Mike's. I decided to stop persuading Mike to 'save little bits here and there', nor to chide him further about his inability to save any of his daily chocolate rations.

Whenever the slightest hint of a southerly wind showed itself we tried to sail but we were invariably blown off course to the west, in which direction lay the Forrestal Mountains and the likelihood of further crevassing.

On one sailing attempt Mike fell heavily and lost the spare

compass which I had lent him soon after we set out when he discovered he had not packed one. Whenever the sun shone we navigated without compass aid but, from now on, in poor visibility conditions, it would be necessary to hand over our single remaining compass every time we changed navigation roles.

There were many nights when I failed to establish communications with Morag due to polar cap absorption, solar flares and other ionospheric disturbances. The problem is that lines of force from the earth's magnetic field curve inward at the poles and draw down, from outer space, electrically charged particles given off by the sun. These interact with other charged particles that are present in the ionosphere. When this happens the ionosphere loses it normal ability to reflect radio waves from one point on Earth to another, in our case between our tent and Morag in Patriot Hills.

A week before Christmas the solar flares behaved themselves and Morag was able to send us a message from our Patron, the Prince of Wales, in response to one I had previously sent him with condolences about his recent separation from his wife. His response showed that he had not lost his sense of humour: 'I had rather hoped that you might be the one person who would *not* hear the sad news.'

During the sixth week there were days of no wind and hot sun for the solstice was close. Inside the tent, since we always positioned the door away from the prevailing wind and since that was invariably from the south-east, it was possible to tell the time when waking at night merely by noting the position of the sun against the orange semi-spheroid of the tent. Often I was warm whilst Mike was cold when the sun shone on 'my' side of the tent. It was difficult to think of Christmas at home but we tried, by way of passing the time.

At the beginning of a day of hauling through the clinging, wet cement of snow-crud, it was truly difficult to master your thoughts and banish the insistent desire to halt because the whole huge task was simply *too hard*.

There is a piece from *Pilgrim's Progress* that runs: 'Now I saw in my dream that they drew near to a very miry slough that was in the midst of the plain and they did both fall suddenly into the bog. The name of the slough was *Despond*. Here they wallowed for a time and Christian, because of the burden that was on his back, began to sink in the mire.' To avoid the mire and our slough of Despond was not always easy when parts of the body shrieked their pain, and hours of jolting sastrugi, falls with crossed skis, or worst of all the slow grudging drag of the sledge, made you think of the horrible distance, the unthinkable hours, yet to be faced.

I often wished to scream my feelings to the sky. Cherry-Garrard wrote, 'Sometimes it was difficult not to *howl*. I *did* want to howl many times every hour but I invented a formula instead which I repeated to myself constantly. Especially, I remember, it came in useful at the end of the march with my feet frostbitten, my heart beating slowly, my vitality at its lowest ebb and my body solid with cold. Then I would repeat "Stick it. Stick it. Stick it. Stick it."'

I used several alternatives to Garrad's 'Stick it'. One was: 'Slowly the snail reached the oak.' Messner imagined erotic fancies. I tried this but failed. I found food more easy to conjure up than sex. Mike agreed on this. Perhaps the English really are colder fish than others, South Tyroleans (like Messner) for a start. Steger, the American, commented, 'My thoughts begin to resemble our trail food; boring repetitive and stale. My mind is exhausted by lack of outside stimulation. Even escaping into my mind has become difficult.'

Zen masters explain: 'All Zen practice requires detachment from thought. This is the way to save energy. Just detach yourself from emotional thought and understand there is no objective world.' This sounded like excellent advice but I had obviously not practised enough since it proved unattainable hogwash when put to the test. Maybe I should have spent my time training to be mindless instead of jogging and eating pasta.

I would watch Mike's fractured sledge travelling over sastrugi bumps and note how easily the runners snaked along. 'Perhaps,' I would think, 'I should cut *my* sledge laterally in two to get rid of its rigidity.' Some aspects of Mike's behaviour, or some chance phrase, would lodge itself in my mind unbidden and the more I chewed the cud the more it would rile me. This I found an especially useful thought-tactic, for *where there is anger there is no room to brood.*

By Christmas Eve we had staggered to 6,000 feet above sea level. That afternoon, for the first time, a southerly wind allowed us to sail through mists and weirdly convoluted banks of sastrugi. We both fell heavily many times but, by some miracle, escaped injury. The wind picked up again on the morning of Christmas Day, but in a short while veered well to the west and we quickly packed away the sails.

My diary: 'Mike looked bitterly sad, so I said, "Never mind. If we had sailed, we might have broken our ankles. So it's just as well. There's a silver lining to every cloud." Like a crotchety old woman he responded, "If that's what you think about sailing, we'll never succeed." "Heavens," I said. "It was only a joke to cheer you up." "If that's a joke," he replied, "it's a very bad one." He was obviously in a downcast mood. To try to keep him happy and optimistic when he's on one of his "downs" may be a waste of time.'

By noon my stomach, loose all morning, was in sharp revolt. I felt weak and sick and was forced to squat, bare-bottomed, beside my sledge in a bitter south-west wind. The terrain was as foul as ever with wet-cement, or drag-anchor crud, clinging all day to the sledge-runners.

Christmas lunch was a bitterly cold affair sitting side-by-side and hunched against the wind to crunch two squares of chocolate and gulp down a pint of tepid glutinous soup.

Our mitts had to come off in repeated combined attacks to unscrew the frozen lid of the vacuum flask. We eventually battered it off against the hull of my sledge but by then we both had cold hands which took an hour of hard hauling to recover.

Whenever I felt my core temperature drop, the alarm bells rang and I would pull harder. At such times Mike would drop behind until, recovered from 'the shivers' and remembering my polar plod policy, I would slow down again. One side of me would fiercely condemn such wimpish behaviour . . . Why limp along when capable of greater speed? But a more cautious voice would prevail – 'There are over a thousand miles to go . . . You are too old, sick, tired and hungry. Keep plodding. Never stop, but never race. Forget the urge to compete with him. Don't pander to pride. Think long-term. If he wishes to squander his energy reserves, let him go ahead.'

Often I found myself scuffing back my jacket sleeve to check the time. I sorely missed having my watch but I knew that Mike would miss it even more. He was happy chopping and changing our navigation periods from day to day and loved being time-keeper. So I let him keep the watch except at night, since my job was to wake us up in the mornings.

When we camped at the end of Christmas Day I rummaged in my sledge for two of my remaining Mars Bars. These we munched with enormous relish and then played chess with the pee-sample pawns.

I tried to contact Morag but reception was poor. I traced this to a loose antenna connector, but by then Morag had moved off frequency. That evening I recomputed the magnetic bearing and local noon time, for we had strayed well west over the past week.

On Boxing Day, determined to cut weight after nine hours of spine-wrenching climbs, we agreed to bury any spare items of clothing or kit we could find. We saved three pounds apiece.

135

The snow surface was again sticky, our runners shrieking and whining over the sharp crusted rime. Although the wind was Force Four or less, we both felt bitterly cold. My eyes began to show signs of their old retina troubles. The knife-like wind had penetrated under my goggles and I could not focus.

Mike's diary: 'The willy-warmer extra padding that I sewed into my underwear last night gives little benefit and the end of my penis was markedly swollen . . . we are exhausted . . . Day Fifty: Desperately hard day. Ran finding it very hard to cope with going slower than I although, in reality, it is not that much slower and both of us are now feeling as though we are running on empty. I think that our steadily pushing up the hours to approaching ten haul-hours is getting too much and we need a break . . . I think I can say that today was the first time that my legs were tired even when I left the tent in the morning. Day Fifty-One: A terrible day of crushing morale, physical decrepitude and difficult terrain. Last night I weighed us. Ran has lost forty pounds and me thirty pounds. Twenty per cent of our body weight.'

When Mike broke the news of this further weight deterioration, I made up my mind to counter future enfeeblement by drastic changes. In only fifty days of eating *exactly* the same food as Mike I had lost twenty-five per cent more weight than he had. I refused to ask for extra food to cope with my greater bulk so I asked him to begin using more rations off his sledge over the next few days. This should, I hoped, even out our rate of bodily weakening.

Whenever I kept well ahead of Mike, he would remind me that I was heavier and longer of leg. He maintained that both these physical attributes were an advantage.

Yet, in scientific papers that he had previously written, he held the opposite view as regards heavy, bulky manhaulers. Of the death of Scott's heaviest team member, Evans, Mike wrote, 'Sheer starvation with consequent emaciation might

136

have been the more significant factor [of their death]. For example, Evans was the biggest man in Scott's team and could have lost over thirty pounds by the time he reached the Pole, let alone what he lost on the return journey . . . Of course the other men would also have suffered from only slightly less devastating weight losses.' Mike's study on the three men on the Mear/Swan 1986 South Pole Expedition led him to realise that the heavier member of that team lost far more weight than the lighter *despite* eating more. This he now chose to ignore.

In terms of my long legs or his own shorter, stronger legs, he again knew from his 1986 experience that the slightest member of that team proved the most capable manhauler. Of Scott's manhauling team the two smallest men, the short, stocky Scott himself and the 5 foot 4 inch Bowers, were by far the most powerful pullers. Messner and Fuchs found similar results in the stature-versus-performance stakes.

I told Mike firmly that I simply would not hack any pace faster than my polar plod but that, on the other hand, there was no way I could face 'giving up'. We *must* somehow try to slow down this inexorable debilitation. The obvious way was by eating more of our food but that was also to 'give in' since it would cut down our total travel days.

Because of my recent bouts of diarrhoea I was again suffering on the march from haemorrhoids. The only benefit of this was a tendency to forget the pain of my feet due to the new aggravation.

Mike was keen to increase our food intake immediately and suggested gradually cannibalising eight of our ration bags over the next few weeks. We reached a fair compromise. We agreed to cut to only half-rations at some point on the far side of the Pole, to counter the extras we would consume prior to the Pole. He agreed to cut the 'forward loan' to only six bags.

To help morale, I unpacked my map of the Beardmore Glacier and started to plan our detailed descent route through its myriad crevasse fields. It was helpful at least to *think* about terrain where there would be features to see other than endless white wastes.

Mike produced two small bottles from his science pack and we each drank the contents, which consisted of very expensive water. He explained the purpose.

'This stuff is deuterium and is made up of heavy hydrogen and oxygen 18. Like atomic *heavy water*, but non radio-active. Each bottleful costs hundreds of pounds, so don't spill any.'

'So what good does heavy water do us?'

'None at all. It just gets mixed up with all the other water in our bodies which we will slowly rid ourselves of and I will slowly collect. My pee-samples do have uses other than as chessmen. The oxygen 18 will come out partially in the form of carbon dioxide. We will burn everything up sooner or later but the oxygen 18 disappears first. I can use the differing disappearance rates revealed by analysis of our urine samples to measure our daily energy expenditure.'

I never ceased to admire Mike's dedication to his research work. However sick he happened to be feeling at the time, he would never skimp the tiniest detail of his science schedule.

On our fifty-third day Mike slowed right down, so that even my polar plod overhauled him. He wrote: 'A desperate day for me. The pulling seemed so hard that I very nearly gave in to the wish to have a rest day . . . I diagnosed a state of near-terminal, physical decline.'

In the tent I offered Mike my spare chocolate saved from previous weeks. He was grateful and said he would think about it. We passed a most uncomfortable night in a wild sastrugi field with nowhere flat for the tent. My diary: 'Mike seems to think my sledge is now twenty-five pounds lighter. In fact the difference is ten pounds but there is no point in arguing the point and we are too tired to unload the sledges to check what is, anyway, academic since nothing short of fifty pounds makes a noticeable difference.'

The next day, after two hours of steep, yard-by-yard progress, Mike was forced by another diarrhoea attack to stop and drop his trousers 'by the roadside'. A few minutes later he told me he could not continue. He must rest.

I was furious. We erected the tent and made tea. After Mike had rested for an hour or two I told him we must get going. He was angry and said I was boorish and graceless; in short a prick of the first order.

Mike's diary: 'I began to feel ill early and got diarrhoea after two and a half hours. Ran was unsympathetic, angry and a right sod.'

I told him that the mounting number of delays caused by his halts were costing us vital time. The few minutes of difference between our relative speeds were of no consequence since our time-keeping methods simply prolonged our marching hours to cover any such difference. This was not true of his stops. I stressed, in my anger, that if he could not take it, I would go on without him and that we must be hard not soft in our approach to every side of our schedule, or we would never reach the Pole never mind the Beardmore Glacier.

This outburst further soured poor Mike and certainly did not increase his readiness to break camp. I settled back to accept the inevitable and to wait for his recovery. After a couple of hours and more hot tea, we set out again, but, after a further three hours, his track began to curve from side to side and then he collapsed into the snow and lay still.

I drew up beside him and waited. He recovered in a few moments and stood up. I took over the navigation but, fifteen minutes later, he suffered further stomach upsets and told me he must stop.

In the tent I apologised for my previous anger and by the time the evening meal was over the atmosphere was clear of tension. Mike took Lomotil pills and operated on my foot by making further incisions in the swollen area over the bone. Although this helped me sleep without painkillers the swelling recurred, and by noon, the next day, I had to stop en route to take off my boot and cut a hole out of its insulated inner bootee at the point of pressure on the wound. This helped for a while.

My diary: 'Extremely cold all day so I had to abandon the polar plod. This put pressure on Mike who tonight complained he could not keep up and must re-adjust the weights back to square one.'

He wrote: 'I think that over the next few days we will slowly get the weights back to equality but I find this hard to suggest to Ran because he is in considerable pain from his right foot.'

The hard work, the cold and the injuries seemed to have been with us for months. Mike wrote:

> Fifty-Eighth Day: At day's end we were both pretty buggered and, although Ran ascribes the shortfall in our 'miles-done' to the climbing, I'm not sure that it doesn't reflect increasingly chronic fatigue and further deterioration in performance. Day Fifty-Nine: A grim day mentally. Early on I felt like throwing it all in. It's unbelievable that we've done this for sixty days . . . The thought of another fifty or sixty is untenable . . . Ran mutters about temperature and climbing but really it is *us* going downhill . . . Kagge is at the Pole and 'the race' is being played up . . . Very difficult to keep going. Each day now gets more fatiguing. I daren't think how they [the dark thoughts] will feel beyond the Pole with *so far* to go. We need a helpful wind. Only in that way will morale and chances be lifted enough to carry on with this psychological nightmare.

We had reached 8,500 feet above sea-level and I was feeling increasingly tight-chested. I eased off my shoulder straps as much as possible but *any* constriction of the lungs led to heavy breathing and the noise in my ears of blood rushing to my

140

head. It became difficult to eat chocolate squares on the move because any interruption to the breath-taking process had me gasping for air. Even to bend over to tighten a ski-binding made me breathless and weak. At night I experienced mild panic from time to time when I woke with air hunger.

Although we did not then know it, and Mike continued to assure me that altitude would not affect us, I learned later that the relatively low air pressure near to the Poles markedly increases the effect of altitude on humans. 8,500 feet here gave the same conditions as 11,500 feet on, say, Mount Everest.

At 11,500 feet the thinness of the air and the consequent lack of oxygen causes many people to suffer from altitude sickness; shortness of breath, dizziness, even nausea and confusion. One of Scott's men collapsed from altitude sickness at 9,000 feet, and Amundsen, although ten dogs hauled his sledge, found 'it was hard work and breathing was an effort'.

I saw huge hill features up ahead but thanked God when, hours later, they turned out to be part mirage, part cloud formations.

Morag had worked hard to erect special antennae outside her tent at Patriot Hills. For several days, she told us, the world press had reported in banner headlines that Kagge had 'won the race'. I could hear Morag but she could not distinguish my words. I needed to ask her to explain things to our London sponsors, who would be livid with the erroneous reports, so I tried to contact the American 'South Pole' science base. I tried for three hours to no avail.

On our sixtieth day Mike had a very bad time and told me he must be wrong about the effects of altitude. He was worried within himself about his ability to continue fending off negative thoughts. 'If things go on like this beyond the Pole, I can see myself wanting out. I simply don't have the same resolute resolve as you do.' He wrote: 'Last night I did express to Ran my fears of not being able to hack it if things go badly. Needless to say I got a sort of "we will be tough" type talk rather than true understanding. He gets *his* strength from "*God and family and the whole clan here inside me*". All very useful but I know it won't help me if I can see the whole chance of success slipping away and us just slogging on . . . Day Sixty-Two: I am a bit down about this Kagge/race business. Why did he have to turn up and complicate matters? . . . Day Sixty-Three: With nausea and abdominal pains through the first hour, the day was long and hellish.'

That night I gave Mike two chocolate squares and he seemed to appreciate the gesture. I am not good at being sympathetic. I knew that Mike was agnostic and did not expect him to gain any mental help in that direction. I had hoped, however, that he might be able to invoke his family and the knowledge that they were all 'gunning for him', but he seemed to scoff at this as too contrived a mental aid.

My practice was to 'hype up' my mind during the first hour of every day, when the pain from my feet was at its worst, by simply remembering that I was not alone in facing the dreaded hours ahead. I pictured my grandfather who had trapped in northern Canada and fought for his country all over the world. I thought of my father and uncle who were killed in the two World Wars. I pictured my wife, my mother and my sisters, and I imagined that all of them were right behind me helping to suppress the ever-lurking urge to put a stop to the pain and the cold.

The surface became so sticky that the sledge-loads seemed to double in weight. We removed our sealskins, by now threadbare and oft-repaired, and found that our 'bare' skis could grip the surface, such was the toffee-like grasp of the snow.

When fresh snowflakes fall they have a beautiful hexagonal shape, but the snow crystals that we sledged over had often been damaged by repeated collisions with other crystals as they were blown about the plateau. Once settled, individual crystals or flakes start rounding off and turn into granules as

142

small as one millimetre. Air is gradually expelled from each granule as others settle from above. Melting where they touch each other continues until nearly all the air is expelled and, at the stage they become impermeable to air or water, they can be called ice.

The conversion from snow to ice can take about ten years on a European glacier but more than 3,500 years in Antarctica. Some parts of the high Antarctic plateau, which we were now traversing, are relatively free from strong winds so the snow crystals can lie loosely packed and, from our point of view, horribly soft. A Soviet tractor expedition over the plateau reported that 'a metal drum of fuel fell under the tracks of a tractor and was pushed into the snow to a depth of five feet without receiving a single dent'.

Even in Scott's day the effect of the temperature on snow crystals and therefore on sledge-runner behaviour was well known. Cherry-Garrard summarised the phenomenon:

> The general trend of friction set up by a sledge-runner upon snow of ordinary temperature may be called true *sliding* friction: it is probable that the runners melt to an infinitesimal degree the millions of crystal points over which they glide: the sledge is running on water. Crystals in such temperatures are larger and softer than those encountered in low temperatures . . . In *very* low temperatures the crystals become small and very hard, so hard they will scratch the runners. The friction set up by runners in such temperatures may be know as *rolling* friction and the effect is much like *pulling a sledge over sand*.

On the sixty-fourth day we unpacked our sledges and found our respective sledge-loads to be precisely the same, at 250 pounds each. Sadly, there was nothing else that we could eliminate. The temperature continued to drop and the surface to deteriorate.

At one soup-stop I found it impossible to get my mug

anywhere near to my mouth due to an eight-inch-long ice-spike formed on my chin.

We both experienced increasing troubles with fogged-up goggles. A white-out at 9,500 feet produced conditions which defeated all Mike's attempts to maintain a compass bearing. He doggedly tried again and again but each time I had to shout 'Go left' for, like an uncoiling spring, he invariably veered to the right within a few yards of putting away the compass.

Sometimes the mists would clear and the wind drop away. Then the world was a place of wonder. Every now and again, usually emerging from the tent to adjust the antennae or fetch an item from a sledge, I would forget the trauma of our existence, the fragility of our hopes, and feel, fleetingly, the silent peace of this great untouched land.

One morning Mike announced that he had lost three of his skins. They must have somehow fallen off. 'Never mind,' I told him, 'you have a spare still and I've got three spares so we've got four skins.' Later in the day, on realising what I had said, we laughed. But at the time the wretched pettiness of our thought-processes precluded any attempt at humour.

Mike's diary:

> A very hard day with sticky cement surfaces and hills
> including the worst period of pulling we have ever had. I
> wanted to try to sail despite Ran's foot pain. When I thought
> I had lost my skins, I was pretty pissed off with myself and
> said to Ran, 'The loss of my skins is likely to prove a worse
> problem than your foot.' He seized upon this as being as
> 'graceless' as his rather more considered response to my
> previous diarrhoea stop . . . I am not sure that they equate!
> Anyway we laughed off these stresses and had a steady but
> exhausting day . . .
> Day Sixty-Six: Ran blew up at me in a big way for going
> too fast although he was only 150 yards behind at the end of
> my ninety minutes. I told him his tirade was pathetic and

144

we soon both ended up apologising. However, he really
seems to believe that my speed will burn up my calories.

The last 200 miles before the Pole involved us in climbing
above 10,000 feet. The altitude effects added to our debilitation
and the heavy loads were beginning to change us in many
subtle ways. Mike said later, 'I had all day these endless
thoughts about how to give up, on what excuse. I was on the
point of calling Ran and I was going to say "This is it." On the
day before we got to the Pole, when it was within sight, I was
going to give up – but because I *wanted* to give up not because
I couldn't take it.'

That was on our sixty-seventh day. The wind chill factor
was −84°C with thick fog. In such conditions it is all too easy to
make some small error that can quickly lead to serious trouble.

Over the weeks of gradually-dropping temperatures we had
each modified our clothes with needle, Dentafloss, and
patches cut from such items as the tent bag. Mike was still
unhappy with his trousers. I have always held it as vital that I
can undo my trouser zip when wearing mitts and accordingly
fix a long loop of plastic wire to the zip-toggle. Mike had a
complete pee-flap which required ungloved hands to
manoeuvre.

I was unable to adjust my face-mask that morning to protect
my nose without causing fogged-up goggles. Frequent
attempts to scratch all the resulting grime off the lens had
failed and, short of pitching the tent, it was dangerous to halt
for more than three or four minutes in such conditions to
make radical face-mask alterations. I therefore asked Mike to
navigate in my place since he could still see reasonably well.
This was the only stint that Mike navigated 'my hours' during
the entire journey and the timing could not have been better
for it certainly saved his life.

During the second hour of the morning Mike stopped to
have one of many wayside pees and fumbled the job of

145

fastening his trousers. His hands, colder than usual, would not fit back into his oiled wool Dachstein mitts. I stood waiting behind him, cursing silently as my swollen foot seemed to vibrate with shafts of pain. Less than fifteen miles away in the frozen swirling mists, the South Pole waited.

Mike turned round, a cumbersome business wearing skis and in harness, but he needed to face away from the bitter south-easterly wind.

I knew he was in trouble when I heard him moaning, then sobbing with pain and fear. I knew what he was experiencing, the anguish that comes with allowing your fingers or toes to go that touch too far down the road to frostbite and permanent loss.

Mike had been trying to force hands with no feeling into mitts that were slightly too tight. Because both hands were now senseless lumps of bloodless meat he could no longer do anything with them. In his moment of blind panic he forgot the most obvious answer.

Normally we do not spring to each other's aid. There is an unspoken pride in being self-sufficient and it can be irritating fending off attempts at nursemaiding. If and when one of us is quite obviously about to drown (in the Arctic), or fall further into a crevasse (in Antarctica), then the other does what is necessary, but day-to-day hazards are coped with individually.

When I saw that Mike was on the point of losing his fingers for good I wrenched off my fogged-up goggles, removed my clumsy Canadian Army mitts, and tried to force Mike's frozen hands into his Dachsteins. My own fingers cooled in seconds to the point that they were of no help to Mike so I thrust them back into my mitts and screamed at Mike to shove his hands into his crotch.

Even this was difficult for him but desperation gave him added strength and, still whimpering through gritted teeth, he managed to force the hands which he could not feel down

146

between his sledge-jacket and his trousers to the only warm place (other than *my* crotch) within fifteen miles.

Forcing his thighs together, Mike gradually squeezed blood back into his hands and eventually down to his fingertips but not before five of his fingers were badly nipped. This was to lead to further troubles at a later date but at least the current danger was averted.

By the time we were ready to move on, both of us were extremely cold, our body core temperatures lower than at any time on the journey so far.

Knowing that Mike was the more prone to hypothermia, I lent him my outer mitts and took his own Gortex outers which, normally excellent, were less than adequate in such conditions.

The delay had rendered my own hands unworkable in terms of trying to de-fog my goggles and the only feature I could see in the near white-out was Mike's indistinct silhouette eight yards ahead of me. His tracks were invisible.

After an interminable time, during which I bitterly regretted the fact that I had not brought a second watch with me, I came to an abrupt halt as my ski-tips struck the rear of Mike's sledge.

Normally when he halted to announce that ninety minutes were up and it was my turn to navigate, he would shout the word 'Time' loud enough for me to hear above the screech of my ski-sticks.

There had been no shout and, as I came alongside to detach the compass from Mike's chest-harness, I noticed something unaccountably different about his behaviour.

My standard practice, having clipped the compass to my own chest-strap, was to move a few yards ahead of Mike and check the correct bearing before setting off for my next ninety-minute session. It was not my habit *ever* to look back except in a zone of crevasses or other hazards, and if, on this occasion, I had followed my normal procedure, Mike would certainly have died.

As it was, some aspect of Mike's stance, perhaps just a total lack of movement, alerted my subconscious and, removing my near useless goggles, I peered at his face.

I could not focus for a while as the cold wind whipped at my tear-ducts and Mike's face gave me no clues through his goggles and balaclava. Ice spikes poked horizontally from his chin as from a grotesque clown's mask.

'Are you okay, Mike?' I screamed at him, and struck him on the shoulder.

There was no response at all and his head seemed to loll.

I remembered seeing him once before in this state, somewhere in the Siberian Arctic, and realised he was about to succumb to hypothermia. Because my fingers were numb and a steady Force Seven wind made things awkward, I spent several minutes unpacking and erecting the tent. When the inner tent was up I shouted to Mike to go inside and start the cooker whilst I fixed up the fly sheet.

A couple of minutes later I found that Mike was still kneeling in the snow and staring vacantly into space. I hustled him through the door-flap and, unpacking his sledge, threw his mat and bag inside.

Once the cooker was going, Mike began leadenly to remove his clothes as though in a trance. He said nothing but accepted a mug of tepid soup from the Thermos. He slept for an hour and when he awoke spent some time staring at the tent ceiling. His memory, which had entirely gone as far as the last few hours were concerned, gradually returned. I made him two cups of tea and he ate two of his chocolate bars.

My mind was in turmoil. I had little doubt but that he was pushing himself far too hard. Time and again I had tried to make him see the sense of the polar plod policy but he suspected my motives, believing I was merely protecting my own interests, and could not bring himself to manhaul at less than his maximum capacity. This, I believed, was both eating into his reserves of muscle strength and rendering him the

148

more susceptible to poor conditions. For days now he had suffered from a 'down' mood and I began to fear, as he did, that he would decide to 'pack it in' somewhere along the plateau between the Pole and the Beardmore Glacier, a region where the altitude and the decreasing temperatures of oncoming winter were likely to tax both our resolve and our remaining strength.

My great fear was that I would face an ANI bill of over US$100,000 should we call for evacuation due merely to breakdown of our resolve and not because of a life or death situation. Only given the latter circumstances would I stand a chance of a successful insurance claim to cover Search and Rescue costs.

Since an ANI flight was shortly due to remove Erling Kagge from the Pole, I realised that I must urge Mike to make up his mind *now*, before we reached the Pole, as to whether or not he wished to continue our attempt to cross the continent and then try to reach the Seaquest ship on the edge of the Ross Ice-Shelf.

When I had urged Mike to push on despite diarrhoea I had, in my pique, said I would continue the journey without him if necessary. Both he and I knew this was nonsense since the whole basis of our venture was to be *unsupported*. If either of us dropped out at any stage the remaining party, even if successful, could never claim an *unsupported* crossing. If Mike decided to evacuate to the Pole, I would have to do likewise. There would be no point in continuing alone, since I had already crossed the continent *supported* back in 1981. To leave from the Pole even on an existing ANI aircraft (rather than at some later point on a dedicated flight responding to a 'non-lethal' call) would save me facing a bill far in excess of what I could possibly hope to pay.

Mike saw this point and probably sympathised with my predicament. He said he *hoped* he would be able to carry on. He had already begun to persuade himself that his current

149

attack of hypothermia was entirely due to his mitts problem and not to his 'speed surges'.

Later in the day the wind dropped, the mists cleared and we carried on. Towards the evening I screamed at Mike, 'Look ahead. Over there. There's a *thing*.' For the first time in over 700 miles a man-made object was visible in the snow. We had a two-part wager between us. Whoever spotted the first sign of the Pole would get a free hamburger snack and, for sighting the Pole itself, a free 'slap-up' lunch.

The *thing* turned out to be a half-buried meteorlogical balloon and its presence was a definite boost to morale.

At 7 p.m., glancing ahead as I topped a slow rise, I thought I saw movement. Removing my goggles and squinting to focus, I could just make out a series of dark, blurred objects; five or six black marbles dancing on the shimmer of the southern horizon.

I turned back and shouted to Mike. It was a rare moment of sheer elation. The journey was far from over but we had dragged to the Pole *just* enough stores to allow us to cross the continent and survive. If our luck held.

Chapter Eight

'The icy fang that bites and blows until I
shrink with cold.'

Shakespeare

I carefully checked the navigation notes from my 1981 Antarctic crossing. The sun-and-watch method of direction-finding is fine when one is heading due south *towards* the Pole but a touch tricky when leaving the Pole for a 250-mile featureless journey which must end up at *exactly* the right point in the heavily crevassed Hinge Zone above the mighty glaciers of the Trans-Antarctica Mountains. Bearing in mind the likelihood of days, or even weeks, of mists which would obscure every feature in the Hinge Zone, I was especially keen to handle all the navigation myself.

I asked Mike if he would object. 'I'd be very unhappy,' was his response.

Deciding to let the matter lie until, and if, we reached the distant mountains, I desisted from further talk on the matter. I was navigator and I would navigate when I felt it necessary and that was an end to it. But now was no time to confront an issue that might never arise.

We had approached the Pole along the longitude or time zone of between 35° and 50° west of Greenwich and I had seldom needed to apply a magnetic correction of more than 20° nor a sun-time correction of over four hours.

From the Pole, once again at the suggestion of Charles

Swithinbank, I intended to follow the 167° east of Greenwich line of latitude. Midday at the Pole station was at Greenwich noon plus thirteen hours. Since I needed the sun to be directly *behind* our backs in the middle of our travel hours and since the sun would be due north at local midday on *our* chosen longitudinal line at 13.00 hours Greenwich Time, we had by good fortune no great time adjustment to make beyond remembering that, the instant we traversed the exact point of the geographical pole, we would cross the International Date Line and lose twenty-four hours. At one moment the date would be, say, 6 p.m. on 16 January, the next 6 p.m. on the 17th.

I would alter the compass variation from 30° to 154° the moment we reached the Pole and, should we later stray to the west of the chosen advance line, I would *add* magnetic variation accordingly. Mist or no mist, we should reach the top of the Mill Glacier so long as we kept carefully to this chosen route.

The American Pole station, known as Amundsen-Scott Base, was ten miles from the point where we first glimpsed its buildings. A series of rising steppes kept hiding the site but, after seven hours hauling on 16 January, we topped the final rise and came to the first of many isolated science domes at 17.00 hours Greenwich Time on the eighty-first anniversary day of Scott's sad arrival there.

All the isolation of the past months fell away. The polar site had vastly altered even in the twelve short years since my last visit. Strangely-shaped installations on jack-up steel legs reared monstrously in every direction from the main central feature, the black-roofed dome, in which over-wintering scientists live and work.

Constructed over an area of two square miles, the site no longer resembled the moonscape of my memory with its small huddle of Earth Stations. We were now confronted by a film set vista as of a long-deserted industrial estate, littered with oil

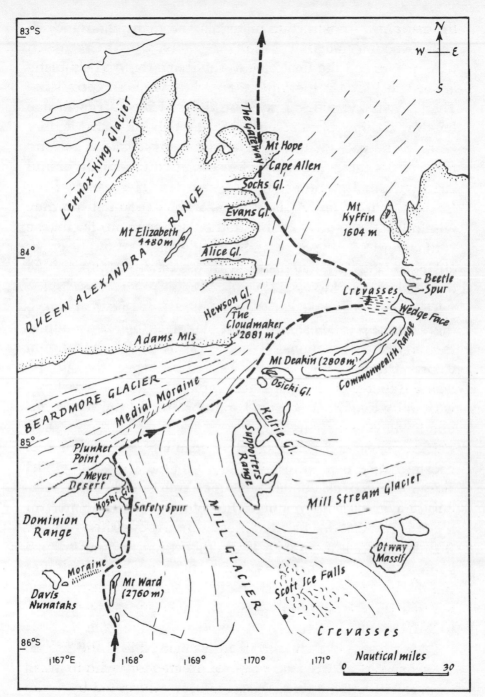

Route through the crevasse-fields of Mill and Beardmore Glaciers

drums, pipes, construction materials and many thousands of large, wooden crates.

As we hauled the final mile to the dome the ANI ski-plane arrived to pick up the Japanese and American expeditions. Then a VXE-6 Hercules landed on the ice runway: one of five US Navy cargo planes specially adapted for cold weather work. Skis, coated with Teflon to stop them sticking to ice, are fitted to slot under the wheels for soft landings. Each year and strictly within the short summer season, the Hercules fly from Christchurch in New Zealand, a hazardous 1,488-mile journey with no landing strips other than the Pacific Ocean. Their base is MacMurdo on the Ross Ice-Shelf, the largest and busiest of all the ninety Antarctic bases with a summer population of over 800 men and women.

The same year that Fuchs and Hillary crossed Antarctica, the Americans established the Pole station as their contribution to the 1957 International Geophysical Year. When Admiral George Dufek of the US Navy landed to inspect the site, he was the first person there since Captain Scott. By 1971 there were forty-two other occupied stations around the continent, operated by ten nations.

The 1957 station was soon crushed under snow-drifts and became dangerous. In 1975, the present base was built with its aluminium geodesic dome, sixty feet high, and housing various caravan-like living units. The rounded shape of most of the Pole installations helps to prevent burial by drifts.

I had no wish to stop at the Pole beyond the need to take sponsor photographs of the sledges and our jackets in front of the dome. I knew that relations between private expeditions and the US polar authority, the National Science Foundation, had deteriorated since my previous stay at the Pole. In 1985 the Mear/Swan expedition ran into open NSF hostility and, subsequently, all US polar personnel were instructed to avoid contact with private ventures.

This was an understandable reaction since 'explorers' in

trouble would inevitably endanger the Hercules crews who would feel morally responsible to search for them. Airplanes of all types are at risk in such an environment. During my last visit a DC10 with 257 tourists from New Zealand had crashed into Mount Erebus. There were no survivors. Several US Hercules have ended up abandoned in crevasses, which is bad enough for the American taxpayer without their planes being involved in the transport of stranded non-scientific adventurers.

The VXE Hercules *have* over the years saved many lives at remote bases. In 1985 an Australian was seriously burned by exploding gases which he inhaled. The nearest medical unit that could help him was in New Zealand and his *only* hope was an US Hercules. He died en route but the US flights had at least provided a *chance* of survival.

On the other hand, during my Transglobe Expedition, when six South African scientists were lost and one killed, neither the Americans nor any other nation were able to send any rescue airplanes and only the presence of our own expedition Twin Otter and the courage of the pilot Giles Kershaw (founder of ANI) saved the South Africans from certain death.

Back in 1980 Ollie Shepard, Charlie Burton and I had reached the South Pole just before Christmas on our three sledge-towing snowmobiles. After a great deal of wrangling between the UK Foreign Office and the US National Science Foundation, we were allowed to spend four days at the Pole whilst waiting for Giles Kershaw to fly my wife Ginnie, who was our base leader, and the rest of the team across from the Atlantic side of the continent.

Memories of that sojourn came flooding back as Mike and I neared the dome. The 1980 station commander, an ex-US marine captain, had allowed us all to eat in the dome's canteen providing we helped his cook with the dishes and chores. One of my duties had been to replenish the canteen ice-cream machine. It was definitely the best chocolate ice-cream I have ever tasted.

Time-wise, Mike and I arrived at the Pole well before the station's working day began, but a huddle of nine figures in full polar clothing stood waiting beneath the colourful array of national flags at the world's most southerly point.

A ragged cheer rose briefly as we gave a token spurt for the last few yards to the flags. The reception committee consisted of the four members of the American Women's Team and the crew of the ANI Twin Otter. The girls had arrived two days before us and, with two of their number sick or injured, they had decided to abandon their crossing attempt.

For some minutes we stood with our sledges by the Pole. I felt curiously remote and devoid of feeling. I looked across at Mike. Half an hour earlier we had noticed Kagge's tracks approaching the Pole and Mike, with unusual vehemence, had commented, 'Why does the bastard continue to say it's a race?' But now Mike's face was a picture of conflicting emotions. He leant forward briefly on his ski stick and there were tears in his eyes. He was clearly elated. I felt pleased for him, knowing that he had tried for so long and so hard to reach this place. Back in 1985, when Roger Mear turned him down and chose Gareth Wood in his place, Mike had admitted, 'Not going to the Pole is hurting, hurting like hell.'

Beneath the wind-frayed international flags, a football-sized silver globe marked the Pole's approximate position (*very* approximate, for nobody had moved it an inch since I had stared at it twelve years before). The globe and the whole polar station are slowly floating away from the Pole like flotsam in the sea.

To walk around the silver globe is to walk around Earth with minimal effort. Mike noted the heavy plywood sheet conveniently placed under the globe so that the 'round-the-world walkers' do not tread out a deep circular rut in the snow. Here at last was a solid surface on which to weigh

156

ourselves with Mike's miniature electronic scales. We erected the tent on this board and, stripping off to our underwear, rushed out to the scales. By balancing on one foot like a couple of Peter Pans, we at last obtained accurate weight readings.

We asked the Americans to join us in the tent for tea. They all piled in and, on seeing our tea mugs scummed with spaghetti and porridge, all but Sue Giller politely declined. Sue managed one gulp. 'Tibetans would love that,' she commented.

They told us the highlights of their journey and I marvelled at their strength and endurance. They all looked incapable of shifting a coal sack yet they had hauled 200-pound sledge-loads and received only two resupply flights en route to the Pole. Tendon and bronchial troubles had respectively troubled Anne and Sunniva. Both Sue and Ann Bancroft wanted badly to continue their crossing attempt but could not raise enough funds from sponsorship to go further than the Pole.

Ann Bancroft had become the first woman to reach both North and South Poles on foot. I hugged her as we took our leave and was amazed at her size, as light and apparently fragile as a teenage ballet dancer. She gave me a note which said we had helped and inspired them. It wished us good luck with the words: 'Our strength and courage and hearts are with you. God bless. Love Sunniva, Ann, Anne and Sue.'

In a few hours' time the Japanese team were due to arrive, having hauled their 200-pound loads unsupported from Patriot Hills in sixty-six days. I left a message of congratulations for their leader, Kenji Yoshikawa, and we continued on our way less than two hours after our arrival.

Warren Randle, the ANI Twin Otter pilot who would fly the Americans and Japanese back to Patriot Hills, warned me that I must give him at least ten days' advance notice should we get into trouble and even then he could not promise that the weather would allow him to reach us. To locate and land at the South Pole station was one thing. Some unknown spot either side of or *on* the Beardmore Glacier was quite another, especially if we stayed on into February when, he warned me, bad weather would close in for weeks not days.

Unbidden thoughts of the food available inside the dome canteen tripped about my taste buds as we forced ourselves north from the station.

A technician was working by a packing crate in the porch of the last lonely shack that we passed. He looked up and I was aware we must have presented a weird image. His was the last hut for nigh on 1,000 miles of hostile terrain. I raised my stick in greeting but he did not reply.

A mile beyond the Pole we entered a region of snowquakes. Without warning I heard a crashing roar and felt an instant of extreme panic as the solid snow surface under my feet dropped away.

Mike later told me he had never experienced such giant quakes as those close to the Pole. When snow builds up into a patch of wind crust several inches thick, whether as big as a sports arena, or merely room-sized, the pressure of even a dog's foot can be enough to trigger a sudden collapse of the whole suspended mass. Never more than a few inches, but enough to petrify the ignorant passer-by and to spark off thunderous sound waves for several seconds.

By the time we made camp in thick mist we had hauled over ten miles despite the two-hour delay at the Pole. I cut my last Mars Bar in half and we silently savoured the exquisite taste for a minute of luxury by way of self-congratulation for reaching the Pole.

My lasting memory of our brief visit to the Pole was disappointment that the Americans had let such a sacrosanct place deteriorate into an ugly, cluttered dump. Not long before, with my wife and some friends, I had joined a package tour rafting down the Colorado Grand Canyon. The success of the Canyon conservationists was heartening and impressive. Exactly 15,000 tourists are allowed down the canyon annually yet, in ten days of boating and camping within its narrow and spectacular confines, we never spotted a single trace of previous human visitors. No litter and no bush latrines; a tribute to all involved.

The National Science Foundation could learn a lot from the Canyon authorities. Greenpeace has for years tried to embarrass the NSF and others into non-pollutive practices in Antarctica. Two years previously, at a Soviet base, they found that 'since the base was set up in 1971 each occupying team had copied their predecessors' and thrown their empty drums and general waste, only partially incinerated, over the edge of a cliff. Although some was half buried in snow, large quantities were still visible. Plastic and glass refuse was dumped down a crevasse and, on a nearby slope, a number of old tanks had leaked oil. The whole site was littered with empty fuel barrels and old abandoned trucks.'

The American base of MacMurdo initiated a major clean-up in 1989, costing US$30,000,000. 6,000,000 pounds of waste, thousands of drums of oil and solvents, old transformers containing PCBs, asbestos explosives and chemicals were removed. A decade previously the US had belatedly kow-towed to Treaty dictates on dangerous wastes by shipping their nuclear-powered desalination plant back home.

Most of the coastal bases have been discharging their sewage direct into the sea, in some cases for over thirty years, and, by 1990, were just beginning to consider biological treatment plants.

The worst pollution threat to Antarctica's wildlife is posed by the ever-increasing number of cruise ship tourists. They come to photograph penguins, seals and other wildlife colonies and they disrupt breeding patterns. One of the ships carrying tourists, the Argentinian naval transporter *Bahia Paraiso*, with 200,000 gallons of oil on board, ran aground in 1989 off Palmer Station. The US base commander there reported: 'The krill are jumping out of the water to try and escape the oil. The birds are going crazy seeing this food and are diving to catch them, getting oiled up as a result.' The ship still contained 64,000 gallons and was expected to release this any day when the hull finally broke up.

Morag sent us news soon afterwards of an oil tanker disaster off the Shetland Islands with countless seal and bird deaths. I prayed that mankind would have enough sense *never* to allow oilfields in or off Antarctica.

My thoughts dwelt only briefly on pollution. I was worried by our body weight figures. I had weighed in that afternoon at eleven and a half stones (161 pounds) and Mike at nine and a half stones (133 pounds). We had each lost some twenty-five per cent of our body weight, in my case forty-nine pounds, and Mike now forecast that I would probably lose a further twenty-one pounds over the next thirty days.

Neither of us could afford this sort of weight loss since the colder temperatures now setting in with the imminent onslaught of winter would cut right into our body cores. Normally our body fat would have provided natural thermic protection but we were already devoid of fat and, especially in Mike's case, vulnerable to hypothermia.

Unless he settled down to a sensible polar plod I could see Mike running himself into the ground. He refused to accept this and, since *he* was the doctor, I stood little chance of persuading him. Since his erroneous diagnosis of the effects of altitude on our performance, I no longer considered his cold weather theories as omnipotent.

I told him that since I was losing more weight than he was, but naturally did not expect to eat more than my half-rations share, the only sensible course I could suggest was that we use up more of the rations I was carrying so that I lightened up by twenty-five pounds before he did. This should continue until he moved at the same slow plod as I did, even on flat surfaces and in easier temperatures.

160

Mike naturally revolted against such a suggestion. Why, he queried, should he carry more than someone who had talked of going on without him and muttered, 'We must be tougher,' when he, Mike, had wished to pause through sickness.

All our previous sufferings were as nothing compared with the days which followed the Pole. Much of this was my fault for underestimating the extreme cold at 11,000 feet above sea level and the effect it would have on our battered bodies. I should have obtained and packed *more* protective clothing and I should not have suggested abandoning our down jackets and outer sleeping bags. We were now suffering for these mistakes, and the immediate future looked grim.

We were working at an effective altitude* of 15,000 feet above sea level. The wind blew day after day at a fairly steady Force Five, exacerbating the daily-decreasing January temperatures. As Cherry-Garrard recorded, 'A low temperature when it is calm is paradise compared to a higher temperature with a wind and it is this constant pitiless wind combined with the altitude and low temperatures which has made travelling on the Antarctic plateau so difficult.'

Only now, beyond the Pole, were we discovering the true meaning of *cold*. Our conditions in terms of body deterioration, slow starvation, inadequate clothing, wind chill temperature, altitude and even the day of the year, exactly matched those of Scott and his four companions as they came away from the Pole. On 17 January 1912 Scott's friend, Doctor Wilson, a leader of 'the worst journey in the world', wrote: 'It blew from Force Four to Six all day in our teeth with temperature minus twenty-two degrees, the coldest march I ever remember. It was difficult to prevent one's hands from freezing in double woollen and fur mitts.

'Thin air, low pressure and oxygen deficiency reach a point, at about ten thousand feet, above which even well-fed, fit

---

* 4,000 feet greater than the *actual* altitude.

humans will be affected by altitude "sickness". It is best not to exert yourself but, if you must, you will find every movement is an effort. The pulse rate races away and to breathe is to gasp as your lungs and heart fight to pump oxygen around the body.'

Additionally, because both our vacuum flasks were broken, we were drinking too little liquid to replace the enormous amounts we lost daily through hard work at altitude and in great cold.

Amundsen's men were less stressed than Scott's since their loads were hauled by dogs, but this did not stop Bjaaland, their fittest member and a national ski champion, from declaring, 'I wish to God we were down on the ice-shelf. Here it is hard to breathe and the nights are as long as the Devil.'

Two days out from the Pole, Mike wrote: 'I had a desperately "black" period during the first four hours and very nearly stopped then and there. I even considered various medical emergencies that might be put on.'

I could sense that Mike was in a bad way despite his continued 'power surges'. I knew that even now he would never recognise that his pace was his own worst enemy. He looked to be near the end of his tether and I feared that any further attempts by me to 'bully' him into copying my polar plod, any further 'gracelessness' should he again need to camp early, might prove to be the final straw. I resolved, from now on, to compromise with him over matters of pace whenever necessary.

That afternoon, on a high place that could have been the summit of Mount Everest without the view, for all its wind-blasted, frozen hostility, Mike stopped at the end of our fifth hour. We slumped, breathless and weak, onto a sledge and feebly tried to crack the ice jamming the top of our Thermos. Gulping at tepid soup, we agreed that something would have to change.

When Mike tried to get off the sledge, his legs crumpled and he fell backwards. On his third attempt he stood up swaying. We both laughed or at least emitted sounds which I took to be laughs. I was surprised at such signs of muscle deterioration in Mike who has amazingly powerful lower limb muscles in terms of sheer effective pulling power.

That night we reached an agreement that Mike would slow himself down by taking rations for the next three days off my sledge, and that we would eat the last of the six cannibalised rations over the next ten days whilst still under maximum altitude stress. If we could only survive as far as the Beardmore Glacier and start to lose height, *then* we could compensate by cutting to half-rations.

Mike unpacked a sterilised scalpel and lanced my infected foot in several places, releasing quantities of surface poison. That side of my foot was now death-white, spongy and hyper-sensitive.

On our seventy-first day we sailed for seven or eight miles but the wind dragged us too far west, which upset my navigational plans. At that time, our Magellan position locator was inoperative, confused by our proximity to the Pole. The cold was intense and a Force Five wind did not help. Mike wrote, 'Getting the tent up and camp made was pretty desperate.'

One of the antenna wires came loose and my numb fingers fumbled for several minutes simply trying to tighten a wing-nut. We made faint communications with Morag, still at Patriot Hills, who told us that Kagge had said to the press, 'The Brits have guts.'

Even inside our tent, with the cooker rehydrating the spaghetti, it was intensely cold. I forced myself to take down my trousers in order to apply haemorrhoid cream to various places, including the raw regions of my crotch, scabbed lips, nose and chin.

'I don't believe it,' Mike exclaimed staring at my legs. 'You can't pull anything with *those*. They're Belsen-like.'

We tried to keep warmer in the tent by applying an old

Arctic trick of Ollie Shepard's. Instead of stacking cut snow blocks to be used for water outside the tent door, we filled the tent stuff-bag with them and kept it down by our feet. Although the bag emanated cold, we at least avoided the need to keep unzipping the door flap.

The following day was purgatory. Mike wrote: 'Cold is an understatement . . . it became very unpleasant indeed and I nearly blew it by delaying putting on my outer jacket in the morning. I suffered both general cold and severely cold hands as a result.'

Mike wanted to try sailing. I was against it as my feet were both in a bad way. Red-hot pains accompanied each sideways contact with either of my rigid boots. I was increasingly wary of heading too far west. I made it clear to Mike that I had no wish to discuss even trying to sail on weak winds which involved painful footwork and endangered our correct route towards the head of the Mill Glacier.

By the morning of the seventy-third day, Mike's sledge was ten pounds heavier than mine and he was holding to a sensible hauling pace which I felt sure would benefit both of us.

That day he wrote:

> A desperately cold day, perhaps −40°C with a stiff wind
> that kept us deeply chilled despite wearing all our clothing
> and going as best we could. My hands were very bad and,
> after each pee, they took thirty minutes to recover. Even
> then they would still be weak which led to further problems
> at the next pee – a vicious circle. My morale was not too bad:
> just a brief spell of 'Let's get out now with an illness/injury'
> phase and, the rest of the day, just quiet recognition that
> after seventy-four days of this it's not much fun. Still, Ran
> has calculated that, at this pace and with no help from the
> wind, we should make the glacier top in seventeen days.
> Surely I can last that long . . . Ran and I have such a
> profoundly different approach to planning and coping. He
> finds it necessary to be as pessimistic as possible and then
> work up from that point while I do the opposite. It is

164

strange to have him trying to help me mentally (for he is being as attentive as he can in this regard) by putting a *black* picture of success. All *I* want is a *white* picture of what could be, to keep me going – although I do accept that knowing even the black one will give us something is worthwhile.

My own diary was beginning to lapse into a mere record of impressions. 'New kind of chisel-hard, hoarfrost surface in sudden patches. It is now horribly body-cold. I feel as though naked. When waiting for Mike, I have to clasp my arms around my torso and jump and sing or swear. We have run out of glue for our skins. Every six days now the average temperature drops two degrees. Today, at the end of the morning, our goggles both rimed up badly. We strain to see through ice-up at white-out and pray there are no holes.'

The next day we sailed but gained two miles at best to the detriment of our southerly heading. Sometimes I stopped to gasp for air and was forced to loosen my chest harness. This I hated for the waist strap immediately began to chafe my hip-sores along the edges of the plasters which I had placed over the original raw areas.

My stomach churned all day and bouts of dizziness came and went. Two explosive attacks of diarrhoea involved taking my trousers down and squatting clear of my skis. This re-opened my haemorrhoids which in turn made leg movement a misery. I dislike people who whinge when they are uncomfortable, and now I started disliking myself, for my thoughts dwelt increasingly on my various sources of bodily discomfort. Since the wind chill factor was around −85°C I pulled my trousers back with alacrity and without careful attention to detail. This soiled my trousers and mitts but the excrement quickly froze solid and was easily knocked off.

Mike came up alongside and said, 'We can stop if you want.' My churlish response, which I regretted as soon as it was said, was 'I don't stop for diarrhoea.'

165

I spent the next hour ruminating on how extremely unpleasant I must be as a travelling companion and ended up quite thankful that Mike was not carrying the revolver which in the Arctic was usually his responsibility. On earlier journeys he had admitted nursing thoughts of using it when I left him way behind and his morale had dropped to rock bottom.

We travelled for ten hours, pausing only for my diarrhoea attacks, so there was no sustenance from the Thermos. We knew the conditions were too cold and a pint of tepid soup would not be worth the frozen hands.

On the seventy-fifth day I woke from a night of throbbing foot pain with an almost phobic dread of my rigid ski-boots. If some modern-day Gestapo had threatened me with the torture of squeezing my feet into those boots, I would have told all and sold my soul to avoid the experience. As it was, there was no such option. The porridge gruel and coffee were ruined by having to count down the minutes to execution, the moment when I must gingerly draw my socks over the mess of my feet. As the textile hairs brushed against the damaged areas, I would grind my teeth together. Then came the unyielding pressure of the boots themselves and the beginning of the twelve-hour ordeal during which I would have only one thing in mind; the moment of release from the boots.

Painkillers tended to make me drowsy – not a good state to be in when working in cold places, so I had fought against taking them for the past two months. Mike now gave me two to take at breakfast along with antibiotics to stave off gangrene. At the time I was on Erythromycin and the mixed effect of the pills was a general feeling of gut sickness.

As we set out, Mike commiserated about my feet but then he surged off for ninety minutes of hard haulage. I arrived nearly two minutes behind him and remonstrated once again at his uncontrolled pace. However, as the morning progressed, the wind picked up and cut through our clothing. Out of self-defence I had to abandon my pace control to save my core temperature from dropping dangerously low. This made it difficult for Mike to keep up with me. I was caught on the horns of an unusual dilemma. At the day's end Mike hissed, 'That is definitely the fastest pace of the entire expedition.' My only defence was to stress that, given such extreme cold, a fast pace actually saved calories by maintaining body warmth.

Mike tried hard to stop the poison spreading in my foot but, as he explained, the safest treatment in addition to antibiotics was immediate prevention of any further trauma to the damaged areas. His diary commented:

> This morning Ran actually said 'I feel like chucking it all in' when talking of his foot. Although he never would, I welcome such signs of weakness which are so familiar to me, although he has my every sympathy since I find it hard enough and I am essentially pain-free.
> Day Seventy-Six: Eleven thousand feet now. Ran was in great pain to start with and went terribly slowly in the second hour. He apologised and said he just felt weak. Later he needed to stop and have a crap and it may well be that the antibiotics have stirred up his stomach. Hence the weakness. I am therefore suggesting that he stops them and I start him on Lederfen and painkillers. His ear is quite badly frostbitten from yesterday.
> Day Seventy-Eight: I was desperately hungry today.

The following day Mike diagnosed possible 'deep-seated infection in the foot bone' and put me on Metronidazole and Flucloxicillin. Unfortunately we were running short of those antibiotics which seemed most effective. The cold in the afternoon and evening was so penetrating it had the excellent effect of taking my mind off my feet. Mike said I had hauled 'incredibly fast', which naturally made me feel both guilty and hypocritical.

*

On 28 January, with the ANI camp at Patriot Hills about to close down for the winter, Morag was flown out to Punta Arenas from where she continued to organise all our communications and to answer the flood of international enquiries as to our whereabouts and problems.

A Chilean mountaineer, Alejo Contreras, who worked for ANI, remained at Patriot Hills to close up the base and help bury the Cessna ski-plane in an under-snow hangar. When communications were briefly reasonable, he warned us that the Americans were also beginning to close down their operations and withdraw all aircraft and ships from the continent. Soon only the Twin Otter would remain. ANI were extremely and understandably keen that we should quit Antarctica as soon as possible. Only twenty days remained for us to cross the continent and then reach the Seaquest ship on the far side of the Ross Ice-Shelf.

Alejo asked me if I thought we could make it.

'Impossible to predict,' I told him.

The great unknown of the Beardmore, if we ever reached it, would determine the outcome.

In the night I woke to stabbing pains from one frostbitten toe. Mike was asleep so I tried to emulate his scalpel incisions with my penknife. That seemed the best way of relieving the pressure. A good deal of pus and tea-like liquid escaped but the pains continued, so I swallowed two painkillers and eventually slept. I woke a few minutes later, or so it seemed, with a head full of rats. Mike checked the infected foot after porridge and squeezed it successfully.

'This is only local pus,' he assured me.

I cut out square-inch patches from my bed mat and plastered them all around the wound. This certainly helped the first few hours of travel by about three on a pain-scale of ten.

My problem was the ongoing tunnel of pain which made

168

me irritable. If only it would go away at least some of the time. I found the sharp feel of it trying to wear me down.

I realised now how lucky I had been for fifty years of experiencing comparatively little pain. Broken bones and teeth, torn-off digits, frostbite and chronic kidney stones had seemed unpleasant at the time. But now I knew *real* pain and I feared lest it overwhelm me, to my everlasting shame.

I tried to think up ways of attacking it mentally on the basis that, whenever there were lethal crevasses about or when navigational worries were preoccupying my brain, the constant pain receded. The pain behaved like a circular railway track with a steam train chugging relentlessly around it . . . when it went through the tunnels it was still there but less noticeable. So I tried to invent tunnels, by day and by night, to programme my mind with vivid thoughts of past happenings. When this failed, especially after I slipped or caught my boot and triggered raw shrieks from one or other foot, I tried to imagine the pain as a living *thing*. Sometimes as a red-hot poker or an electric drill. At those times I would try to imagine I was part of the poker or the drill and I was working to stoke a fire or drill a gatepost. This would lead me to think of a myriad other 'jobs' that my pain could attack. I never won the fight with these tactics, but nor did I lose it.

On the eightieth day a powerful south wind tempted us to try sailing, an activity made notably unpleasant by the intense cold. The cotton bum-flap of my ski jacket was constantly rucked up by my sail harness and my buttocks began to freeze. That night I tried sewing cut-out patches of the tent bag to the back of my trousers but failed to achieve any improvements.

For the first time the wind was strong enough to pull our sails directly south without the need for painful tacking manoeuvres. But frequent wind surges of thirty or forty knots saw us hurtling over concrete-hard ridges. A single fall at such speeds could cause severe injury not least through a skull or spine crushed by a flying 250-pound sharp-prowed sledge.

169

Because our leg muscles were, to put it mildly, depleted, every yard that we sailed in such conditions was a calculated risk which, given the slightest touch of bad luck, could instantly put paid to the entire journey.

After a day of −90°C wind chills, with no possibility of stopping for long enough to open the soup Thermos, the cooker decided to play up as we squatted in the ice-box of our tent.

Mike wrote: 'On arrival, bone-cold, at the tent, I found the cooker was leaking from our make-do pump seal and for an hour I fiddled with it before achieving a seal and frostbitten finger tips. We now risk further tent fires in more hazardous locations. We have both agreed to accept this risk and carry on. Ran now has nasty frostbite on two toes of one foot and parts of the other . . . I am loath to manhaul if I can sail. I *think* Ran believes we should only manhaul but he has just said, "We both want to make it to Scott Base so there's no more to be said."'

Although scarcely a word passed between us outside the tent, it was then that the mutual feelings of hostility were most rampant. From my side of the fence, my irritation, dislike or sometimes sheer hatred of Mike varied in intensity, whether he was ahead or behind, in direct relation to the pain-scale I was experiencing at any given time.

Once we struck camp and I had chosen a suitable spot for the tent, we hastened to get ourselves and our gear inside, leaving the sledges carefully strapped down against blizzards. However tired we were I made a habit of rushing this part of the day, to cut down every second that delayed the instant when we would be out of the wind, the cooker lit and, moment of sheer pleasure, *my boots removed*. From that point until boots-on time the following morning, however bad the night pains, cracked lips and lack of sleep, I never felt hostility or tension towards Mike.

We would discuss most things under the sun and often found that our viewpoints were utterly at variance.

I commented to Mike that I never thought of sex during polar journeys. He agreed and put this down to a temporary withdrawal of the male hormone testosterone. As with sub-mariners on long voyages, he said, this hormone tends to absent itself when it knows there is no possibility of sexual activity. Reinhold Messner recorded continued erotic day-dreaming during his Antarctic manhaul. 'Time and again I encountered figures of women, living, obstinate, wanton women. I pictured them naked and sometimes as my partner.' Perhaps too many years of high altitude climbing had mucked up his testosterone responses.

Shackleton, on the other hand, would tolerate 'no smut' on his long polar journeys. The only way of dealing with sexual deprivation, he decided, was to pretend that women did not exist.

Food took the place of sex, anticipated with salivating eagerness and savoured to the last lick. In three days' time we must switch to cut rations, to prolong the number of travel days left to us, by making up for the six rations we had cannibalised to date.

Now that the physical struggle of the 800-mile, 11,000-foot ascent was behind us, our calorie expenditure had dropped from an appalling 10,000 to about 7,000 per day. Our standard ration of 5,200 calories per day would shortly be cut to 3,000, which is the amount a healthy male teenager expects to consume in everyday life conditions.

Our current sorry state had largely been caused by the long weeks of calorie deficiency. As Mike put it, 'Our calorie *deficit* has been the equivalent of the total *input* of a normal person. It is exactly as though a normal person had eaten nothing, I repeat nothing, all this time. After several weeks they would get weak and desperately hungry. In fact they would starve. We *are* slowly starving.'

This, of course, was a godsend for Mike's research work. After sixty days of watching Mike divide our daily ration in two and hand me one vitamin tablet, four small-size milk chocolate bars, eight sheets of loo paper (inedible) and one crunchy flapjack, I began to nurse horrible suspicions that he was handing me the smaller of the flapjacks every day. This irked me as I grew more ravenous until, on the sixty-first day, I suggested that we take turns to choose the daily flapjacks. Mike agreed readily enough.

By Day Eighty, to my eternal disgrace, I found myself suspecting a less than mathematically precise division of the contents of the porridge pot each morning. When I could no longer bear the sight of Mike licking even the most innocently 'empty' cook's porridge spoon, I suggested that we take turns at scraping out any porridge remains. Mike again responded with good grace and I felt renewed shame at my greed.

We both talked and thought about food a great deal and I filled up two pages of my notebook with scribbled lists of everything I would devour on my first day back in London.

On 30 January we recorded our first barometric descent of a few hundred feet, but this welcome news was balanced by a potentially disastrous event.

In the morning a gusting south wind soon had us attempting to sail in thick mists and between giant sastrugi. Mike crossed his ski-tips, an easy mistake, crashed down and was dragged along at speed and spread-eagled until his sail lines were snagged by an ice-ridge. Either the ice or his sledge prow struck his shoulder, which remained painful for several days. Worse was to come.

At noon Mike had problems with his sail and caught me up after a twenty-minute delay to announce that both his ski-sticks had somehow fallen off his sledge. He had already scanned his back-track but could see nothing. We could have wasted the rest of the day searching to no avail so I gave Mike one of my sticks and suggested we try to progress with one each.

Early skiers in the Alps and Scandinavia used only a single ski stick but *they* never tried hauling heavy loads behind them. Even on flat stretches we found it exceptionally difficult to progress with only half our previous thrusting power.

I could not help considering the irony that, all this time, we had thought life was about as bad as could possibly be and yet we had had the luxury of *two* sticks. If only we had known how lucky we then were.

Working at only half-thrust, I began to freeze and was forced to step up the pace. Mike lagged far behind and, every time I stopped to await him, I became colder, until my body shook as though with the ague. I would have given anything for more clothes or even some newspaper, or straw, to stuff under my jacket and trousers. I considered cutting up the remaining polythene ration bags and stitching them to the inside of my jacket.

We tried to sail again but both our sails inverted badly, causing complex tangles in the lines. I attempted to sort mine out but only made them worse. Mike had proved himself an expert at this. I admired his dexterity enormously but, this time, even he could not disentangle the lines. His fingers were ragged with blisters, which did not help.

So we manhauled again through a curtain of weird yellow light and cut by bitter winds from the Pole. I estimated a wind chill factor of −90°C. I was plagued by the nagging worry that the morning's sail had taken us far to the west, meaning miles of adjustment to regain our approach line for the correct glacier pass.

Our hauling was now ridiculously slow and especially painful for whichever foot corresponded with the stick-wielding arm. I moved slowly but, nonetheless, Mike dropped far behind and, waiting, I became so cold that my feet went numb. In something of a panic I could think of no answer but to stop early, which was taboo, or to encourage Mike's pace by giving him my remaining stick. This he accepted gratefully and he resumed a much steadier pace.

By pumping my arms to and fro like a marathon walker and by applying the herringbone position with my skis on icy ridged stretches, I found I could keep much warmer and progress reasonably well despite being stickless.

For thirty minutes we advanced through less than ideal wind chill conditions but Mike's speed gradually decreased to a crawl and his head began to loll with exhaustion. I spoke to him and his response was blurred. I grew frightened. He was clearly heading for hypothermia again. Some twenty-five minutes before stop time, I erected the tent and made hot tea which tasted exceptionally good.

Our bodily condition was becoming highly suspect. I was not in the business of leading suicide expeditions. We were approaching the edge of our ability to cope safely with very extreme conditions and this was, we both knew, because we were starving. That night I thought a lot of Douglas Mawson, the toughest of all polar travellers. The journey which tested even his endurance is described in *Mawson's Will* and serves as a warning that leaders should decide to turn back *before* their progress begins to *depend* on good luck. This principle holds good today as it did eighty years ago. Shackleton missed the Pole but saved his expedition, through knowing when to give up. Scott reached the Pole and died, as Mawson nearly did, by tempting fate a touch too far.

After their companion Ninnis died down a crevasse, Mawson and Mertz were left with less rations than could see them back to safety. They resorted to eating their huskies and abandoned their goal of charting the coastline, having, at the time of the tragedy, travelled 320 miles from their coastal base

174

in six weeks. The return journey was to prove unpleasant, as can be seen from these extracts from *Mawson's Will*:

They relished the freedom from the incessant chew-chew-chewing of the meat. They could swallow chunks – ignoring the fishy, foul flavour and the slimy, clinging texture of the canine liver. They had not read the writings of Nansen on men who were reported to have died from eating such livers. Only that year, 1912, was the word *vitamin* first coined . . .

Eight years later the excessive substances in dogs' livers were isolated and named as Vitamin A. In 1971, it was shown by biochemists that four ounces of the liver from a Greenland husky dog contain a dose of Vitamin A that is toxic for an adult man. Mawson and Mertz between them swallowed sixty toxic doses . . .

They had come about half-way back to their base when they had their Christmas meal. They ate some liver; then Mawson heard Mertz ejaculate, 'A moment, still, please.' He plucked at Mawson's left ear. His fingers lifted away a complete skin cast. The entire covering of Mawson's ear drooped between Mertz's thumb and forefinger . . .

Mertz took off his own wet helmet and, inside the wool, strips of skin and small tufts of beard were attached. There were raw patches at his temples. The cracks round his mouth, nose and eyes were opening into red, raw fissures, deep like razor cuts and runny . . .

Mawson ached for food. There was one source he could not ignore – Ginger's head. The two haggard and tattered men crouched in the narrow tent and watched the skinned dog's head cooking. When it had boiled for ninety minutes, they lifted it onto the lid of the cooker. They took turns in gnawing their different sides, biting away the jaw muscles, lips, swallowing the eyelids and gulping down the eyeballs. They scooped out the contents of the skull and then split the thyroid, the tongue and brain into two servings . . .

Mertz was in a dire state. His trousers were fouled from an attack of dysentery, his eyes were wild and rolling and he babbled incoherently. Mawson cleaned his soiled clothing and was shocked to see his legs, his groin, stripped clean of skin, red, raw, rippled with painful folds . . .

Mertz raged. 'Am I a man or a dog? You think I have no courage because I cannot walk – but I show you.' He lifted his left hand; the little finger yellowed from frostbite was thrust into his mouth and Mawson watched in stupefied horror as Mertz crunched his teeth into the middle joint, savagely severing the skin, the cartilage and sinew, tearing away with grimaces and groans of pain . . . then, in disdain, spitting the severed digit onto the tent floor . . .

Mawson lowered his thick underpants and a shower of skin fragments and hair fell into the snow at his feet. Strips of skin had vanished from his legs; his kneecaps were without cover, just roughly rippled flesh, his private parts were red and raw, scarified from the friction of work and walking. Around his waist, on his shoulders, the harness had laid a skin pattern and he found eruptions breaking out like small boils with festering heads . . .

The sight of his feet was a hammer blow. His soles had separated into casts of dead skin, that came away leaving abraded, raw tissue. An abundant watery fluid filled his socks. He replaced the separated soles and bound them in position with bandages.

In this state Mawson, through willpower alone, struggled the final hundred miles back to his base. On one of his remarkable polar journeys in 1909, he had set a record of travelling 1,245 miles without outside support. This journey had stood as the undisputed world record for eighty-four years. Mawson had achieved it partially by killing penguins and seals to save the weight of hauling rations.

The longest-ever unsupported dog-sledge journey *not* feeding off the land was that of Sir Martin Lindsay, Andrew Croft and Daniel Godfrey in 1934 which crossed *1,080 miles* of the Greenland Icecap.

By far the longest unsupported *manhaul* journey recorded, *883 miles*, was that of Mear, Swan and Wood in 1986 to the South Pole although they compromised their claim, as did

Kagge in the Arctic, by contacting outsiders en route and eating food which they themselves did not carry.

Mike and I had by the eightieth day of our journey overtaken the record of Mear, Swan and Wood as well as that of Lindsay, Croft and Godfrey. These teams had been mainly British. The outstanding record distance by the Australian Mawson was still many miles to our north and, at our current showing, might well prove unattainable.

Mike wrote about the loss of his sticks:

> We were both very cold today and I have further frostbitten my fingers. Three p.m. saw us hauling initially with one stick each. But then with me on two sticks and Ran with none (how he goes with none amazes me). Later, on opening up my sledge, I found devastation. The aerial of the Sarsat beacon was smashed despite being wrapped in my sleeping bag. The lid of our remaining Thermos is chipped and frozen soup is all over my bag. I was horrified and so, no doubt, was Ran although he has taken it remarkably philosophically despite real concern about the Sarsat. Much to my guilt, Ran says he can walk without sticks so my great concern there is much lessened (I am useless without arm power). My shoulder is painful but manageable.

I wrote:

> I am worried that this morning's hectic wind sail, a very nasty experience, took us way too far west. I *must* correct our bearing. If over the next 27.8 nautical miles we can keep to 225° on the compass, we *should* locate the Mill Pass. Just now Mike said my feet 'look horrific'. I think his fingers, all bloody and raw, look revolting. He is trying to fix the Sarsat. No way will he succeed as he's well and truly jiggered its antenna. It's amazing how well we get on *once* we take our boots off. I cut my cheek and lower eyelid today: it seems that the plastic goggles rim got too cold and stuck to the skin. Congealed blood all over the mask. My hair is welded to a big weepy blister on my eastern [right] ear.

The next day Mike began to work out a satisfactory way of forcing his sledge to move with just one stick and we carried on at a goodish rate in a lop-sided manner. Our sledge-weights were equal again and, so long as the big winds stayed away, I kept rigidly to the polar plod.

Although the sun was visible for much of the day I constantly checked the compass for I knew we would need great accuracy to enter the Mill Glacier by the relatively crevasse-free route suggested by Charles Swithinbank. The slightest deviation could lead us into vast fissure fields, as bad as any in the world.

Sir Vivian Fuchs, leading the only crossing of Antarctica before my own in 1980, neatly summarised the standard problem of the Pole. 'It was slightly confusing to find that, when we turned north onto our course, the compasses became increasingly useless. For on leaving the Geographical Pole *every* direction was north and we had to travel some fifteen miles before stopping to take sights and decide which way north we wanted to go. Since the Magnetic Pole was still one thousand two hundred and fifty miles *south* of us according to the compass, *east* had become *west* and vice-versa. The nearer we got to the Magnetic Pole the less responsive our compasses, and attempts to use the sun compass were usually frustrated by the generally overcast sky.'

I was uncertain at what distance we would first glimpse the peaks of the Trans-Antarctic Mountains. Maybe twenty miles away or maybe only ten. On my map there were many small peaks with no names which dotted the region to our immediate south.

Early in the day I began to spot fleeting images of dark blips but none stood the test of remaining visible in the same place for a second glance. I suspected polar mirages of trying to trick me and, several times, narrowly checked myself from shouting 'Land!' to Mike. Polar mirages can *lift* objects such as mountains or tents that are on a distant horizon off the surface, so that they float and give false impressions of their distance and location.

When Amundsen's men neared the South Pole, in dread lest Scott had preceded them, they peered ahead. 'Do you see that black thing over there?' one called out. Everybody saw it. 'Can it be Scott?' was one suggestion. Bjaaland skied forward to investigate. He did not have to go far. 'Mirage,' he reported laconically. 'Only a dog turd.'

At last, at 11 a.m., I spotted a definite black peak directly ahead. We both shouted our delight and relief. An end at least to the many hundreds of miles of whiteness where evidence of progress could be measured only at the end of the day.

On seeing the mountain, I determined to take over all navigation down the glacier. I had no personal reason to trust or mistrust Mike's navigating abilities since, on all our previous journeys, I had been sole navigator apart from six days when I was partially blind. Until now, all our Antarctic navigation had consisted of following a simple compass bearing or keeping to a course dictated by the position of shadows, sastrugi or wind direction. From now on success would depend entirely upon selecting the correct tortuous pathway between the myriad man-killer crevasse fields of the second largest glacier on Earth.

I had total confidence in my navigating abilities and no confidence in anybody else's. I remembered a telling incident during a journey made by Mike, Roger Mear and a friend to re-enact Cherry-Garrard's 'worst journey in the world'. The leader was Mear but he had allowed too much democracy to creep into the process of navigating. He was soon to regret this because continued contradictory suggestions from Mike undermined his own vital self-confidence. He wrote: 'We were heading due east when Mike began to urge a more southerly course. In situations such as these decisions have to be made based on something more than correct evaluation of known facts. Much is conjecture . . . Mike was angry with me for once again he felt that his ideas had been treated with contempt. He had suggested, when the uncertainty of our position began to be felt, that we were heading in the wrong direction and it might be safer to turn east . . . It is impossible to be guided by reason in all one's decisions, and yet, because I had lost faith in Mike's judgement, I am forced to treat all my decisions as infallible.' Mear added: 'Indecision caused us to continue blindly on in what had become a howling gale.'

I wanted no such pressures on my instinctive navigation processes on this next, most hazardous and final stage of the continental crossing. On the other hand I did not wish to antagonise Mike, as Roger Mear apparently had, where I could avoid doing so. I could see I would have to be as tactful as was possible once we reached the mountains and I made my intentions clear.

Of one thing I was certain. I would prefer Mike's displeasure to any relaxing of my principles of expedition leadership. I liked to take the idea of democratic decision-making to the brink but no further.

I was alarmed that, about to enter 200 miles of notorious icefall and great stretches of slippery blue-ice, we had no crampons between us and only two ski-sticks, both of which had recently lost their baskets and their pointed ends.

That night, probably some ten miles still from the first rock features but already flanked by fearsome crevasse fields, I began to manufacture crampons to fit our four ski-boots. Using knotted lengths of our safety rope, our last repair wire and the pin-nose pliers, I put together some rough and ready crampons just before we reached the first blue-ice.

To replace our lost sticks was less simple since there were no trees; only rock, snow and ice to be had. We carried a single spare ski and I suggested that Mike cut this down its length with the small saw on his penknife. This might take many hours but, if he started right away, could result in second sticks for both of us in a week or two.

180

Mike wrote: 'This evening the mountains *seem* almost touchable but are still far away. Ran's frostbitten feet are bad in the night as are my fingers. I was very tired at the end of today and couldn't keep up.'

We were both a touch subdued. Grateful to be escaping, as we believed, from the unbearable cold of the high plateau, but apprehensive of the 9,000-foot ice labyrinth below.

Chapter Nine

'And Terror like a frost shall halt the
flood of the thinking.'

W. H. Auden

The eighty-third day dawned cold and clear. Stomach stirrings
of apprehension helped dull the boot pains of the first hour.
Gradually the Otway Massif and the peaks of distant mountains, the Trans-Antarctic Range, floated into view. This massive bastion, that effectively dams a mile-deep ocean of ice, is
2,000 miles long and 200 miles wide.

When the moving sea of inland ice, descending from the
polar plateau, laps against the upper flanks of the range, even
6,000-foot-high peaks seem vulnerable to the surging forces of
ice which have drowned two-thirds of their rock mass.

The scale of rock and ice is massive, the pent-up power of
Nature threatening, the jumble of gigantic tributary glaciers,
contorted ice-falls and deep hidden valleys more grandiose
than anywhere on earth.

Many thousands of great glaciers have forced a path through
this range, tearing away mountain-sides and burying anything and everything in their wake. Of all these glaciers the
Beardmore is king, the second biggest glacier in the world and
twice the size of Alaska's Malaspina which was the record-
holder until Shackleton discovered and named the Beardmore
in 1908.

Ice plays games in Antarctica where God has franchised all
power to its whim. Ice is solid only to the eye, for its sinuous

183

eddies are endlessly renewed, constantly revitalised. Mankind is trivial and of no concern to the ice. Unstoppable and unpredictable, sheering and truncating every solid thing that stands in its way, ice lays a thousand traps and snares for those who trespass in its southern playpen.

Amundsen, who had seen it all, north and south, looked upon these mountains and was awed. Forty years on, Sir Edmund Hillary, already the conqueror of Everest, flew over the Beardmore and wrote, 'As we skimmed over the continuous crevassing and vast areas of ice pinnacles that covered its hundred twisting miles, I thought once again of the courage and hardihood of Shackleton and Scott.'

Mike and I needed to make *no* mistakes from now on. We were committed to the 9,000-foot descent as if in a rubber boat at the moment of yielding to the first pull of a great rapid. Around us the polar ice plunged silently over the rim of the Trans-Antarctic Range, to our immediate west sucked down into the Beardmore Valley and, dead ahead, into the maelstrom of the Mill Glacier's upper icefalls. We trod at our peril through God's most menacing mine-field, a place shot through with fissured snares and hidden plunges. This whorling mass of voids has no guidebook to help those who need to pass by.

My own intention was to use Charles Swithinbank's overall advice but to react flexibly to each new set of obstacles. Reinhold Messner had tried to follow Charles's suggested route but, despite his unparalleled experience in glacier icefalls, had soon become lost in a maze of huge interlocked crevasses.

I knew my main trouble would be going *downhill*. An earlier journey down uncharted rapids in British Columbia had taught me the dangers of travelling with the down-flow. Even major whirlpools and waves of water and ice are only visible *after* it is too late to go back. Cherry-Garrard wrote: 'One of the great difficulties of the Beardmore is that you saw the ice-falls as you went up and avoided them, but coming down you

184

knew nothing of their whereabouts until you fell into the middle of pressure and crevasses, and then it was almost impossible to say whether you should go left or right to get out . . . The Mill Glacier is a vast thing with big pressure across it.'

For an hour we hauled towards the upper gateway of the Mill. The most visible gatepost, my aiming point, was the black ridge of Mount Ward and a smaller peak to its east. Half-way through the morning a fifteen-knot wind caught us six miles from the ridge-line and blowing directly towards Mount Ward. Nervous of the crevasse fields, by now on both flanks of my chosen route, I set up the sail and was relieved when the wind dragged us both north without need for perilous side-tacks.

In an hour I was confronted by the vertical cliffs of an isolated buttress which forms the southernmost peak of Ward Ridge. At this point I could follow Charles Swithinbank's advice and head down the eastern flank of the ridge, where he warned me to expect 'small crevasses'. I looked ahead as best I could and found the view distinctly menacing; in *every* direction the horizon either dropped abruptly out of sight, suggesting very steep and fissured descents, or gave on to middle-distance views of chaotic ice-falls.

Since the wind favoured the unknown western route around Mount Ward, I wasted no time in balancing the two equally unsavoury options, and headed north-north-west as close beneath the black ramparts of Ward Ridge as visible crevasses would allow.

With little warning the hard-packed snow dropped down a long slope of scoured blue-ice and the wind gusted to twenty knots. Dismayed, I clung to the sail, prayed hard and hung on. Somehow I made a mile of breath-stealing, breakneck descent and reached a chance patch of snow-crust where I killed the sail and snowploughed to a thankful halt. The sledge rammed me from behind and dragged me a further thirty yards before I could stand up and check for broken bones.

I was bruised but lucky. Taking the hint, I packed away the sail and tried to ski. This was impossible on the concrete-hard surface, so I tried to walk. At first this too proved useless and I thought about the rope crampons. My hands were by now so cold that I gave up attempting to fit the home-made grips and worked at walking with my one blunted ski-stick for balance.

The sledge repeatedly slid past and knocked me over.

Mike was a long way behind and I shook with cold whenever I needed to stop. It would not do to lose sight of each other since I left no trail behind me on this iron-hard surface.

For two hours we skidded and slid down the ice-clad slopes of Mount Ward until, a mile to the north of its peak, I came to an unbroken west-east wall of boulders deposited by centuries of glacial flow and forming a barrier between the Ward Ridge and the Davis Peaks, three miles to the north-west. I saw Mike a mile or so to the south, and the weather was clear, so I sneaked between many boulders, flinching whenever my sledge-runners scraped over rock chips.

We spent less than an hour manhandling the sledges up and over the moraine. I watched the runners of Mike's sledge curve snake-like over rocks and ice ridges and marvelled at the workmanship of Graham Goldsmith, the designer of the sledge, which had now come over a thousand miles with its two broken segments attached only by two thin runners and a handful of screws.

I noticed that Mike was wearing his rope crampons and working well with them. I envied him his ability, even with blistered fingers, to handle ropes and lines. Even at home in summer I am cack-handed with knots; 'rope dyslexia' I call it. Either I donned my crampons in the tent first thing or it was best to forget them . . . The circulation in my hands is bad and

186

always has been, so fixing rope crampons *al fresco* was not on my menu.

Once over the moraine I took a bearing to the left of the most northerly peak of Ward Ridge and we ascended a gentle snow slope for two hours right up to the rim of a fissure-field that fell away steeply to our front. I pitched the tent some twenty yards from the dip of the first crevasse.

Mike wrote his diary with sore fingers. His entries were getting shorter.

> Down blue-ice which was extremely difficult. It was a vast improvement on foot. Me with crampons and Ran without. The crampons probably had some advantage but it was difficult to compare when I couldn't keep up with Ran who was chilled and 'going for it'. Down we went but, unfortunately, although little was lost, down the wrong tributary and hence the wrong side of Mount Ward Anyway it took us approximately where we wanted to go and we finally camped close to the Swithinbank route having rounded Mount Ward and, after crossing a moraine, joined a bigger Mill tributary. So we have achieved two days' journey in one.
>
> Tomorrow we switch to half-rations and both of us are now walking in pain. My ankle is painful and swollen. I will take Brufen. The radio is very quiet: worrying. The second Thermos is not working.

My diary:

> Very strong wind today. Mike very tired. He fell way behind and I got ever colder. I took an extra ration bag off his sledge. We bury his Thermos. Our sledge weights are now equal although he still doesn't think so. Standing joke! For two days now I set up camp before Mike gets in. Agonising night. Four and a half hours no sleep. I found myself groaning aloud at the sudden stabs of pain from my frostbitten big toe. My eyelid and chin bleeding. Feet got blue cold waiting in the moraine today.

187

Part of the reason for my painful feet was, I suspected, my falling over a great many times and slipping into ankle-cracker slits, mini-fissures, due to the hard rubber soles of my boots. On blue-ice they achieved no grip whatsoever, and forward movement, even without the heavy sledge, required careful balance and extra effort. I was worried about our chances on the great 8,000-foot ice-slope below. I remembered our predecessors' problems.

Mawson's Will: 'Only by wearing the long-toothed Swiss crampons could anyone keep to his feet . . . Since he was falling every few steps, cursing the slippery ice, regretting his desire to lighten his sledge that had led him to throw away his crampons. He had reckoned later to pick up the steel spiked crampons for the steep climb down to our hut. Now he was crashing into the iron-faced ice, jarring his aching frame, the fear of a broken limb coming with every shattering impact.'

Shackleton wrote: 'Without crampons, each step was an essay in uncertainty where "many times a slip meant death."' Scott recorded: 'We have worn our crampons all day and are delighted with them.'

Messner, in 1990, wrote: 'The descent of the Beardmore became ever more difficult. Bare ice. We had travelled a hundred and fifty kilometres over bare ice and our crampons were wearing out. Our knees suffered for this ice was full of irregularities.'

After a memorably unpleasant night Mike and I followed an unnamed tributary that descended steeply into the crevasse-streaked maw of the Mill Glacier. The horizons which now opened to us in slow motion were awesome, a sprawling mass of rock and ice locked in suspended motion. This was the headwater of a *moving* ice-river. Constrictions caused by 15,000-foot-high mountains had formed, and were even now renewing savage whirlpools and mighty maelstroms of cascading pressure-ice. Huge open chasms leered from distant foothills and standing ice-waves reared up at the base of black truncated cliffs.

I found this canvas full of power and wonder and thanked God for this moment of being alive. Nothing else lived here nor ever had since the dinosaurs of Gondwanaland. No birds nor beasts nor the least bacteria survived. Only the deep roar of massive avalanche, the shriek and grind of splitting rock, the groan of shifting ice, and the music, soft or fierce, of the winds from a thousand valleys, moved to and fro across the eternal silence.

Like Shackleton and Scott, we were but temporal and irrelevant shadows against such a backdrop, our personal pains, hopes and grudges as petty as an eddy in the breeze.

I scanned the skies north and south and saw no clouds. So long as I could *see*, I could find the best route. I felt a god-given confidence and, for the first time on this journey, the warm pleasure of challenge. I knew the rules. Never waste a minute. Pause for nothing. Here there could be no place for my polar plod. So long as the weather held we must go like the wind, for every hidden hole, every snow-covered snare, would double in danger once white-out closed down on the glaciers.

This was the region of the monster holes described by Cherry-Garrard as 'vast crevasses into which we could have dropped the *Terra Nova* with ease'.

To avoid the region I most feared, where our approach glacier first met and fought with the main flow of the Mill, I followed a visual bearing on the southern bulk of Mount Henry Lucy, some twenty-seven miles to the north-east, hoping that this would bring us safely onto the Mill's ice-escalator with minimal crevasse-crossing.

For two hours, a rare calm allowed the sun's blessed heat to warm our bodies but then a katabatic wind from the high polar ice-fields rushed down on its way to the sea, intensely cold and unwelcome. We hitched our sails to the sledges and

189

careered, mostly out of control, down the long, steep slopes at the eastern foot of Dominion Range. Mike wrote: 'Much downhill so big problems and some painful falls on my agonising left ankle. We gave up the sails and manhauled. The wind became stronger and stronger and it was very cold.'

We crossed many great fissures by way of their sagging lids, our hearts beating fast, especially on these trapdoors where the danger of bridge-collapse was greatest. Our loads were still in excess of 200 pounds and, at the end of the Antarctic summer, the bridges were at their most fragile, mere crumbling gangplanks spanning unseen voids.

By noon the dark bulk of Mount Tennant loomed to our west and I remembered Charles Swithinbank's warning: 'There are *many* crevasses. You will be best off no more than one kilometre out from the cliffs.'

As we joined the mainstream of the Mill the great width of the ice-valley narrowed to only eleven miles between its cliff banks; this constriction had created wide regions of chaos to be avoided. The passageways between the disturbances were themselves far from idyllic. After five hours we reached descending blue-ice races where skis were useless. Without them I once again faced the need for crampons, but cold fingers kept me from trying to fit them to my boots. Countless crevasses with narrow lips threaded the blue-ice.

Mike wrote: 'Some of the day was hell on rough bare ice with many crevasses. Ran going much faster than me . . . He was very cold. Too cold for any stop. I had one bar of chocolate in ten and a half hours.'

The wind gathered strength through the afternoon. At forty knots the windchill was probably in the minus eighties. I could only keep my balance with one stick and bare boots by maintaining a lop-sided trot, concentrating, with each step, on avoiding the crust-snow traps every few feet between the blue-ice pans. There were many steep descents where our sledges took control and knocked us over and dragged us, teeth

190

clenched, over fragile bridges. My feet and Mike's ankle complained bitterly.

Increasingly I found myself waiting for ten or fifteen minutes, with Mike a distant black spot, often blurred or wiped out by blown snow crystals. I do not remember *ever* feeling so deeply chilled. I stamped and slapped myself and swore viciously at Mike. To my left a second katabatic slammed down the face of the Vandament Glacier. I counted to a thousand again and again, all the while jogging and slapping. I racked my mind for some ingenious way of keeping warm. As the travel hours passed by at a tortuously slow pace, I told Mike, when he finally joined me beneath the great red cliff of Safety Spur, that I would not wait again as I was dangerously core-cold. I would *try* to find a place to camp off the blue-ice and out of the vicious wind. Mike nodded his agreement.

The wind roared against the cliffs in Force Eight strength and, donning my skis, I found it possible to body-sail over lakes of wind-scoured blue-ice. The wind struck my back with enough power to move me, sledge and all, with the blessed bonus of less boot action needed and a corresponding reduction in foot pain. My arms became numb with cold since they were no longer pumping with the rhythm of the ski-stick.

Antarctica is by far the coldest place on earth with still air temperatures of −88°C. In such temperatures mercury turns to solid metal, tin falls apart into granules, the flame of a candle becomes hooded by a wax helmet, and a carelessly dropped steel bar is liable to shatter like broken glass.

For humans in Antarctica the danger is chiefly the wind. Each knot of wind has the effect on human skin of a drop of one degree in temperature.

No wonder explorers reached every part of the world except Antarctica by the mid-nineteenth century. Only modern inventions, like the primus, allowed the first steps towards the South Pole to be taken *well within living memory*. When we talk of the 'early explorers' of Antarctica we mean men who lived in our parents' lifetimes and, in some cases, they were still alive when I first crossed Antarctica in 1981.

The changes in relevant foods and clothing made in the eighty years that had passed between Scott and ourselves treading the Beardmore had unfortunately been minimal. Why is this? Chiefly because research and development is costly and can only be rationalised by the hope of resulting profits. Sadly, the number of people likely to buy the sort of food and clothing that is suitable for pulling very heavy loads in very low temperatures for long periods are minimal, and do not form a likely profit centre.

For this reason we, like Scott, found ourselves starving, freezing and in danger of falling into crevasses without hope of rescue. This indisputable fact flies in the face of the general understanding of the media (not many of whom have pulled sledges in Scotland, never mind in polar regions), who educate the public with the attitude that 'nowadays explorers have it dead comfortable compared with the early explorers.'

Shackleton wrote of suffering from anemo-mania, literally wind madness. His colleague, Marshall, carefully monitored their body temperatures and found them to be two degrees under normal. This is a highly vulnerable state to be in. Marshall wrote: 'All nearly paralysed with cold.' Shackleton agreed. 'The end is in sight,' he said. 'We are weakening rapidly.'

Shackleton's biographer Roland Huntford wrote of Amundsen's men: 'The winds were Gale Force Seven and Eight – thirty knots and more. Under these conditions the landscape seems to be boiling with snow. It is an effort to move on skis; at high altitude every step is a strain. For most people, even well-trained skiers – it is a heavy mental and physical strain.'

As I waited for Mike on the scoured ice sheet and the wind knifed through me, I found my body chattering beyond control with violent shivering seizures. The ever-nagging pain from my feet disappeared, at least from my awareness, with this utterly new experience which had not even accompanied

192

previous Arctic soakings and the subsequent waiting, sodden, with clothes turning solid. At least my *core* resistance had on those occasions been in fighting form.

If only I could revert to my polar plod, I would not have to experience these awful spells of frozen waiting. I tried to plod, but not for long. Unless I reached a certain level of effort and speed, I stood no chance of even partial recovery from the previous period of inactivity.

We were now experiencing the coldest 'flesh' temperatures of the expedition. In forty-eight hours we had dropped some 4,000 feet in height but we were still at 6,000 feet above sea level. This was the worst of conditions, for we battled now against altitude cold *and* katabatics fed by gravity from slopes above. As elevation drops and air 'warms', gusting katabatics are wont to grow stronger. They have been known to reach 200 miles an hour. Tents are ripped into shreds by katabatic gusts, and I knew we must find a camp spot somehow protected from the full blast that polished this blue-ice canyon.

I have met people who have been in Canada or Minnesota and laugh, 'Oh, I was working at −60°C last year. It was easy.' As like as not these polar veterans experienced their 'cold' wearing adequate clothing, with full stomachs, healthy and about to return to a nice warm bed.

Rounding a bend in the cliff-walk I spotted, through the blowing snow, a sudden steep descent of several hundred feet. This was the confluence of the Koski Glacier with the Mill and liable to present too many dangers to attempt at the end of the day in such wind conditions.

I retraced my southward trail and headed straight for the rockface in the hope of finding some nook of protection for the night. Small rocks began to litter the ice floor and these increased in size until we were clambering between boulders, manoeuvring the sledges with care for they tended to jam.

Battered by katabatic blasts, but afforded some shelter by the boulders, we made camp, working carefully together to

193

avoid the tent being torn from our grasp as, with our near-lifeless fingers, we tried to insert the rods into the billowing cotton dome. With considerable relief we crawled into the tent. This was the first of our nights on half-rations. For some reason I remember it as the only night when I smelled a powerful aroma of stale body odour in the tent. Whether the stench was mine or Mike's I am unsure. We never washed in three months.

On the eighty-fifth day, 3 February, I felt dog-tired from lack of sleep. My feet had been unusually vociferous through the long night and I had tried hard to stifle involuntary groans when the stabbing pains were especially excruciating. I twice lanced the ugly swollen lump on my right foot and pierced the worst two frostbitten toes on the other foot. Liquid matter of various hues pulsed out of the new release-holes but the throbbing pain continued and I could not work out a way of dealing with it.

Mike's hands had gradually deteriorated since his mitt problems just before the Pole and now looked quite impressive, for three of the main finger blisters had burst, the dead skin falling away to reveal raw stumps like red sausages. He continued to handle our evening cooking and turned down my offer to help (my fingers were in good shape). What pained him most, it seemed, was the removal of his mitts for their wool sometimes stuck to the raw finger flesh.

Mike was better off in some ways with burst blisters. Cherry-Garrard wrote: 'The blisters on my fingers were very painful. The liquid inside these big blisters, which rose all down my fingers with only a skin between them, was frozen into ice. To handle the cooking gear was agony.'

A well-known mountaineer, Steve Venables, had told me of a photographer friend who, using his camera on a climbing trip, had lost the use of his fingers for eighteen months. It takes only seconds in extreme wind-chill conditions.

In the Arctic I remember long nights and days of extreme finger pain caused by unscheduled swims due to broken sea ice. And a friend, Geoff Newman, with whom I had spent many a dark tent night in the minus fifties, had to give up his polar ambitions after a single failure to re-warm his mitted fingers when driving a snowmobile in dire conditions.

Freezing winds blew all day but the steep descent past Koski Glacier proved no problem due to a patchwork of névé blotches which descended haphazardly to gentler slopes and which gave enough grip to prevent a headlong glissade. A mass of crevasses filled the centre of the valley to our right flank and, to the left, the 6,000-foot cordillera of the Meyer Desert and Browns Butte separated us from the ice-falls of the main branch of the Beardmore.

By midday, with exceedingly painful feet from hours of trotting on ribbed blue-ice and falling into crust-covered holes, we came to Plunket Point where the Mill joins the Beardmore and another breathtaking vista opens ahead. Here the Beard-more is more than thirty miles in width and pours down its valley in a cataract of spectacular chaos, a devil's cauldron with crevasses large enough to devour St Paul's Cathedral if Scott's men are to be believed.

We were about to enter this region of monster holes which, according to Scott's man Lashley, 'goes all the way down to the Gateway with crevasses, great big fellows of thirty feet across'.

To choose the best pathway I intended to try to follow Charles Swithinbank's suggestions but, since this 'route' was simply picked off the map and largely based on his expert knowledge of ice behaviour in general, I knew it would be a miracle if I kept even vaguely close to it. I must also rely on my past experience of glaciers and the rules which most crevasses tend to obey.

Nearly all glacial surfaces are in some way cracked where

flowing ice is deformed or under tension. When stretched, ice splits into slices and the crevasses that separate each slice usually reach 120 feet or more in depth, with sheer blue walls. Different stresses create varying fissures. The retarding effect of converging valley sides cause *marginal* or *transverse* crevasses which extend across the glacier and are generally perpendicular to flow-direction. When glaciers spread out through lack of containing barriers the fracture direction swings to *splaying* crevasses which are parallel to the flow. Where a variety of stresses interact, crevasses will intersect in a nightmare spider's web of tumbling blocks.

Immediately south of Plunket Point, Charles Swithinbank had given me an easily visible clue, a safe entry point to the mayhem ahead. The only other person to have *tried* to follow my intended route was Reinhold Messner who is unequalled in strength, skill and experience when it comes to dangerous ice work.

Within a few hours of leaving Plunket Point, Messner and his colleague Fuchs began to lose the Swithinbank route. Messner wrote: 'The hardest and most dangerous day so far. For the most part we move between and over gigantic crevasses. We have to overcome an ice fall which looks like the upper part of the Khumbu Glacier on Mount Everest.'

The Swithinbank pointer which Messner must have missed was a flow-band which initially led from the long line of rocks and detritus, a glacial moraine, leading from the cliffs of Plunket Point into the very heart of the chaos. These rocks might contain any one of the many minerals known to exist in the Trans-Antarctic Mountains. Copper, gold, silver, cobalt, platinum, manganese and coal are but a few of the hidden riches, and the extremes of temperature cause extensive fracturing. The Plunket Point moraine carried rocks of many colours and varying sizes all mixed up and resulting from centuries of rock-falls from the Dominion Range and other massifs between the Mill and Beardmore glaciers. There is no ostensible limit to the size of moraine rocks nor the distance down a glacier that they can travel. Certainly, many large boulders have been spotted floating around the southern oceans perched on icebergs. One great rock weighing 13,000 tons once travelled six miles down an American glacier.

Like Reinhold Messner I found it impossible to locate 'the curving path of the flow band to the *right* of the medial moraine', which was the Swithinbank instruction.

Mike began to lag again but the colder I felt, the faster I needed to travel. I again gave him my remaining ski-stick but soon regretted this because we entered a region of successive pressure waves where progress became a near-impossibility with no sticks and no crampons.

Scott, in similar conditions, wrote: 'Blue ice showed on the crests of the waves; soft snow lay in the hollows. We had to cross the waves in places thirty feet from crest to hollow and we did it by sitting on the sledge and letting her go: then following a fearfully tough drag to the next summit.'

Like Scott I lay on my sledge and rushed down the ice waves. The trouble was that, unlike Scott, I had no spiked boots nor pointed ski-sticks with which to drag my sledge *up* the bare slopes, and resorted to tearing at the tiniest ledges with my boot edges and mitts to gain some leverage. Often my sledge slid sideways and pulled me back down into the troughs. My knees were bruised and my language was bad but, at least for a while, I kept from freezing.

Mike wrote: 'Whole day on bare ice. Fell innumerable times. Couldn't keep up with cold Ran who finally gave me the second ski-stick. I *still* couldn't keep up but, although *he* thought we were going "unbelievably slowly", our distance belies this and in fact he was near trotting at times. High katabatic winds continue.'

Twice, looking back at Mike, I spotted potentially magnificent photographs of snow blowing in an eerie light and the jagged rock background behind Mike's approaching figure. Each time I desisted for a curious reason.

Both of us had read Messner's book and noticed his tactic of including photographs of his colleague Fuchs some distance behind. By captions or related text, Messner had indicated his frustration at Fuchs's comparative slowness.

Knowing that our relative pace was at the route of *our* mutual frustration, I decided not to take such photographs in case Mike mistook my motives. This I later regretted for such pictures would have been worth any mistaken irritation Mike might have felt at the time. Three times over those months of travel, I glanced up to spot Mike with his camera at the ready and, almost without thinking, I found myself moving out of the 'scenic line'. To anyone who has not personally experienced the paranoia that can be induced by such an experience as our journey, such thoughts and reactions will appear unbelievably petty. They are!

When we had hauled for eleven hours I looked for snow on which to camp and eventually found a scrap of crusted névé, no bigger than the area of the tent floor. We anchored the tent to the sledges since the metal pegs would not drive into the ice. Throughout the night the winds roared down the narrow furrow where we slept between two curving waves. All around, as far as the eye could see, were pressure mounds and cracks. As Shackleton's friend Wild once wrote, 'the view is exactly as one would see from a small boat in a very rough sea'.

This was a bad place and worse lay ahead for the Keltie Glacier debouched into the Beardmore thirteen miles ahead of the tent.

Messner, in this area, wrote: 'You look around and see only crevasses. On a surface of several square kilometres, nothing but upthrust glacier ice and you are in the middle of it with no obvious way out. A false route description by Charles Swithinbank made us angry. After five hundred metres I believed I

198

had found a fairly safe route. We struggled to the left. We found no way out. This cost a great deal of effort. Like blind men we had run into the middle of the abysses and holes, into a labyrinth of ice towers and crevasses which were more than two hundred metres deep.'

Cherry-Garrard, on Scott's team, agreed. 'The Keltie Glacier is a vast tumbled mass. Our last one and a half hours were in big pressure with hundreds of crevasses. With difficulty we found a patch big enough to pitch a tent free from crevasses.'

Fearful of Messner's experience, and unable to pinpoint the Swithinbank route (which, despite Messner's claim, contained no false route descriptions), I decided to follow the line which looked best at the time and kept well away from the turmoil of the Keltie pressure. This proved easier said than done.

At first my attempts to head north-north-east were foiled by monster ice ravines. On a forward reconnaissance without my sledge I came to one bare ice trough at least fifty feet deep and running parallel to the glacier. I found myself forced by insurmountable obstacles to head even further to the north-west. After three hours and at least a mile off my desired course, the succession of pressure waves finally died away and a blue-ice flow band led north, spattered with small crevasses and ankle-snappers, but heading due north.

Mike, from whom I had retrieved my ski-stick, was often out of sight, a tiny black speck on the southern horizon that disappeared as I dropped from every wave crest. We stopped at noon on a high snow bank and I told Mike I would aim for a black rock at the foot of Mount Deakin, some sixteen miles to the north-east.

Knowing there were badly fractured ice-fields in every possible direction, I considered our safety rope, but I was cold and tired and said nothing. My hips were sore from falls and from the old harness wounds so I pulled from the shoulders only.

For four hours the Deakin bearing proved a lucky one for

we sneaked through ugly-looking regions on both sides of us. Then, suddenly, a third of the way across the mouth of the Keltie Glacier, the many hundreds of lightly bridged crevasses that we had been crossing for two or three hours began to converge and to increase in size.

To our left, and for at least twenty miles over a 180° front, there stretched a sea of havoc which I preferred not to contemplate. When one is scrambling in the Alps up features like Mont Blanc and the Matterhorn there are sometimes vertiginous drops close by, and my tactic, as with parachuting, is to close my eyes and concentrate on the solid rock *immediately* in front of my boots. I brought this policy into play as the Keltie crevasse fields closed in.

The crevasses were for a while interrupted with a field of sharp sastrugi. Unable to cross these with my skis on I made the nearly fatal error of unclipping and strapping them to my sledge. Mike was some 400 yards away and himself involved in tricky negotiations of crevasse bridges which I might well have weakened prior to his reaching them.

The very first crevasse bridge I attempted to cross without skis was a minor affair, no more than four feet wide and similar to hundreds we had safely traversed.

My boot broke through close to its far wall and I dropped straight down as through a trap door. Because my harness waistband was unfastened the sledge ropes did not restrain me as they should have done, and my abrupt plunge into the dark shaft was halted only by the thin webbing strap of my ski-stick looped over my right wrist.

I dangled for a moment more surprised than frightened. The fear came as soon as I realised that only my ski-stick had saved me from certain death. The stick had wedged itself at an angle between one wall of the crevasse and a knob of crusty snow on the other. Any movement that dislodged the stick was liable to send me downwards, for the unfastened harness was loosely draped about my neck.

200

The *feel* of the void below my feet brought instant panic and, throwing caution to the wind, I lunged upwards with my free hand and grasped the handle of the stick above my captive mitt.

With one foot scrabbling against each smooth ice wall, I fought to loosen the wrist strap but my mitt was caught so I tore my bare hand free. With my arm strength quickly sapping, I lifted my body high enough to reach the crevasse lip with my mitted hand and then heaved my chest over to safety.

For a minute I lay shaking with relief until, with horror, I realised that my stick and the mitt in its wrist loop were loose down the hole. There was no spare mitt.

Fearful lest I knock the stick, I inched to one side until I could squint downwards. My breath rushed out in a sigh of relief as I spotted the ski-stick now loosely lodged some four feet down the hole. Using my boots as grabs, I thankfully retrieved both the stick and the vital mitt.

Mike arrived and his eyebrows rose as he saw where I had been. We agreed to fix up a safety rope between us since the region was clearly lethal.

Should we keep to my bearing on Mount Deakin despite the worsening state of the route or try to veer to the centre of the Beardmore away from our current Keltic problem area? Mike took one look at the gigantic upheaval to our left flank and voted to continue for Mount Deakin no matter what lay ahead.

With extreme care we edged our way through a formidable crevasse field. Whenever I moved too fast, Mike shouted so that he could keep our rope manoeuvrable but taut between us. My route was tortuous and very unsafe. We both broke through on many occasions and the rope often enough spanned two separate gaping holes at different points along the zig-zag trail between us. Had there been *any* way of avoiding such a nightmare route, we would have taken it.

By good fortune we had found the very narrowest point of

the upheavals where the Keltie meets the Mill, and, some two hours after entering the disturbances, the crevasses began to separate into individual features which could be more easily circumnavigated. As we reached the first unbroken flow band, deep soft snow layers covered every trap and we breathed again.

At night our tent vibrated to the steady roar of winds from the heights of the Keltie. I again lanced my toes and the festering side of my right foot. With four painkillers I slept well. Mike's fingers were showing signs of improvement.

Attempts to sail early the next morning and beneath the high tumbling walls of the Osicki Glacier were doomed to failure since the local wind currents altered every few minutes boxing right around the compass.

Pulling hard in soft snow, we made heavy going and crossed many well-bridged holes. Once the heights of Mount Deakin were behind my right shoulder, and following Swithinbank's advice, I set 210° on the compass and headed out towards the central fields of the Beardmore.

Cold side-winds cut under my goggles and gave me focusing troubles and the long shadow of Mount Deakin added to the difficulty of spotting dangers well ahead. For five hours we snaked between huge open crevasses climbing 200–300 feet as we moved west. At length a flow band which looked free of trouble took us north between cracks like the streels of doom. The mouths of these monster cavities appeared to lead to the very centre of the earth.

Mike's ski-skins were threadbare and loose. Because the slopes between some of these giant mid-glacier holes were steep and long, he had great trouble hauling his sledge up at all. I do not know what was going on in his mind at the time but, although he later wrote in his diary, 'Ran leading all the time. This is selfish and egotistical. But this obviously means much to him so I can cope', he also congratulated me on taking what he described as an 'excellent route'. The discrep-

202

ancy between the given events on any one day and Mike's diary record of it is a point of interest because, as soon as an explorer has decided to write a book about his experiences, what he writes in his diary tends to become doctored, selective and artificial. He or she knows that whatever is written can thereafter be taken down and used in evidence. By this time, although I was not then aware of it, Mike had indeed decided to write a book of our various expeditions together and presumably made his diary entries with this in mind.

The whole subject of travellers and their diaries fascinates me and I had long since reached the conclusion that I should avoid basing a later account of my relationship with a colleague on any single diary entry. That way I could hope to avoid undue emphasis of the extremes of hostility I felt when unbalanced by temporary stresses.

If, for example, I were to write what a mean, idle bastard X was when he had made some innocuous comment in the tent three hours after I had been attacked by a polar bear, my immediate diary entry about X might be most unflattering but not a true reflection of his real character or my *normal* feelings about him.

Roland Huntford, in writing his biography of Scott, used the standard and well-accepted method of quoting from the diaries (or letters) of Scott's team-mates, often written on the heated spur of the moment. One of Huntford's most useful posthumous pawns was Titus Oates, a stern critic of Scott through the medium of confidential letters written to his mother. He intended the comments only for his mother and he recognised that they were flawed in that he had not been his normal, balanced self at the moment of writing. Oates said, at the end of one of these letters, 'Please remember that when a man is having a hard time he says hard things about other people which he would regret afterwards.'

Messner wrote of his Antarctic manhaul: 'My diary functioned as Father Confessor for me. With the making of notes

I got rid of everything: my anger, my tiredness, my despondency. Whatever I didn't want to scream in Arved's face, I jotted down so as to unburden my soul. It was not Arved's fault that we were too slow, it was simply a fact and it made me boiling mad. In the evening, after writing up the diary, I was free of anger . . . Arved did likewise in his diary.'

Huntford, who revered Amundsen as much as he reviled Scott, is inconsistent in his attempts at praising Amundsen's accurate diary-keeping. 'In what he [Amundsen] tells, there is no tampering with the record. "Simplicity" and "sincerity" recur in reviews of this book.' Later Huntford says that Amundsen 'misleads without the lie direct', and 'it was Amundsen's style to play down difficulties and draw a veil over circumstances that suggested plans going awry'. But surely this *is* tampering; by selective omission.

We camped at the mouth of the central crevasse field, relieved to be free of the stomach-gripping dread that is never far away when one is tip-toeing over such masked holes of death.

Next day, we sailed for two hours through no man's land between the snow-capped leviathans of the Commonwealth Range and the giddy walls of the Queen Alexandra massif. The 8,000-foot-high ramparts of the Cloudmaker were, unusually, clear of mist, and for three blessed hours I felt merely chilled instead of unutterably cold. To our immediate west lay an area through which some of Scott's men 'tumbled into the horrible pressure above the Cloudmaker'.

The wind took us gently too far east until, after an hour of traversing huge but well-drifted 'bomb crater' fissures, a sudden katabatic struck from the south-east and in seconds we were hurtled towards the distant ice cliffs of Siege Dome. There was only one thing to do and that was to cling to the sail line with one hand and the sledge ropes behind with the other. With knees well bent to absorb the shock of ribbed ice and sudden sastrugi, we sped on at some fifty degrees off-course and fearing imminent disaster.

Within minutes Mike, who was having difficulty with his sail, was drawn three to four miles further east. Since he could not gain ground back west whereas I could easily, though reluctantly, yield to the wind and follow him, I did so, fearing separation otherwise. I found the unaccustomed speed exhilarating but, in the back of my mind, I remembered Charles Swithinbank's warning of a giant crevasse field opposite the Cloudmaker.

Some three miles south of Mount Patrick, in the teeth of a Force Eight wind-storm we collapsed the sails and, bitterly cold, I took a bearing some 20° west of Wedge Face buttress.

At first the wind-blown ice-fields ahead, dark and forbidding in the shadow of Wedge Face, were simple enough. At this point of Reinhold Messner's descent he wrote: 'We go two miles to get one mile north. From above we have no view of the route. We try to reach the middle of the Beardmore by crossing side-streams. We go three hours with crampons on bare ice and come to a widely shattered ice-fall marked on no map. We get stuck. We go back. In part the crevasses are so big one could put a church inside.'

Scott wrote of this place: 'There were times when it seemed almost impossible to find a way out of the awful turmoil. The irregular crevassed surface giving way to huge chasms closely packed and most difficult to cross.'

I knew we should soon be stopping, having travelled for over nine hours, but Swithinbank's warning coupled with the fear of imminent bad weather forced me to continue in the desire to camp where I could see beyond the Wedge Face to the fjord mouth below.

The wind was spinning spray from distant peaks and lifting snow. The sun played about with the mountain shadows and I gasped as I saw, or thought I saw, the ravaged face of the land ahead.

For a moment I considered turning back and starting a wide ten-mile loop, perhaps more, to circumvent the pock-marked ice cauldron to our front. Tiredness or idleness overcame common sense and, with Mike twenty minutes or more behind and my body shaking with cold, I hunched my shoulders and promised myself we would rope up if things became really bad. Too late, apprehensions turned to the realisation that I had made a mistake.

More lines from *Pilgrim's Progress* ran vaguely through my head: 'From the place where he now stood the way was all along set so full of snares, traps, gins and nets here, and so full of pits, pitfalls, deep holes and shelvings down there that, had he a thousand souls, they had in reason been cast away. And I saw in my dream, that at the end of this valley lay blood, bones, ashes and mangled bodies of men. Death also doth spread his wings over the place. It is every whit dreadful being utterly without order . . . There is dangerous quag into which, if even a good man falls, he can find no bottom for his foot to stand on. And oft times, when he lift up his foot to set forward, he knew not where or upon what he should set it next.'

Mike said of the place that we now entered: 'The crevasses were huge and the combination of icy surfaces, slopes and changes of direction totally knackered me.'

Such turbulent confusion is difficult to convey. To plot any route through its midst or indeed to fix upon any less convulsed region as a goal of safety was impossible. In such conditions you can turn back or rush on. I looked back at Mike who seemed to be progressing well and, strapping my skis to the sledge, slid twenty feet down a narrow ramp between two ninety-foot-deep sink-holes. They might have been deeper.

My hands were numb, incapable of donning my rope crampons. I hoped that Mike would be able to affix his own. Towering walls of grey ice loomed above and around me. For some while I could not work out my intended direction for my

206

tracks were invisible and high ridges encompassed me on every side.

Of these conditions Cherry-Garrard wrote: 'I cannot describe the maze we got into and the hair breadth escapes we have had to pass through today. Fathomless pits fell away on each side too numerous to think of. Often and often we saw openings where it was possible to drop in the biggest ship afloat and lose her.'

So it was with Mike and me on our eighty-eighth day but, unlike Cherry-Garrard, we had no crampons nor pointed sticks to help grip the ice as we crept along slanting, slippery crater rims and knife-end ridges between deep, dark craters.

Mike was especially at risk since, although I had lost more weight than he, he was still the lighter of the two and so more prone to succumb to the nerve-racking behaviour of our sledges. At moments when, with dizzy drops on both sides and virtually no traction, we traversed slanting gangplanks, our sledges would sometimes slip sickeningly sideways, and their weight, heavier than our own bodyweight, would try to tear us from our precarious foothold.

In one way I was thankful that Mike was far behind and could not hear my gasps of terror as I fought to keep my balance and struggled, veins bulging, to fight the pull of my sledge down to some waiting maw. But then I feared that, where hard ice hid my tracks, Mike might take a wrong turning through the maze. Then we would be in serious trouble. I began to beckon him on. My chief dread was being caught in this awful place in a white-out.

The whole breadth of this Wedge Face crevasse-field stretched over many miles and, after an hour within the maze of its fractures, I climbed an ice hillock which at last gave me a glimpse of the far side. For another mile, if we could only continue to avoid culs-de-sac, there was a steeply-descending shoulder to the north-west, riven with fissures but leading to gentler slopes and, eventually, the edge of the troubled zone.

During the last hour I often found it necessary to descend slopes which I knew we would not be able to renegotiate should my route lead to a dead end. That this never happened was due to exceptionally good fortune, for a more zig-zag rabbit warren of a journey would be hard to devise. Mike kept lagging way behind and, partly to keep warm, partly to speed him up, I gesticulated with both arms. I suspect this had little effect but to annoy him.

When at last we emerged from that perilous place, we had travelled non-stop for twelve hours and I pitched the tent on a patch of snow crust amidst a spider's web of narrow ice crevasses.

Mike wrote: 'I was definitely hypoglycaemic at times . . . The weather this evening is quite different and it may be that we're in for trouble.'

Next day, the glacier and the weather both relented. There were crevasses in plenty but all were adequately bridged and the winds died away leaving us blissfully warm by comparison to previous days. I took the opportunity of reverting at once to a comfortable polar plod and spent the day imagining feasts of food.

Being on half-rations after so many weeks of slow starvation brought about a state of ravenous hunger which I found difficult to control. Determined efforts to conserve my two small bars of chocolate over the entire day met with abject failure.

At every step my thoughts refused to concentrate on *anything* other than the chocolate in my pocket. Eventually, I decided to eat *all* the chocolate at once and at one sitting, so that the mental conflict would cease. This policy graduated into one of eating both bars within the first ten minutes of each day.

Mike wrote: 'We are both very hungry and I definitely felt hypoglycaemic in the afternoon which is not helped by my eating two-thirds of my chocolate supply in the morning. What life will be like in another few days or after further food reduction, I hate to think.'

All that day the wondrous fairyland floated, inch by inch, past our goggles. Progress was not apparent for the panorama was simply too huge. The 13,000-feet-high snow queen, Mount Elizabeth, reigned with majestic serenity to the west, wreathed in ever-changing veils of cloud, whilst, to the north-east, the soaring red cliffs of Mount Kyffin marked the very edge of the Antarctic Continent. Mike recorded: 'Only two days from crossing the continent, an amazing thought.'

At this point we had travelled hundreds of miles further than any of our unsupported predecessors, including Scott's men. But we were sorely debilitated. Mike was hovering, as is evidenced by his own diary, on the edge of a dangerous hypoglycaemic state. We had both lost nigh on one third of our body weight and were already in a state of extreme vulnerability to the cold. Nothing, I felt, could now stop us reaching the very edge of the continent, but beyond that point our chances of reaching the Seaquest ship were, to put it mildly, remote. I decided to think no further than the coastline some forty miles ahead.

Scott's team, at this very point, were cheered by sighting the Beardmore's western gatepost, Mount Hope, but their morale was dashed by their largest and strongest member, Edgar Evans, who, concussed from crevassed falls, badly frostbitten and more affected by starvation than were his smaller colleagues, died of hypothermia. They buried him by the entrance to Socks Glacier, named after their pony that had died down a nearby crevasse, and some six miles north of another spectacular glacier to which they gave Evans's name.

We camped some distance short of Mount Kyffin and, on our ninetieth day, heavy cloud banks warned of possible weather change. I feared the onset of the white-out conditions and storms for which the snout area of the Trans-Antarctic glaciers are well known. Our immediate vicinity was one where good visibility was vital. Wild described it as 'an awful place exactly like a rough sea in appearance but in every hollow there was a crevasse. The strain on one's nerves was greater than on the muscles.'

I did not trust the weather anywhere in Antarctica however 'settled' it appeared. There is no region of the world with so fine a balance between calm, happy weather and the onset of violent storm conditions.

Keen to progress as far as possible whilst we could still see to avoid holes, I tried to sail whenever a breeze stirred the air. Mostly this was useless but three reasonable periods took us past Mount Kyffin and, hours later, to the coarse, granite pillars that hide the main bulk of Mount Ida.

Once we had rounded the Granite Pillars, so named by Shackleton, we passed through a number of small crevasse fields in misty conditions. I tried to steer east of these obstacles without much success but all minor troubles were forgotten as we entered the pass which separated the island of Mount Hope on our right from the mainland's foothills to the west. This three-mile passage, the Gateway, involves a steep climb to the summit of a giant snowdrift several hundred feet high.

When Shackleton discovered this narrow corridor to the Beardmore Glacier, he had found one of the very few negotiable routes to the polar plateau from the Ross Ice-Shelf.

The Gateway was also the spot where Roger Mear's dreams of making the first *unsupported* South Pole journey were dashed in 1985. He wrote: 'As I approached the col I saw a figure eight hundred yards away. I pondered what this awful event might mean. To have the isolation destroyed by this unexpected encounter made the four hundred miles we had walked an exercise without point or reward . . . Gareth Wood cursed and was in tears when the tents came into view.' They all then approached the tents and met the US scientist occupants. 'I hope you chaps have got some spare

210

food, 'cause we're powerful hungry,' Robert Swan said, and that evening they were invited to dinner, the first of many US-supplied meals over the next two days. Mear wrote: 'Our greed was an embarrassment which did nothing to convey to our hosts the tight control we had exercised during the previous forty days . . . but the encounter destroyed the mystery and doubt that had hung over the remaining four hundred and eighty miles to the Pole. Gone was the knowledge that we were engaged upon an unsupported journey of unique magnitude.'

Mike and I were lucky. There were no strangers in the Gateway, so we could continue our ninety-day starvation regime untempted by hamburgers. Mike at this point felt 'cold and ill'. He wrote: 'Another sail took us to crevasses opposite the Pillars. These Ran circumvented to the east before turning in towards the Gateway. He is very quick on the sail/manhaul turnround. I don't know how he does it although unblistered hands must help.'

I waited for Mike in a wide desolate basin, rough with sastrugi. He looked weak and complained that he 'felt terrible'. Fortunately a forty-knot wind picked up from nowhere and we sailed the mile up the giant snowdrift and over its seaward slopes.

Mike wrote: 'A good wind took us up and through the Gate. Then a desperate couple of miles where I kept having the sledge catch me up . . . Ran somehow avoids this.'

With many halts for Mike, anxious when he failed to appear over the summit of the Gateway's col lest he had gone down a crevasse, I at length reached a steep slope some 500 feet above the edge of the Ross Ice-Shelf and pitched the tent in a rising wind.

Mike's diary: 'I felt pretty rough for the first half of the day despite eating all my chocolate early on. We had our soup stop half an hour early because I had big cramps and felt rough – and that is after only six days on half-rations. But, if not elated

211

now, after a very long twelve-hour day, I certainly recognise that we have achieved something very special.'

I tried to plot a route following original advice from Charles Swithinbank and remembering his warnings of ice chaos immediately below our current camp spot. The outward flow of the Beardmore onto the ice-shelf causes many miles of turbulence through which there is but a single feasible route.

We took stock of our rations and fuel. Ten days. The blizzard season was imminent, during which a single storm can prevent all travel, on foot or by air, for two or even three weeks without a break.

With 360 miles of the Ross Ice-Shelf between us and the ship our chances were razor-slim. The most sensible course was probably to count our blessings, already far greater than we could ever have counted upon only three months before in Chile, and ask ANI to try to locate us whilst the precious good weather still lasted.

On the other hand, manhauling out on the ice-shelf was an unknown factor when applied to our current state. Until we tried it, we could not accurately summarise our remaining chances of reaching the ship and, from my point of view, avoiding possible bankruptcy.

I took two painkillers from our dwindling supply and tried to sleep. However uncertain the future, we were within half a mile of walking over the highest, coldest, most inhospitable continent on Earth from Atlantic to Pacific.

Chapter Ten

'One never notices what has been done,
one can only see what remains to be
done.'

Marie Curie

We would need two ski-sticks each for the last hurdle of the Beardmore and Mike had been slowly slicing our single spare ski down its length with his penknife saw, completing four or five inches a night.

I spent two hours splicing a handle onto the end of each ski-half by cannabalising existing materials. I then fashioned metal tips and baskets from ice-screws, the sawn-off top of a fuel bottle and a broken tent pole.

I also completed my *twelfth* repair to my woollen mitts, using patches cut out of my woollen socks.

The Ross Ice-Shelf which we shortly hoped to 'board' is a remarkable feature, larger than Texas and hinged to Antarctica's coastline. Any part of this shelf could theoretically break away from the continent, and large tabular bergs are constantly calving from its seaward edge. The whole shelf moves north some four feet each day due to pressure from feeder glaciers like the Beardmore. The Ross Shelf is itself pitted with crevasses including the huge Steers Head fracture system which I had taken great care to avoid back in 1981.

As the Beardmore moves away from the hidden coastline beneath it, a huge chasm or shear-crack forms, and this caused delays to both Shackleton and Scott. Shackleton met the crack at a point where its width was eighty feet and its depth 300 feet. Cherry-Garrard, approaching the Beardmore from below, described its base as 'a great white line of jagged edges, the chaos of pressure which this vast glacier makes as it flows into the comparatively stationary ice of the Barrier'.

I lay awake for an hour at this, our last and ninetieth camp on the Antarctic Continent. Should we try to continue on over the shelf? How much further did we stand a chance of surviving? Since all our main aims were now achieved, the only practical rationale for continuing must be to reach the ship before its departure in eight days' time. 360 miles in eight days meant forty-five miles daily. This *might* just be possible given steady southerly winds from now on. I decided that this factor alone warranted at least an attempt to progress further in the hope of picking up such winds over the next day or two.

The nine days wasted in Chile back in November 1992 had now come home to roost with a vengeance. Long before leaving England, I had sent our sponsors my calculations of likely progress. These predicted arrival at the Beardmore's snout, our current position, on the eighty-sixth day. Although we had done slightly better than I had dared hope back at the Pole, we were, nonetheless, five days behind schedule in addition to the nine delayed days.

Everything would now depend on quickly picking up the right wind over the next day or two.

I said nothing to Mike since I was increasingly aware of his mental struggles. Half the time he spent in black moods looking as though he wished to accept the continental edge as our final target, but then, mercurial as ever, his mood would change and he would swing the other way. His thoughts and his motives were complex and contradictory. It seemed to me that he feared that I would secretly seek to blame him for any decision to abort, *whenever* such a decision might occur.

This would place him in the highly awkward position of needing continually to demonstrate his strength and not give in to a deteriorated state which, in other circumstances, he would quickly have identified as potentially lethal. I felt he needed *somebody else* to make the decision to abort and, further, to do so for reasons unconnected to his own vulnerable state.

Should anything happen to Mike at this stage I would, as leader, be held responsible. The question would then be asked: Why had I risked further travel after it was blatantly pointless from most aspects?

I did a good deal of tossing and turning and eventually concluded that, even if I *should* be calling for evacuation right now, we would still need to traverse the turbulent ice to our immediate front in order to find a safe place for the ANI skiplane to land. Nine days of food remained. Without wind help and on half-rations it might be possible to reach the science base at the far edge of the ice-shelf but *not* in time to catch the ship. Such a journey lacked the clearly delineated goals which had driven me and probably Mike as far as the edge of the continent.

One factor which did help motivate onward travel, even for a few miles, was the knowledge that thousands of pounds were pledged in Britain for *every* mile of our progress. Set against this was the personal awareness that I alone might have to pay for ANI rescue costs which were already mounting by $3,000 daily since, but for us, ANI would have shut up camp four days previously and gone home.

After a bad start caused by a cooker fire, we set out in a semi-white-out, not ideal conditions to thread our way through the complex labyrinth of fissures around the glacial shear-zone. I used the compass and chart with great care but Mike twice spotted deep crevasses narrowly avoided. We zig-zagged through the gloom along three distinct bearings, switching from one to the other at set times. After three hours the worst of the ridges and rifts fell away until, some five miles out from the Gateway, we came to a deep trench that stretched away to west and east as far as the eye could see.

I found a narrow spot where giant ice boulders offered a precarious crossing point. Mike said he would prefer to continue following the course of the rift until we reached a safer bridge, because he felt it unfair to his wife and children should he come to grief at this last hurdle. I fully concurred with this view and, some hundreds of yards further to the west, we crossed a giant causeway formed by a snowdrift. In our weakened state, even this took time and effort.

After four hours of concentrated travel we cleared the last obstacle. From now on the ice-shelf should be free of trouble and as flat as the Filchner. Remembering Mike's resentment at my decision to navigate the entire Beardmore, I immediately handed him the compass, set for 203° magnetic.

Now that the going was flat and easy, I reverted thankfully to the polar plod for the first time in almost two weeks and noticed with relief that Mike also seemed to be 'plodding'. This was a pleasant surprise for any flat going normally saw him hauling as hard as he could. But now he slowed down until, some five hours into the day, he came to a complete halt with his head drooping forwards.

Recognising the signs of imminent hypothermia I grew fearful and erected the tent immediately, for there was no wind. Mike's lisping attempts to talk were inaudible. He sat listlessly on his sledge and I asked him in a loud voice to collect snow for tea. He hit the plastic shovel against one of his fingers and whimpered with pain.

As I waited for tea to boil, the foolishness of continuing to travel in so vulnerable a state and for so fragile a purpose was rammed home by Mike's collapse after only five hours of travel in comparatively friendly conditions. I determined to take the sensible decision as soon as I could without upsetting Mike's sensitivities. Many a time after past expeditions he had told me how much he had regretted my decisions to abort. Mike had always worried lest it should be thought that I had based my thinking on *his* state of health. I knew that now, more than ever before, any decision to abort before our scheduled end, however sensible and responsible, would be anathema to him.

Yet, I grew suddenly more worried that I would be powerless to help should his obvious susceptibility to hypoglycaemia take him 'over the edge'. I remembered five or six occasions when I had guided Mike into the tent just in time. A person with hypothermia can die quickly even during a weekend hike in wet weather. For someone semi-starved and debilitated, the dangers are great.

Scott wrote of Evans, who died of hypothermia on the Beardmore, 'We got him on his feet but he sank down again. He showed every sign of complete collapse. We went back for the sledge but when we returned he was practically unconscious and when we got him into the tent, quite comatose.'

Hypothermia and hypoglycaemia, to both of which Mike was increasingly vulnerable, involve a fairly small lowering of body heat. Roland Huntford wrote of Shackleton's expedition: 'They were starving. They were not only growing thinner and weaker, they were not eating enough to maintain their body heat. Adam's temperature was nearly four degrees below normal. Under ordinary circumstances he would have been nearly dead.'

I was in a no-win situation. Either I told Mike we *must* abort before he died – in which case he would never forgive me for terminating due to his fallibility, for making him look weak – *or* I kept going with the ever-present danger that, the next time he fell hypothermic, I might be navigating and fail to notice his absence until too late.

I wondered to myself which his wife and children would prefer, a bold Mike who had never 'given in' until it was too late, or a live one who had swallowed his pride and known when enough was enough. That night, even as Mike wrote in his diary, 'Ran is considerably supportive,' his worry that he must not be the one to 'yield' made him add, 'But nice for him.'

Since I did not know what Mike was writing in his diary until after the end of the expedition, I could not at the time be sure how weak he was feeling. If I had known then what he wrote that night, I believe I would have overruled his request for 'one more chance' and taken the responsible course to abort no matter how much he would undoubtedly have damned me thereafter.

He wrote:

> A very black day. Debilitation seems to be knocking me down and there's nothing I can do about it. I only lasted five hours before I went gaga in my head and had severe cramps in both legs. I was cold but I don't know how much was hypothermia and how much hypoglycaemia. The cramps are probably a lack of some food for the muscles. It's just like Siberia. Anyway, tent up, tea and chocolate and I was much better.
>
> Since then there has been the talking. Ran sees me as chronically deteriorated with no hope of recovery and he's almost certainly right. He would therefore think it best to radio for the aircraft now.
>
> I, however, have great difficulties in being 'the cause for failure' although I do feel what we have already done is beyond expectations. I, therefore, have determined to try again tomorrow although I already know that, if it gets too tough, I have a 'let-out' that he will accept and so I am concerned about the psychological aspects of forcing myself on. Anyway we shall see . . . I dread turning round and counselling the end (although I would also love it!).

That night I spent two hours repairing a ski-binding which Mike had partially broken. I also tried to make our ramshackle ski-sticks more wieldy.

My diary:

Mike says my sledge is now eight pounds heavier than his. It makes no difference to the drag of the thing. He feels it is *very* cold. I agree. But we both know it's really our dwindling lack of resistance. I fear for him if we continue. When he 'goes', it's with little or no warning and I will be blamed, perhaps rightly, by his family if he 'goes' once too often. He accepts that my 'conserve energy' policy has now paid off for me. He is always exhausted but he *cannot* see that it is largely due to his totally unncessary pushing himself on the flat stretches.

Starving and inadequately clothed, we are feeling the cold horribly. We must push ourselves when the cold *forces* us to, but otherwise we should keep to the most non-taxing form of progress possible to conserve every calorie.

In his phobic desire to outdistance me, even by a few hundred yards, he has convinced himself that any complaint from me is selfishly motivated and not for his own good. We human beings are pretty weird when you think about it.

On the ninety-second day, clear of the crevasses, we hauled for ten and a half hours on flat soft snow. The wind, so vital to our chances of catching the ship, stayed away and, far from making the necessary forty-five miles per day, we just managed thirteen.

Mike wrote: 'Three months today with no re-supply! Quite a feat by any standards. It was a delight to have a stick in both hands again. My bed is getting bonier every night.'

Mike's bed was, of course, his quarter-inch, closed cell mat, and the only thing that was getting 'bonier' was his body. With no fat layer left, his hipbones were sticking into his skin.

We were in the same state as Scott and his men at this stage with two major exceptions. Our mileage had been obtained with *no* help from storage depots en route. Secondly, we *could* call for a ski-plane and Scott had no such easy option. He, therefore, did not need to agonise about what was or was not responsible behaviour. His team could only keep going, and this they did until an early blizzard stranded them a mere thirteen miles short of one of their food depots. As is common with such storms on the ice-shelf, it raged for over a week. Their death warrants were signed.

I was aware the blizzard season was already upon us and we could easily end up in exactly the same position as Scott, since no ground or air search-and-rescue unit on Earth could, or would, assist us during an Antarctic blizzard. Conditions in 1911 and 1993 were unchanged in this respect but, unlike Scott, we had no food depots on the ice-shelf, only the eight days of rations left on our sledges.

Scott's men organised a search party and eventually found the death tent. One of the searchers, the Norwegian Tryggve Gran, wrote: 'It was a horrid sight. Scott clearly had a very hard last few minutes. His skin was yellow, frostbites all over. I envied them. They died having done something great – how hard must not death be having done nothing.'

Gran's colleague Williamson said: 'Scott's face was very pinched and his hands had been terribly frostbitten . . . Never again in my life do I want to behold such a sight as we have just seen.'

Cherry-Garrard wrote of the burial service: 'Perhaps it has never been conducted in a more magnificent cathedral and under more impressive circumstances – for it is a grave which kings must envy.'

They could not bury Titus Oates for they failed to find his body. I contemplated whether, in Oates's skin, I would have found the courage to act so selflessly. I knew that I would not. His suffering must have been horrific. Gangrene had set in to his frozen feet. He was exhausted and could envisage for himself a carbon copy of Evans's awful fate. Yet somehow he faced up to a suicide totally alien to his nature and likely to prove about as pleasant an experience as crucifixion. Since it would have taken him two hours of painful manoeuvring to put his boots on, he crept out to die in his socks.

Shackleton had, by the skin of his teeth, avoided the same

220

fate on this same ice-shelf by taking the decision to abort *just* in time. I decided to give us one more day in which to catch the wind or, in some other miraculous way, improve our mileage. Failing this, any continued travel would be tempting the Devil in his own playground.

Mike wrote: 'My legs were sore as hell at times and I had distinctly blurred vision all afternoon with some lightheadedness in the evening. Towards the end of the day I thought a lot about giving up and thought that I would raise it seriously in the tent tonight. However, I haven't and I guess that I won't since, *in* the tent, everything still looks possible despite my knowing that we are eating hopelessly inadequately and are very vulnerable to both hypoglycaemia and hypothermia. It certainly seemed strikingly cold today although I'm sure in fact that it wasn't.'

On 12 February, our ninety-fifth day of travel, the last US aeroplane left Antarctica to escape the imminent winter blizzards. In five days' time, at 7 a.m. precisely, our ship would steam out of the Ross Sea. We were still 289 nautical miles from Ross Island and there was still no wind. The time for procrastination was over. Now we would need to achieve fifty-eight miles each day for the next five days to catch the ship. We were struggling to manage even twelve miles daily; there was no point in continuing up a cul-de-sac.

After two hours' travel Mike again tried to push his pace and, as before, I remonstrated with him at the following compass change-over. But I knew it was pointless. I must bring our increasingly aimless progress to a halt without further delay. As on previous polar journeys, I experienced a dread of the actual moment of decision. Once I broached the subject of stopping, I must have *no* later regrets. Crying over spilled milk is the most pointless of all exercises. Time and again that morning I said to myself, 'Let's do just *one* more mile for the multiple sclerosis coffers. Then I'll call it a day.'

But, as with the dreaded *instant* of letting go in an aircraft door, before jumping into space (with a parachute), I instinctively backed off.

At 1 p.m. I made up my mind to delay no longer and turned to tell Mike we must erect the tent to discuss calling it a day. I dithered and explained my halt as merely to suggest curtailing the travel days from now on to combat the alarmingly decreased resistance to the cold that we both acknowledged.

I immediately cursed myself for giving in to procrastination and, two hours later, I finally crunched the bullet. We put up the tent having hauled some forty-one miles since crossing the Pacific coastline.

Within fifteen minutes, Mike had agreed that the realistic course was to call a halt. Our key hope was that the ANI skiplane reach us before a long period of bad weather arrived on the ice-shelf.

Our satellite transmitter was irreparable so I laid HF antenna wires on the ice and made contact with ANI. I was fortunate since, given bad solar conditions, several days might have passed without communications.

Mike told me he had found himself falling asleep that morning simply standing beside his sledge and, despite feeling so cold, it was 'like having no clothes at all'.

In his diary he wrote: 'Every day begins, continues and ends in pain.' He was delighted and relieved that *he* had not made the decision to stop even though he agreed with it. 'The decision,' he wrote 'is only hours old and already I feel regrets. I hope I can live happily with this achievement. It's too late to change now. At least Ran precipitated it . . . I want to get out very quickly to family . . . When the wind blew it was as if we were naked . . . However hard we worked the cold gnawed at the bone, and hands and feet cried out for release. Clearly sailing would be impossible. Our bodies are lean and emaciated. Did we "bottle out" or did sense prevail?'

Mike was desperately keen that his own state of health

should not appear to be the cause of our halting. He wrote: 'I *fear* Ran may make my vulnerability the scapegoat. *His* feet and the dangers of up-skiing sailing *are* the biggest risks.'

He set out in his diary what he considered the pros and cons of having continued would have been. He summarised the only advantages as avoiding future regrets and the faint chance of reaching Ross Island. The main negatives he listed as the very real frostbite dangers if we tried to sail (far colder than manhauling), the fact that reaching Ross Base was highly unlikely, the serious consequences of our remaining food supply (six days) in the event of the blizzard season's arrival, and the risk of hypothermia.

The weather held and the Twin Otter ski-plane which had dropped us off three months before on the Atlantic coast now picked us up from the ice forty miles 'out to sea' on the Pacific ice.

Only when back in the diesel-fumed warmth of 'civilization', the little aircraft's narrow fuselage, did our bodies begin to show the full state of their debilitation. Within hours our legs became horribly swollen, as with dropsy, we felt sick, giddy and disorientated, and concentrated effort was required even to rise from the lying position. Neither of us could focus our vision.

Most fatal climbing accidents happen during the descent of the mountain. Our highest mountain peak had been the moment of crossing the continent.

Our resolve had long been focused on the Gateway. Once we reached the ice-shelf, I should have delayed no longer but, then and there, called a halt to our undertaking and remembered Shackleton . . .

Within an ace of reaching the South Pole but aware each further mile would overstretch his eventual chances of survival, Shackleton had not wavered but turned around to head back for the Ross Sea. Whether or not his team were grateful to him, he saved their lives. When his wife asked him how he had found the strength of mind to turn back (an act described by Roland Huntford as 'one of the bravest acts of polar exploration') Shackleton had replied, 'I thought you would rather have a live donkey than a dead lion.'

Whether or not London Insurers would pay for the ANI costs of retrieving us would depend on their definition of our state of health when found. Mike's medical summary included, along with details of various wounds, a description of my feet as 'toes infected and ulcerated due to frostbite with large areas of devitalized tissue', and 'eroding ulcer on right foot, present for seventy days but increasing in severity since supplies of appropriate antibiotics finished'.

He described his own debilitation: 'Rapidly increasing vulnerability to cold demonstrated by an episode of hypothermia two days prior to pick up. Additionally, episodes of mild hypoglycaemia, due to starvation and high levels of exercise, are increasing in frequency and severity and posing the probability of a very dangerous situation.'

We will never know how much further we could have continued because there are too many ifs and buts. If, like Scott, we had no option but to battle on, it is my opinion that we would have died short of Ross Island.

If the winds had picked up, the risk of hypothermia/hypoglycaemia would have increased enormously. If we had used such hypothetical winds to try to gain mileage by sailing, we would have become still more vulnerable because our main defence against the cold was the bodily activity of manhauling.

On the other hand, *without* sailable winds, our food would have run out, even on half-rations, after, at best, some 150 miles, a distance many miles short of Ross Island and providing we suffered no storms or white-outs.

If we had carried more food, perhaps we could have reached Ross Island and survived. There will always be such 'what ifs'. Cherry-Garrard wrote of Scott's tragedy: 'With some tins of extra oil and depot'd pony meat, the polar party would probably have got home in safety.'

Scott's modern detractors make much of his 'narrow-minded stupidity' in championing manhaul travel over the use of dog teams. Amundsen's colleague Hanssen is often quoted as concluding, 'What shall one say of Scott and his companions who were their own sledge dogs? . . . I don't think anyone will ever copy him.'

All attempts for a century, whether by Norwegians, Soviets or Americans, to cross the continent unaided and using snow-machines, or dog teams, had failed miserably.

In hauling our own loads across this area, greater in mass by far than the United States, we have shown that manpower can indeed be superior to dog-power and, in doing so, have partly exonerated Scott's much-abused theories on the matter.

Based upon careful chart-keeping by our Aberdeen radio base operator, Morag's husband Laurence, our completed mileage from start to finish was 1,487.48 statute miles or 2,380 kilo-metres in ninety-five days. Amundsen's teams of world cham-pion class skiers and the strongest of husky dogs managed a total of 1,615 miles in ninety-nine days. The dogs' overall average was 16.3 miles per day and ours was 15.7 miles per day. However, the dogs' loads were considerably less than ours because of Amundsen's system of positioning many food depots along his outward route, some of which were installed the previous year.

Laurence Howell's 1,479 miles and Amundsen's 1651.5 miles are cut by 125–185 miles if the two journeys are measured on charts in straight lines instead of recording totals of each day's mileage. Therefore the 1993 *Guinness Book of Records* now states: 'The longest totally self-supporting polar sledge journey ever made and the first totally unsupported crossing of the Antarc-tic landmass were achieved by R. Fiennes and M. Stroud. They covered a distance of 2,170 km (1,350 miles).'

Back in Punta Arenas a week later, I joined Mike and Morag buying Chilean trinkets for our families. I reflected that it would be difficult to find two better people, one a doctor, the other an engineer. Both are very 'normal'. Cherry-Garrard wrote of Scott's team: 'If you are a brave man you will do nothing. If you are fearful you may do much, for none but cowards have need to prove their bravery. Some will tell you that you are mad and nearly all will say "What is the use?" For we are a nation of shopkeepers. And so you will sledge nearly alone, but those with whom you sledge will not be shopkeepers.'

What are we then, those of us who like to dangle in the void and test the cutting edge of our ability?

Are we eccentric? I think not, for I am always put off by individuals showing signs of abnormality. Nine out of ten of all those I have selected, during twenty-five years of expeditions, have been conventional people with everyday jobs and families.

I seldom look for people with particular skills. The ideal criteria are level-headedness, patience and, above all, good nature towards fellow human beings. Under stress these characteristics will be sorely tested whether the strain comes during a polar expedition, a marriage undergoing a difficult period or a business challenge.

As far as determination is concerned, any human being, however meek and unambitious they may think themselves, can develop and nurture a single-minded desire to fulfil a particular goal. The quantum leap is the moment of instigation, that first push to make the stone roll.

Thereafter all manner of undreamed-of outside factors will fall into place. In the words of the Scots philosopher William Murray, 'Until one is committed there is hesitancy, the chance to draw back, always ineffectiveness. Concerning all acts of initiative there is one elementary truth, the ignorance of which kills countless ideas and splendid plans . . . That the moment

226

one definitely commits oneself, then Providence moves too. All sorts of things happen to help one that would otherwise have never occurred.'

Once the stone is rolling and the die cast, most people will find they can keep going against the odds which Providence will also supply, to balance Murray's theory.

I am no philosopher. I do agree with Murray, but I would add that a great deal of luck (or, if you are religious, help from above) is also involved. The frozen continent that we crossed is, after all, ruled by the untamed might of Nature. A single storm could have wiped us out, mind over matter notwithstanding, but Antarctica suffered our passing as a giant that allows a fly to crawl across his face.

Appendix I

The Expedition

Discipline, Leadership

In conditions of war where instant, blind obedience is required by many men responding to the sometimes questionable orders of a single leader, whom they may not respect, discipline is a *sine qua non*. Armies make discipline possible in such circumstances by application of the stick as well as the carrot.

Soldiers are educated to appreciate that the best leaders are those who *first* learn to accept the principles of loyalty to other leaders. The British Antarctic Survey (BAS), where Mike Stroud received his polar baptism and training, and most other such Antarctic working communities, understand the sense of this tenet of leadership. Doctor Phillip Law, the famous Director of Australia's DEA Antarctic Division, their equivalent of BAS, wrote, in the 1980s: 'Nothing is so important as the appointment of a first-class leader and nowhere are the qualities of leadership subjected to more gruelling tests than at an Antarctic station . . . One quality is fundamentally essential to any team. It is loyalty. A man must be loyal to the expedition, loyal to his leader and loyal to himself. Some men are naturally loyal; some are fundamentally antagonistic, critically outspoken and disloyal.'

Knowing this, it would seem sensible for a leader, in choosing his team, to seek out naturally loyal individuals rather than knowingly to lay up trouble for himself or herself by taking self-avowed critics.

Roland Huntford, biographer of many polar leaders, says: 'Few leaders find it easy to tolerate stronger men under their command . . . Shackleton, feeling his way to leadership, instinctively avoided anyone whose authority might be a challenge to his own.'

Amundsen, where practical, did likewise. He avoided the great antagonisms between Scott and his ship's captain by becoming the skipper of his own vessel. Polar explorers, in the days before aircraft could reach Antarctica, had to depend on sea-captains for a key part of their journeys. Amundsen neatly side-stepped this division of authority by passing his skipper's licence.

Shackleton's physical strength was an adjunct of leadership which he did not hesitate to use. When a recalcitrant crewman on his ship refused to obey him, he hit the man repeatedly until he did as he was bidden. Such tactics have never been part of my armoury and I have never been tempted to 'get physical' on any expedition. My policy has always been to choose self-reliant, strong characters for my team since they are more likely to push themselves against great odds. The down-side of such people is often that they are, in Dr Law's words, 'fundamentally antagonistic and critically outspoken'.

Mike Stroud was of just such a persuasion. He openly disapproved of 'leadership *per se*' and felt strongly that all decisions on an expedition, especially with a small party of only two or three, should be taken by democratic agreement.

When we returned to Britain after the Antarctic crossing, Mike told the press: 'All I'd heard about Ran, until I first joined him, was that he was extremely difficult to get on with and a real problem as a leader. In fact we get on very well: we're both easy-going and, if any problems do arise, we can forget it.'

When I asked Mike where he had heard that I was a difficult leader he could not identify the source but admitted he had read the books I had written of previous journeys, in which I had clearly expressed my very undemocratic views on leadership. This was anathema to Mike, yet he has knowingly subjected himself to my leadership on five extremely successful expeditions and has stated his willingness to go on others in the future.

The tragic situation between Amundsen and his number two, Hans Johansen, could very easily have repeated itself, at least in part, with Mike and me. Roland Huntford, Amundsen's biographer wrote: 'Amundsen had to tread warily with Johansen for within them lay the seeds of conflict. And in those circumstances that meant lives in danger. The mountaineer on the rope; the explorer with his sledge, to anyone in an extreme environment, the strain of personal conflict is a mortal hazard. Johansen posed a threat to his authority, trying (consciously or not) to assume the psychological leadership . . . In a crisis this could cause division and disaster. Mutiny, in the deepest sense, was a possibility.'

The clash between the men led eventually to a show-down. Amundsen was forced to be heavy-handed and Johansen, never able to forget the humiliation that followed, finally committed suicide.

One day, conversing peacefully with Mike in the tent, not jlong before we reached the Pole, I told him I was surprised that, in 1985, Roger Mear had not selected him for their attempt on the South Pole. Mike was clear in his mind about this: Roger feared that Mike would be, in his own words, a 'threat to my control'.

'Why,' I asked Mike,' since you were desperate to be chosen did you not show yourself to be more amenable?'

It transpired that Mike had initially read Roger's mind wrongly. Less experienced than his rival, Gareth Wood, Mike decided, during their polar trials, to show the others not only how physically strong he was but also that he 'could actively and intelligently participate in decision-making'. This was his undoing, but he could hardly have taken any other course, even had he seen through Roger from the outset, because Mike was fiercely proud of his independence. At every opportunity he was wont to propound his preferences for leadership by mutual consent and he would have found his inclination difficult to conceal.

Dr Holmes-Johnson, the physiologist who studied all the Swan/ Mear team, described Mike as 'seeing himself as undisciplined and dominant, aggressive and stubborn. His type,' Holmes-Johnson summarised, 'may slow up group performance and upset group morale.'

'Expeditions without a single clear leader who is not afraid to impose his will undemocratically on others,' I told Mike, 'are asking for trouble. You have only to look at your own group troubles back in 1985 . . .' Because Robert Swan, the initiator and self-nominated 'political leader' of the 1985 Expedition, had failed

233

clearly to establish his position at the outset as *the leader*, he had found it almost impossible to establish overall control once the team reached Antarctica.

At one point this reached the stage where the 'field leader', Roger Mear, could consider actually selecting a team which excluded Swan; and Swan himself (who was subsequently to style himself as *the* leader) wrote in his diary, 'Roger Mear is the man to back and follow now.'

For all Mike's insistence that he hated leaders who imposed their will on others, he himself has written: 'Roger had not imposed himself as "the leader" and so there was a lot more room for dissent between three strong wills, dissent which under the coming trial was to be inevitable.' And, whatever his averred protestations and no matter how much Mike may silently have disapproved, he never on any occasion confronted my leader-ship. On many occasions he may have been irritated, even furious, with my failing to solicit or follow his advice, but he kept such feelings to himself and, as a result, our actions were never stultified by indecision born of dissent.

However much he objected to my 'graceless' pushing to continue travel at times when he felt weak and ill, he appreciated my motives. On our last day on the ice he said quite simply, 'You never stopped for health reasons once in all the journey. That's pretty good.' He would probably squirm at the thought of being considered loyal in this sense, but, by his forbearance, he would have scored well with Dr Law, who wrote, 'It was made clear to all our men that to back up their leader when they agree with him is no test of loyalty. It is when they disagree with him that they must stand behind him.'

In the Army, officers are taught to lead from behind. Amund-sen, Steger and many other polar leaders followed this sensible tenet but I have always led from the front in physical terms, and that involves handling all the navigation and setting a sensible travel pace. In the Arctic the leader/navigator should be able to go much faster than the rest of his team because he has to locate the best of many alternate corridors through sea-ice rubble and he will make mistakes that cost valuable time if the others are all bunched behind him.

On the Antarctic plateau this is not the case; indeed, the reverse is true. Navigation and route-finding are simple and, before we left England, I had readily agreed to Mike's request to navigate from time to time to alleviate boredom. Had I refused his wish, I might have caused him to become bitter but it would at least have forced him to maintain a sensible pace. This might well have prevented the various hypoglycaemic attacks which he suffered when he navigated and punished himself by maintaining too gruelling a pace.

Over the years, with different groups, I have slowly learnt to keep my antennae alert at all times to the cross-currents of atmosphere, the ever-changing under-currents of people's moods and topics to be avoided. In isolated communities under stress, even imagined mole-hills easily become great mountains and vicious storms blow up in tea cups of hurt pride.

I need to have my own way, but secretly so. I must appear to be democratic, to listen to advice, patiently to discuss criticisms to my suggested course of action and, whenever a better course *is* suggested, to go with it at once and to give open credit for it.

Sarcasm must be avoided like the plague.

Integrity, within a team, once compromised, is gone forever and is not replaceable. An argument usually produces plenty of heat but little light. After disagreements the hatchet should be buried and the handle *not* left above ground.

Charlie Burton, the most courageous and the wisest of men, taught me many lessons, and the greatest was that God gave men two ears but only one tongue. Think about something and chew it to death before you spit it out as abuse, for the greatest remedy to anger is delay.

I believe that it is best to forecast with intentional pessimism. When things go badly, perhaps dangerously wrong, the team will be less angry with their leader if he argued the case for his actions up-front and painted a negative picture of likely outcomes which, after the setback, he can regurgitate.

In order to carry your chosen way through the hurdle of 'democratic discussion', you need to be one hundred per cent certain that your method is clearly the best and that you have already considered in depth all lesser alternatives and contributory factors. There is no place for false modesty. I *believe* I know more about travel over polar ice than any man alive and that we will go faster and more safely through problem areas if I am leading from the front. To state such an outrageously conceited self-belief to Mike, or anyone else, would be asking for trouble, so I don't, but this basic belief is the root of the confidence necessary for leadership.

Press Relations

Of his book on his journeys with Scott, Cherry-Garrard remarked:

> There are those who write of polar expeditions as though the whole thing was as easy as possible. They are trusting in a public who will say 'What a fine fellow this is! We know what horrors he endured, yet see how little he makes of all his difficulties and hardships!'
>
> Others have gone to the opposite extreme. I want to do neither thing. I am not going to pretend that this was anything but a ghastly journey, made bearable to look back upon by the qualities of my companions. At the same time I have no wish to make it appear more horrible than it actually was: the reader need not fear that I am trying to exaggerate.

I echo Cherry-Garrard's sentiments and believe they hold good of this book. Mike Stroud may well have seen many things from a different angle but, thanks to his lending me his diary, I have been able to quote his viewpoint throughout my story. After a traffic accident it is well known that no two people remember the event exactly the same way. This may hold true of us. It is all too easy to be accused of exaggeration, and to avoid this I have been careful not to try to recreate long-forgotten conversations, especially where possibly contentious points need to be covered. The only safe method of accurate recall is the use of diaries, so I have done my best to quote from Mike's diary and my own wherever possible.

When we returned home from Antarctica in 1993, Morag, Laurence, Mike and I were invited to 10 Downing Street to chat with the Prime Minister who congratulated us, as did our Patron, the Prince of Wales, at Kensington Palace. Mike and I were awarded OBEs and I was sent some 4,000 letters by members of the public. One of these enclosed a news cutting which read: 'It is one of the symptoms of this age of nerves and hysteria that we magnify everything, that our boasts are frantic and our scares pitiable, that we call a man who plays well at football a hero and that all successes are triumphs. Just now, when we are feeling a little downhearted at seeing our supremacy in sport and in more serious matters slipping away from us, it is a moral tonic to find that in exploration we are still the kings of the world.'

This was, in fact, a cutting from the *Sketch* newspaper following Shackleton's return from Antarctica in June 1909.

Plus ça change . . .

There were also the usual carping columnists in 1993: Anne Robinson in the *Mirror* – 'That tiresome and unnecessary trek across Antarctica nearly cost them their lives,' and Margaret Maxwell of the *Independent* on 'how pointless it all was'.

Few people bother to counter-attack columnists unless they feel very strongly. Several letters bounced back in the letters columns this time, including:

> How wrong and foolish of Ms Robinson to pour scorn on Fiennes and Stroud. These fearless men who risked life and limb for a worthy charity are what this country needs; *and, from Lord Hunt, the leader of the first ascent of Mount Everest –* In these depressing times, I derived some comfort from the rejoinders to Margaret Maxwell's denigration of the trans-polar journey. It ill becomes Ms Maxwell to question the motives underlying this astonishing feat of human endurance and courage which was also concerned for people who suffer from a particularly sad and intractable illness. Surely at a time when, as never before, we need to develop these qualities in the young generation, this story should be accepted at its face value, as a shining example to Britain's youth.

Various letters flurried between the polar pundits as to precisely what had been the previous record. Dr Geoffrey Hattersley-Smith, a great polar traveller of the 1950s, wrote: 'Shackleton's party, without support, covered a distance of 1,215 statute miles. They picked up depots laid by themselves on the outward leg of the same march. It is this record that they have broken. All honour belongs to both Sir Ernest's and Sir Ranulph's parties, men of different eras whose achievements approached the limits

237

of endurance. Comparisons are superfluous if not impossible to make.'

When Messner returned to Europe from his supported crossing of Antarctica he received heavy criticism. This he summarised as coming from 'citizens who were indirectly angry with themselves when they saw one person living out his dreams to the ultimate. But I understod better the criticism of my neighbours who considered my activities irresponsible. That somebody should think it right to evade his middle-class responsibilities was an affront to their morality. That I, despite my family commitments, for months escaped from day-to-day pressures, in order to follow my private ambitions, was for them not justifiable.'

When Reinhold Messner, the world's greatest mountaineer, and Arved Fuchs, Germany's top polar traveller, completed their journey they were reasonably friendly, but things changed once they returned to the civilised world and the temptations of the media. Messner wrote:

> With a single news article, and through no fault of ours, a quarrel broke out which would forever affect relations between us. Once he had let himself appear the quiet hero of this quarrel provoked by others, Arved suppressed the facts more and more. It pleased him to play the role of the oppressed . . . I had made the speed and track in order to save the expedition. Now, suddenly, all that had been Arved's tactics.
>
> Was I supposed to be the 'fall guy' twice? First used, then slandered? Was Fuchs so sly? The quarrel with him made me ill and sleepless. I was hurt as after a broken love affair. The breach of trust gave me so much pain at first that I needed a long time to recover.
>
> This argument was not the first with my touring partners. Time and again I had been publicly slandered by 'comrades', always *after* the relevant expedition, always only *after* a great success. Thus one or other managed to come out from under 'my shadow' on the title page of magazines or daily papers.
>
> *Stern* utilized the 'media lust' of some of my 'quiet, oppressed' climbing partners shamelessly, in order to concoct a story out of falsehoods, half-truths and distortions, which I was able to expose as deliberate character assassinations. Nevertheless some of it stuck with

238

the readers, above all because Fuchs knew how to disguise the facts.

Over fourteen years of polar expeditions, mostly with Charlie Burton and Oliver Shepard, we had survived exactly the same post-expedition strains that Messner listed. Both Ollie and Charlie were loyal and honourable men. They had their grudges, as I did, but they kept them to themselves and we have remained the most solid of friends as a result and despite constant rumours to the contrary.

After their 1985 South Pole journey, Mear and Swan erected a screen over the intense antagonisms between themselves. 'It was part of the rules,' Mears wrote, 'that an outward pretence of cohesion be maintained.' In their joint book they were open and honest about one another's failings and their relationship did not degenerate into a mud-slinging match that would ruin whatever mutual feelings of respect had withstood the journey itself. Sensible partners in marriage or business do likewise.

The Director of the Scott Polar Research Institute, Dr John Heap, told me that he considered that Mike and I were 'a marriage made in heaven, with your initiative and drive and Mike's scientific ability'.

After our return, Mike's sister, Debbie, told a reporter, 'When I heard that Mike nearly died through hypothermia, I didn't know whether to run up to Ran and hug him for saving my brother or whether to shout at him for putting him in that danger in the first place.'

Mike told the press that we had got on 'extraordinarily well' together and, when asked if he would consider another expedition with me, replied, 'I can think of nobody I would rather do these things with.' My own responses had been on similar lines when asked about Mike and Morag.

Five peaceful months after our return from Antarctica, a tabloid reporter produced a full-page article which claimed to be based on Mike's writings, which began: 'The smiles and mutual back-slapping that marked the return of Fiennes and Stroud, from their record-breaking Antarctic expedition, was a sham and their 95-day trek was peppered with bitter arguments.'

Mike phoned me the very evening that the article appeared, apologised profusely and explained that he was furious with the newspaper which had completely misquoted him. So no harm was done between us. He wrote back to the newspaper to say: 'I have been bitterly hurt by the allegations that the smiles and handshakes on our return were a sham. It is not true – worse, it is unadulterated rubbish. I feel so bad about what was printed, I had to apologise. Despite difficulties and immense hardships, we came back smiling and acting like friends, because that is what we are. There were some arguments on the expedition – but that is hardly surprising when you have just one man's company for so long. They were not frequent, they were not bitter and they did not spoil our relationship. We have since hinted at another expedition together. Both of us would be more than happy to go on another expedition together, and personally, I hope we are able to do so.'

I have referred above to a side of expeditions not often discussed so that expeditioners perusing these notes prior to making their own plans can take heed. Forewarned is forearmed.

Notes on Equipment and Rations

Clothing

My opinion, after years of polar manhauling, is that the heavier the weight towed, the more difficult the selection of clothing. I have never managed to keep warm at all times. The principle is to move as fast as is commensurate with conserving energy yet keeping the blood circulating. Avoiding perspiration is my chief aim when selecting clothes. Trapped perspiration is a great danger, especially when there are inadequate facilities to dry out clothes in the tent.

Even the most up-to-date so-called breathable fabrics are *not* 100% breathable. The very best material for prevention of sweat entrapment is 100% Ventile cotton. I wear a loose-fitting outer sledge jacket and trousers of Ventile directly over thin wickerway underwear. Even at −27°C wind chill this keeps an active body lightly but bearably chilled and unlikely to perspire even towing very heavy weights.

I have been criticised for wearing Ventile not Goretex (or other such hi-protection from wind gear) because Ventile has been around for decades. But that which is new and indisputably excellent for cold wear, when mountaineering, does not apply to the vastly more strenuous work of heavy manhauling. In 1913, in his then 'modern' Burberry gear, Scott wrote, 'One continues to wonder as to the possibilities of fur clothing as made by the Esquimaux, with a sneaking feeling that it may outclass our more civilised garb.'

Steger wrote of his husky-drawn Antarctic crossing, 'Moisture is our mortal enemy; drying is our saviour. The colder it gets, the harder it is to rid your clothes of dampness. Moisture dampens your insulating layers and allows the cold to seep to the bone. We string our wet clothing in nets on the tent ceiling and pump up both our cookers.' Unlike Steger, we had no fuel beyond what we needed for cooking purposes. For this reason we could not choose clothes to keep us 'warm'. Ours had to keep us cool.

Scott and Shackleton were in fact sensible in *not* using fur jackets and trousers (which were unbeatable for the dog-sledging of Amundsen's teams) *but* they wore Burberry garments which they had designed too tightly fitting and, a key point, without fitted hoods. A typical clothing 'weight allowance' for both men's expeditions consisted of twenty pounds per man in addition to a sleeping bag. Mostly they carried spare underwear and mittens, spare socks, felt overboots, reindeer skin Eskimo boots to wear in the tent, sennegrass insulation for their feet, snow goggles, felt hats for hot sun and face masks for low temperatures in high winds.

Because their clothing was tight-fitting and lacked adjustability for varying temperatures, they sweated a lot, the moisture froze and made the clothes heavy, uncomfortable and less insulatory. Like us, they lacked sufficient fuel to dry their wet clothes.

Modern Antarctic scientists, when required to do field work, always take plenty of extra fuel to dry out damp clothing.

British Antarctic Survey field workers wear: cotton briefs, long-johns and long-sleeved vest of synthetic material, wool and synthetic tartan shirt, cotton 'moleskin' or fibrepile trousers, heavy duty wool and acrylic sweater, fibrepile jacket with full-length zip, extra-long tail and sleeves and high collar, 'breathable' waterproof jackets/trousers for wet/cold *or* heavy-duty lined nylon jackets/trousers for sea work *or* windproof cotton Ventile anoraks/over trousers for dry cold and an extra layer of down-filled jacket/trousers for extreme cold.

241

Vapour barrier sleeping bag liners (inner and outer) and vapour barrier socks are slimy and uncomfortable, but necessary if there is no fuel for drying out socks and moisture-filled sleeping bags.

Clothing

Ran	Mike
Merron Coverplus fleece jacket (stops at waist) (and Damart adapted hood)	Dawson Duofold fleece jacket with hood
1976 Army outer cotton trousers	Goretex overtrousers
Underclothes (wickerway) long sleeve vest and longjohns	Ditto
Nil	Fibrepile Salopettes
Meraklon headover (roundneck)	Black cotton scarf
Light cotton balaclava and thick Damart balaclava	Ditto
Separate lip protector mouthpiece	Nil
Scott ski goggles/Messner glacier glasses	Ditto
1 pair thick white woollen socks	Ditto
1 pair thin Helly Hansen socks	Ditto
Merron Coverplus vapour barrier socks	Nil
1 pair Dachstein Mitts	Ditto
1 pair Phillips Army gauntlets	Outer ski gauntlets
Nil	Thin Damart gloves
Nil	Woollen hat

(no shirt, sweaters, briefs or inner trousers.)

Tents

The pyramid tent invented by Koettlitz, one of Scott's men, eighty years ago, is safe, easy to erect in a storm and almost indestructible. Unfortunately, it is heavy compared with most other models.

The geodetic dome shape, which I have used for the past twelve years, is light and safe but difficult to erect in strong winds with poles that are easily bent. I would recommend it above all tents for use with sledges long enough to accept the four 'unbroken' tent poles. However, a backpacking expedition should beware of the long elastics which allow each pole to be 'broken' into six segments. In extreme cold this elastic goes floppy and the poles become dangerously difficult to slot together at the most vulnerable moment of any sledging day.

Amundsen preferred dark tents for ease of identification against snow, rest for the eyes when tent-bound and superior absorption of the sun's rays to heat the tent. This still makes good sense.

Skis/Footwear

The rigid plastic double-boots (which clipped to the plate bindings of our touring skis) provided poor insulation and being inflexible were unkind to our feet. However, the less rigid canvas boots and langlauf-type bindings that I used on previous polar journeys were not supportive enough to give us leverage when towing such heavy weights. The fact that we were able to pull our fully laden sledges *at all* was due to our correct choice of boot. The down-side was bruised, infected and frostbitten feet.

Our skis and bindings were excellent as were our chunky metal ski-sticks with their tailor-made steel baskets. The latter lasted for over a thousand miles of punishing treatment, just a few miles of which would have rendered useless any standard stick.

Windsails

Scott, Shackleton and Amundsen all used sails when the wind allowed and in 1990 Messner recorded, 'As the wind began to fill the sail, it wriggled, rustling across the snow, then rose 8 metres in the air and was away. Our speeds, when pulling the sledge conventionally, were 2 mph maximum, when skiing and sailing 4 mph and when sailing alone, 5 to 8 mph.'

Overall I believe we were better off taking our sails because, on those *rare* occasions when a following wind was neither too gentle nor too fierce, we made better mileage than when merely manhauling. However, there is an argument that we would have been in a far better physical state had we not taken sails.

My feet were badly mauled by trying to ski and sail at the same time. Mike's fingers were severely nipped trying to sort out inverted sail lines. We carried a total of twenty-three pounds extra for over 1,000 miles during which there was no sailing. By far the greatest risk of injury of a nature that would quickly have stopped the journey was the chance of a bad fall when trying to sail. Our worst and most lethal crevasse problems were the direct result of sailing. We were rendered weak with cold and I received badly frostbitten toes during attempts to sail.

All in all I could not recommend sails without strong reservations. For an expedition that happens to strike a 'windy' year they could be well worthwhile. Otherwise dubious!

The difference in energy expenditure between manhaul and doghaul as far as the effect on humans is concerned is marked. After fifty days of manhauling, I was using up 10,000 calories per day and Mike 8,500. After 170 days of dog driving at the same heights, Steger found it difficult to 'cram in 6,000 calories a day'.

It is important to prepare the body for a specialised diet well in advance. We began to eat large quantities of complex carbohydrate some six months before leaving the UK.

Scott, Shackleton and Amundsen all knew of the dangers of scurvy and how best to prevent scorbutic symptoms. Indeed Captain Cook learnt to conquer scurvy two centuries earlier.

Slow starvation was Scott's greatest enemy as it was ours, and for the same reason – an inability to progress at a fast enough speed had we carried more food and had correspondingly heavier sledges.

General Gear (As at start)

| | Weight (lbs.) | |
	Sledge 1	Sledge 2
Sledge and traces	27.5	27.5
Skis and skins	11	11
Ski sticks	2.5	2.5
Spare skins and glue	2	2
Spare ski and binding	5	1
Tent (7). Pole (1) inc. 6 alloy stakes (inc. 1 spare pole and alloy sleeve) and tent bag	8	1
MSR cooker on steel base in cooker box (wood) inc. 2 mugs, 2 spoons, brush for floor, 2 cook pots, windproof matches	9.5	1
Spare MSR with spare parts and 1 cook pot	—	1.5
Sleepbag outer/inner/vapour barriers inner and outer	13.5	13.5
Karrimat closed cell roll-up (2)	2	2
Rucksack (empty) (Géant Karrimor)	5	5
Windsail in bag	11.5	11.5
Rope (60 ft.)	—	6.5
Para-cord length (100 ft.)	1	—
Jumars (1 pair) (w. loops)	1	1
1 icescrew 4" and 8 karabiners	1.5	1.5
Ice axe	—	2
Snow shovel, plastic/alloy	0.5	—
Personal bag inc. small adjustable spanner/pin nose pliers/needles/thimble/Zippo lighter/ flints/Dentafloss/thin cord/twine/superglue/ some screws/wire/diary/pencil/Velcro/chart/ map/compass/Swiss army knife/spare socks/ mitts/goggles/personal medical items	8	7
Pee bottle	1.5	—
PLB beacon and 2 batteries	1	1
Magellan and AA batteries	6	6
Sarsat beacon and 3 batteries	—	10
HF radio and ancillaries	13	—
2 HF radio batteries	4	4
Medic kit	—	4

	Weight (lbs.)	
	Sledge 1	Sledge 2
Science kit	—	6
Sony video camera and 9 tapes and 2 batteries	—	8
Olympus 2000 camera and 10 Kodachrome II films	2.5	2
Thermos (2) (full)	8	8
Ski mountaineer boots/inners/gaiters	8	8
Sledge jacket (Ventile cotton)	5	5
Harness and fixtures	2	2
51 foodbags (5200 cals each man) 5 lbs.	255	255
31 Sigg fuel bottles (1 litre) @ 2.3 lbs.	72	72
TOTAL:	485.5	484.5

Medical Problems

Our medic pack weighed 4 pounds and was based on our previous journeys. I suffered from haemorrhoids so we had cream for this. Likewise hand cream for cracking fingers, lip cream for UV affected lips, amethocaine drops for sun blindness, Canesten powder for crutch rot, Bonjela gel for mouth ulcers, antiseptic cream for wounds, plasters for blisters, cuts and rubbed raw patches of skin, drugs and painkillers, Lomotil for diarrhoea and anti-inflammatory pills.

None of our ailments were new to polar travel. Amundsen suffered badly from haemorrhoids. Edward Wilson, despite the lack of an ozone hole, wrote in 1908, 'Our lips are in a horrid state. The Captain's and mine have been raw for many weeks now.'

Although Amundsen used for eye protection a wide visor with ventilation slits on top like modern ski goggles, his men and Scott's suffered sun blindness on many occasions. Dr Wilson (who, like Mike, had trained at St George's Hospital Medical School in Tooting), wrote, 'My eye was so intensely painful that I could see nothing and could hardly stand the pain. I cocainized it repeatedly. I never had such pain in the eye before. All I could do was lie still dropping in cocaine from time to time. We tried ice and zinc solution as well. After two hours of misery I gave myself a dose of morphia and slept well.'

Mawson also used this treatment and tannic acid from tea leaves. Mike had two opium derivatives, pethidine and morphine but, sadly, no cocaine.

In case of the need to operate Mike also packed various forceps, scalpels, hypodermics and stitching needles. There have been a number of field operations in the Antarctic wastes and not all performed by doctors. Under one of Shackleton's upturned boats, two of his men amputated the frostbitten toes of a third. But the first recorded operation, by Shackleton's Doctor Marshall in 1904, was the removal of the eye of somebody struck by a boathook.

Following the end of our days on the ice, we found it difficult to focus. Eric Arnott, one of Britain's top opthalmic surgeons, diagnosed this as a temporary derangement that he had previously only diagnosed in long-range bomber pilots who flew for many hours staring at very little. The natural ability to focus can, it seems, get 'rusty'. As he advised, our vision was to clear up after a few weeks back in England.

Within two months we had returned to our normal body weight and our frostbitten areas were largely recovered, although two of my toes and the main wound on my right foot are, five months later, still intermittently painful when walking in anything but soft slippers.

How many more days could we have survived before one or both of us succumbed to the cold? There are too many ifs and buts to answer such a question. To me it is enough that our minds and our bodies thankfully held out for long enough to cross the continent.

247

Comments on expedition rations over eighty years
(All: 1 man/1 day ration)

	1910 Scott (manhaul)	1910 Amundsen (dogs)	1985 Mear/Swan (manhaul)	1992/93 Pentland S. Pole (manhaul)
	grms	grms	grms	grms
Biscuits	454	400	205	—
Pemmican	340	375	—	—
Butter	57	NK	148	125
Sugar	980	NK	— Acc	— Acc
Cocoa	24	NK	100	20
Chocolate	NK	125	120	208
Cereal	NK	NK	—	213
Raisins	NK	NK	—	—
Tea	20	NK	— Acc	— Acc
Dried Milk	—	75	— Acc	— Acc
Corn Oil	—	—	28	—
Oatmeal block	—	—	95	—
Salami	—	—	85	—
Soup	—	—	43	128
Freezedry meal	—	—	58	170
Freezedry veg	—	—	24	85
Bacon bar	—	—	50	—
Flapjack bar	—	—	—	80
FATS %	39	NK	57	57
CARBOHYDRATES %	42	NK	34	34.6
PROTEINS %	19	NK	9	8.4
			(inc acc total)	(acc total = 63 grms)
TOTAL WEIGHT	980	975	956	1092
TOTAL CALORIES	4430	4560	4795	5200

(NK = Not Known)   (Acc = As Accessory)

Physiological Investigations

In August 1992 Doctor David Drewry, the Director of the British Antarctic Survey, wrote: 'I have been approached by the South Pole '92 Expedition to be led by Sir Ranulph Fiennes in respect of their physiological research. The British Antarctic Survey has undertaken a review of this project through its Medical Unit. I am pleased to report that we have found the project credible, interesting and addressing a topic of importance.'

By August 1993, at which time this book went to print, the analysis of all Mike Stroud's work was not completed by those working on the various samples and related figures. The bodies involved other than Mike and his staff at APRE include the Universities of Surrey, Nottingham, Southampton and Cambridge. In the absence of any definitive paper, I have put together the documents, illustrations and tapes that Mike has given me to date and edited the data to suit the layman rather than the scientist.

Research by Dr M. A. Stroud

The research involved examining the physiological effects of three months' sustained exercise with inadequate nutrition and an adverse environment. The three areas studied were:
a) energy balance and body weight control
b) nutrition
c) exercise physiology

Energy Balance and Body Weight Control
Despite many decades of intensive study, the mechanisms by which man regulates energy balance and his body weight are not understood. In part this is because it is difficult to conduct prolonged studies of exactly what an individual is eating and exactly how much energy he/she is using.

We ate a fixed diet of known composition for many weeks whilst performing a repetitive form of activity. Since we *could* measure the diet contents, knew *exactly* what exercise we were taking each day, and could measure our changes in body weight and metabolism, we could obtain information as to the interaction between energy expenditure and body weight change.

249

Our daily intake was worked out by analysis of our ration composition and notes taken of any rations *not* eaten or temporary diet changes made. We therefore had good records of what we had eaten in terms of fat, protein and carbohydrate over the entire ninety-five-day period.

We measured energy expenditure by looking at the weight losses that occurred on this known diet and we measured our weight changes in body fat. This gave information as to how much fat and muscle we were losing; information backed up by more accurate tests of body composition when we were weighed *underwater* before and after the expedition.

Underwater weighings gave information of body density which was directly related to how much muscle and fat we possessed.

Both of us lost a great deal of weight, amounting to nearly 3½ stone (49 lbs) in Ran's case and slightly less in mine. Interestingly, more than half of our weight losses turned out to be *muscle*. It is not clear why this should be so but information still awaited may provide an answer.

The results of the above measurements show that over the course of the expedition, our average daily energy expenditure was just over 6,000 calories each. But this *overall* figure masks the very high levels of energy expenditure early in the expedition, especially when climbing to the high plateau, when Ran had energy expenditure levels approaching 10,000 calories per day and mine of 8,500 calories. These are enormous and *greater* than any shown by previous measured experiments.

As well as measuring our energy expenditure in the above way, we also made measurements using a technique involving isotope labelled water. This requires water to be drunk which contains heavy isotopes of hydrogen (deuterium) and the heavy isotope of oxygen (oxygen 18) instead of normal oxygen 16.

We drank doses of this abnormal water at the beginning and half way through the journey and then collected urine samples nightly to show how rapidly the abnormal isotopes were disappearing from our bodies.

The deuterium comes out in all forms of water including sweat, urine and vapour in the breath. However, oxygen 18 comes out in both water and carbon dioxide in the breath and therefore disappears relatively faster than the deuterium and the *difference*

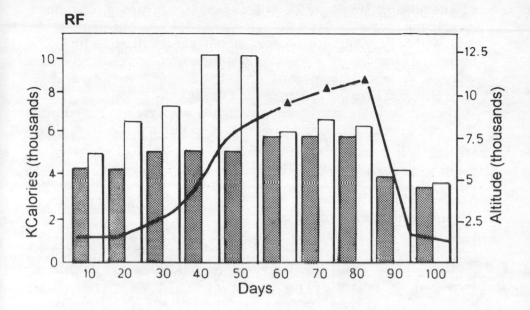

RF

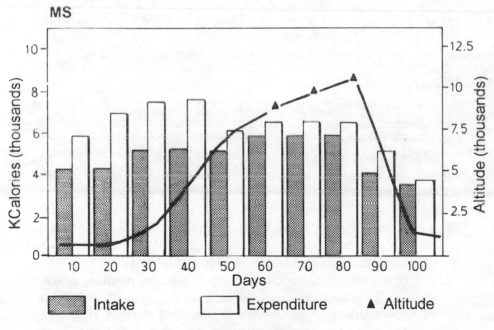

MS

Intake   Expenditure   ▲ Altitude

Energy expenditure

in the disappearance rates reflects the total carbon dioxide production.

It is therefore a measurement of all energy that is finally burned. At the time of going to press, the results are awaited but will give more accurate information as to how our energy expenditure changed over the course of the expedition.

In addition to the above measurements, we were interested in how our resting metabolic rate (and its response to a meal) would alter over the course of the expedition.

Normally if people are losing weight, the resting metabolic rate (and the response) declines quite quickly. This is one of the reasons why attempting to lose weight by dieting *alone* often becomes unsuccessful quite quickly.

In our case, following the expedition and despite our having lost a great deal of weight, we found that both our resting metabolic rate (and the response to food) were markedly increased, the opposite of normal findings.

This serves to emphasise the important effects of exercise on weight control (in addition to mere dieting) by stopping the fall in metabolic rate. We were an extreme example of this where losing weight by exercising a great deal seems to have increased resting metabolism. Quite why this should have happened is not clear. The results of analysis of our blood samples showing levels of hormones that regulate metabolism are still awaited.

Nutrition
Because we needed to eat as many calories as possible with as little weight as possible, we consumed a very abnormal diet containing fifty-seven per cent of energy from fat.

Because we were going to sustain this abnormal diet for a long period, we were interested in whether we could adapt to it, and so, before and after the expedition, we had a standard test meal where a high fat composition meal was followed by blood sampling every fifteen minutes for six hours.

The preliminary results of this experiment show that we have remarkably adapted our ability to absorb fat from the gut and move it as a fuel supply into the bloodstream: an unusual finding which has not been previously documented.

We were further interested as to whether sustained exercise would eleminate any adverse effects of the high fat intake on our

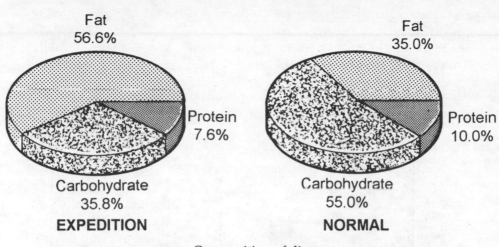

Fat
56.6%

Protein
7.6%

Carbohydrate
35.8%

EXPEDITION

Fat
35.0%

Protein
10.0%

Carbohydrate
55.0%

NORMAL

Composition of diet

serum cholesterol and tri-glycerides. The results of these tests are also awaited and are taking time to process since the tiny samples that we returned have all to be meticulously analysed by hand.

Another area which we were examining was the interaction of our diet and exercise and our protein requirements. Although most people believe that a lot of exercise requires a high protein intake, this is generally untrue.

However, the levels of exercise, sustained for so long, might indicate other effects, so we were interested in measuring the amount of turnover in our muscles as we ate dietary protein and then either used it for building muscles or burned it for energy.

To do this, we took doses of an amino acid called Glycine which were labelled with an abnormal isotope called nitrogen 15. We did this on several occasions throughout the expedition and followed each dose by collecting twenty-four hours' worth of urine to analyse for the clearance of the abnormal amino acid. These results are also awaited and should give us information as to where and when we lost so much of our muscle bulk.

Exercise Physiology
Although one would expect three months of sustained effort to have a dramatic fitness effect even on robust individuals, we were interested in the effects of exercise taken whilst eating inadequately.

253

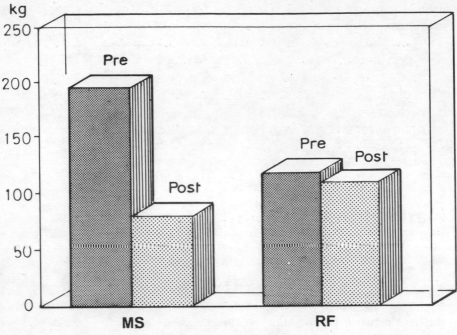
Lower limb strength, compared

Measurements were made of our aerobic capacity, the ability of our heart and lungs to move oxygen around the body and for our muscles to use it, before or after the expedition. These showed a *decline* in both of us which probably reflects that we had lost heart muscle as well as skeletal muscles.

We also took measurements of muscle-strength in different muscle groups which showed considerable declines in the strength of both of us although they were more marked in me than in Ran.

This loss of strength would have been associated with a loss of muscle bulk. Interestingly, the muscle biopsies that were taken also showed that the enzyme levels in all parts of the muscles' systems were markedly reduced.

Conclusion
At the time of going to press, five months after the expedition, we have yet to get the full picture of the physiological changes that we underwent during the course of the expedition. Nevertheless, the results that we have to date have proved immensely

interesting and unusual. They will prompt further investigation into man's responses to such extreme conditions.

When the work is fully collated, it will be published in open scientific literature and presented to learned societies.

I gratefully acknowledge the assistance of the Department of Physiology, the University of Nottingham, the Dunn Nutrition Unit, Cambridge, the Department of Nutrition, University of Southampton and the Department of Biochemistry at the University of Surrey.

Dr M. A. Stroud, M.R.C.P.

Daily Progress Chart

Date (1992)	Location	Wind Comments	Height above sea level	Surface Comment
09 Nov	78°19.08N 43°46.94W	From Berkner to Filchner floor. No wind.	Approx. 50 ft.	Good. Hard. Small (3 ft wide) cracks.
10 Nov	78°28 43°45	White-out partial.	NK	Saggy crevasses.
11 Nov	78°36 43°45	Very slight SSW wind.	NK	Many very large part-covered crevasses. Good surface.
12 Nov	78°44 43°45	Strong wind 20 k from N. Semi white-out.	295 feet	Big open crevasses.
13 Nov	78°57 43°45	Partly windless and clear sky.	NK	Big crevasse field.
14 Nov	79°05 43°13	Good. Then semi white-out. Some falling snow from SSE wind.	NK	Crevasses bad and big all day. Surface not so good.
15 Nov	79°10 43°00	White-out (semi) 55 knots from W. Heavy drift.	NK	Crevasses all covered but wide and saggy.
16 Nov	79°20 43°05.1	Part semi white-out. Later good. Windless.	NK	Major crevasse field. Opened up as we passed.
17 Nov	79°28.8 43°00	Near white-out. Small wind from SE.	NK	Slow climb. Good surface but ridges and drifts.
18 Nov	79°36 43°00	a.m. bitter SE wind, changes p.m. to good, clear, windless.	NK	Now close in to Berkner island coast. No crevassing. As for yesterday.

Daily Progress Chart (*continued*)

Date (1992)	Location	Wind Comments	Height above sea level	Surface Comment
19 Nov	79°46 43°00	Semi white-out. Strong wind from SE.	NK	As before.
20 Nov	79°46 43°00	Semi white-out. Some clear periods.	NK	As before.
21 Nov	Nil	White-out. 70 knots from SSW.	NK	In tent in crevasse field in white-out. 70 knot blizzard.
22 Nov	80°02 43°00	Good clear sky. 15 knot N a.m. later windless.	NK	Surface getting sticky.
23 Nov	80°10 42°30	White-out a.m. Clear p.m. Light breeze from S.	NK	Surface now drags due to drifting.
24 Nov	80°19 42°00	15 knots from SSW. Sunny.	NK	As before. Can still see Berkner Island behind.
25 Nov	80°27 41°12	12.4 miles from SSW. Clear.	NK	Surface flat but some drifts.
26 Nov	80°36 41°18	Zero to 15 knots from ENE. Some sun, wind, semi white-out.	NK	As before. Good surface.
27 Nov	80°45 40°29	Similar.	NK	As before. Good surface.
28 Nov	80°55 39°51	5 knots from NE. Mostly sunny.	NK	Approaching coastline. Best going.
29 Nov	81°05 39°43	a.m. 5 knots NE breeze. Clear day.	NK	Best going.
30 Nov	81°15 39°36	5–10 knots from E. Clear skies.	1,735.5 feet	Cross coastline. First sastrugi. Soft crust.
01 Dec	81°25 39°29	18 knots from ENE.	1,624 feet	Sastrugi. Soft crust. Some patches of grey hard ice surface.
02 Dec	81°36 39°23	2 hours 5 knots from E. Then no wind. Hot.	2,297 feet	Bad sastrugi »4ft. Big climbs. Blue-ice for 2/3 miles.
03 Dec	81°47 39°23	Clear. 3 knots from N.	3,000 feet	Big hills running N/S to our E. Blue-ice valley stops. See solitary Bogman Peak to W.
04 Dec	81°58 39°13	10–20 knots from E.	3,000 feet	Bad sastrugi all day.

Daily Progress Chart (*continued*)

Date (1992)	Location	Wind Comments	Height above sea level	Surface Comment
05 Dec	82°09 39°07	10 knots from E.	3,700 feet	Big climbs in waves. Follow 3 mile-waves of covered crevasses running SSW.
06 Dec	82°35 39°23	3 knots from NNE. Clear sky.	4,160 feet	Worse sastrugi and ridges. Many falls.
07 Dec	82°46 39°	10 knots from N.		
08 Dec	82°51 39°	15 knots from E.	NK	Climb heavy. Big sastrugi.
09 Dec	83°02.7 39°24	Clear. Slight breeze from SSE.	3,900 feet	Big sastrugi. Soft crust.
10 Dec	83°13 39°27	20–30 knots from SSE. Blowing snow.	4,630 feet	Harder surface. No climb.
11 Dec	83°23 39°25	40 knots from E all day. Very cold.	4,170 feet	Big drag on sledges from blown snow.
12 Dec		40 knots from E. Clear sky.	5,190 feet	Saw small peak to SW. Climbed grey ice re-entrance. Steep.
13 Dec	83°44 39°48	Semi white-out all day. V warm + snow. No wind.	5,220 feet	Good surfaces.
14 Dec	83°55 39°46	NE wind 8 knots. Good visibility.	5,350 feet	As before.
15 Dec	84°06 40°04	Thick white-out. Clear last 2 hours.	5,500 feet	Soft crust. Drifts.
16 Dec	84°18	6 knots WNW. Clear.	5,600 feet	Soft crust but some ice patches. Big region of huge filled-in crevasses and hills.
17 Dec	84°31 41°52	10 knots from W. Good visibility.	NK	Very good flat surface. Downhill.
18 Dec	84°43 42°48	8 knots from NE.	5,250 feet	Bumps, sastrugi. Sticky surface. Drifts.
19 Dec	84°54 42°41	2 hrs of 6 knots from E. Very clear.	5,830 feet	Steep hills with many 3 ft sastrugi.
20 Dec	85°05 42°43	Very good visibility. 2 knots from E.	5,530 feet	Good surface.
21 Dec	85°15 42°35	Clear. No breeze.	5,390 feet	Good surface.
22 Dec	85°27.4 42°36.3	2 knots from N.	5,875 feet	No sastrugi. Flat crusty surface.
23 Dec	85°40 44.58	5 knots SE breeze.	5,710 feet	Good flat surface.

257

Daily Progress Chart (*continued*)

Date (1992/3)	Location	Wind Comments	Height above sea level	Surface Comment
24 Dec	85°54 47.00	15 knots from ESE.	5,500 feet	Sastrugi. Some hills.
25 Dec	86°06 49°00	10 knots from NNE all day. Some mist.	6,000 feet	Sastrugi. Scoured patches. Some climbs.
26 Dec	86°19 51°04	10 knots from NE. Misty.	6,470 feet	Ridges, sastrugi, soft crust. Drifts.
27 Dec	86°31 51°10	10 knots from ESE.	6,350 feet	As before.
28 Dec	86°43 51°22	10 knots from ESE.	7,100 feet	Bad ridges all day. Two big filled-in old crevasses.
29 Dec	86°55 51°33	30 knots from ESE.	7,100 feet	As before.
30 Dec	87°07 51°52	5 knots from ESE.	7,570 feet	As before.
31 Dec	87°19 52°51	5 knots from N.	7,300 feet	As before.
(1993) 01 Jan	87°29 52°54	10 knots from E. Overcast.	8,100 feet	As before. A touch flatter at end of day.
02 Jan	87°36 53°15	Light snowfall from clear sky. No breeze. Some clouds p.m.	8,000 feet	Good surface. Flatter.
03 Jan	87°46 53°24	Overcast. Soft snow falling. No wind.	8,100 feet	Ridging quite bad.
04 Jan	87°57 53°36	25 knots from SE. Clear skies.	8,220 feet	Good surface. No hills. Drifting.
05 Jan	88°08.4 55°05.6	15 knots from SE.	8,200 feet	Good surface. A few sastrugi.
06 Jan	88°18.7 54°52.3	10 knots from ENE. Semi white-out.	8,610 feet	As before.
07 Jan	88°29.4 54°40.8	Clear except overcast to W.	8,920 feet	Mirage of big high hills to S. A steep climb.
08 Jan	88°39.7 54°38.4	6 knots from SE. Clear skies.	NK	Low sastrugi in all directions. Very flat and hard surface.
09 Jan	88°50.4 54°08.4	10 knots from SE. Clear a.m. Part overcast p.m.	8,530 feet	Good surface. Some hills.
10 Jan	89°3.3 57°23.4	10 knots from ESE. Overcast.	8,980 feet.	As before.
11 Jan	89°14.1 57°35.3	15 knots from NE. Overcast.	9,150 feet	As before.
12 Jan	89°24.5 55°0.6	White-out.	9,500 feet	New snow. Soft.

Daily Progress Chart (*continued*)

Date (1993)	Location	Wind Comments	Height above sea level	Surface Comment
13 Jan	89°34.1 53°30.34	No wind. White-out p.m. 10 knot from NW.	9,550 feet	As before.
14 Jan	89°43.8 50°37.8	No wind. Overcast all day.	9,500 feet	Big hill. Good surface.
15 Jan	89°52.4 49°27.6	6 knots from SW. Very cold. Slight white-out.	9,150 feet	As before.
16 Jan	89°57.0N 176°42.7E	Very cold. 10 knots from SW.	9,015 feet	Slow surface. Snow-quakes.
17 Jan	DAY LOST IN CROSSING POLE AND INTERNATIONAL DATE LINE			
18 Jan	89°46.7 165°03	Semi white-out p.m. Rest of day clear. 10 knots from S.	9,160	Flat. Slow surface. Snow-quakes.
19 Jan	89°37.8 167°31.8	10 knots from W. Semi white-out.	NK	As before.
20 Jan	89°18.6 179°25.9	10 knots from NW. Semi white-out.	9,730 feet	Climbs in waves.
21 Jan	89°07.35 176°44.4	10 knots SSW. Part white-out.	9,700 feet	As before. Slow surface.
22 Jan	88°56 175°28.3	15 knots from SW.	9,700 feet	Slight surface improvement.
23 Jan	88°42.3 174°44.4	10 knots from W.	NK	New type hoar frost surface in sudden patches. Big climbs. Breathless.
24 Jan	88°30.4 174°14.4	Mist pockets moving about – 85°C windchill.	10,360 feet	As before.
25 Jan	88°19.3 173°38.2	White-out.	11,100 feet	As before. Better surface.
26 Jan	87°58.2 169°48.3	12 knots from SSW.	11,400 feet	Harder surface. Some ridges and sastrugi now.
27 Jan	87°44.4 170°05.4	15 knots from SSE. Sunny.	10,800 feet	Ridges and sastrugi.
28 Jan	87°30.3 170°12.1	5 knots from SSW. Some overcast hours p.m.	NK	As before.
29 Jan	86°38.4 167°47	5 knots from SSE. Overcast all day all directions.	10,390 feet	As before.

Daily Progress Chart (*continued*)

Date (1993)	Location	Wind Comments	Height above sea level	Surface Comment
30 Jan	86°10.4 164°47.5	25–40 knots from S.	NK	Many sastrugi and ridges. All W/E.
31 Jan	85°59.4 166°55.4	30 knots from S.	NK	As before. See mountains.
01 Feb	85°35.3 167°31.1	5 knots from SE gusting up (katabatic).	8,480 feet	Better surface. Crevasses seen in distance N, E & W. Cross moraine.
02 Feb	85°16.4	Gust from SE (katabatic).	5,980 feet	Descend upper reach of glacier. Many crevasses to flanks.
03 Feb	84°59.3 167°41.2	Strong winds from south (katabatic).	5,350 feet	Windchill at S Pole = −53°C. Surface as per glacier.
04 Feb	84°48 169°18.4	No wind.	4,480 feet	Some v. soft snow. As before. Major crevasses.
05 Feb	84°34.3 170°14.2	Fluctuating winds from side glaciers.	3,185 feet	As before. Major crevasses.
06 Feb	84°10.4 170°55.6	Clear. Clouds over mountains to flanks. 30 knots for 2 hours from S.	2,300 feet	As before.
07 Feb	83°56 170°52.3	Calm all day. Some clouds.	1,930 feet	As before.
08 Feb	83°29.1 170°51	Gusts from 2–20 knots from S (katabatic).	NK	Reached coastline at Gate. Mixed surfaces but no soft snow.
09 Feb	83°23.2 170°35.5	Semi white-out a.m. Cleared p.m. Little wind from SW.	NK	Soft surface. Last crevasses crossed.
10 Feb	83°10.1 170°43.2	High clouds but sunny. 5 knots NE and SE.	178 feet	Soft surface.
11 Feb	82°57.2 170°43.1	5–8 knots NE and SE. Clear skies.	74 feet	Soft surface.
12 Feb	82°50.05 170°48.01	High cloud but sunny. 5 knots from SE.	NK	Soft surface.

Pentland South Pole Expedition Communications

This report details the equipment, operating philosophy, propagational details involved in engineering the communications facilities for the first unsupported crossing of the Antarctic continent by foot between November 1992 and March 1993.

Written and Compiled by Laurence Howell, IEng. MIEIE.

UK Communications Base – Mintlaw Radio, operated by Laurence Howell – UK Communications coordinator.

Antarctic Field Communications base at Patriot Hills, Antarctica, and later at Punta Arenas, Chile, operated by Morag Howell, Antarctic and field communications coordinator.

High Frequency (HF) communications

Communications between the expedition's forward base in Antarctica with the field party traversing the Continent, the expedition's UK radio base in Scotland, the logistic base in Punta Arenas, Chile, and long range aircraft communications, relied for the most part on (HF) short wave radio. The frequencies chosen using the ionosphere as a reflective medium are affected by solar conditions on a hour to hour basis. A daily log of radio conditions was kept by both the radio operators at Mintlaw Radio Scotland and Patriot Hills Antarctica to compare with the issued Ap and or K Geomagnetic Indices for the period. The expedition occurred when the number of sunspots was declining in the eleven year-or-so solar cycle. Solar flux was reducing quickly and this produced an average lowering in frequencies but able to propagate the large distances involved in some of the inter-continental links.

The great circle bearing from the designated UK radio base at Mintlaw, Aberdeenshire Scotland 57° 30 mins North 2° West to Patriot Hills Antarctica 80° South and 81° West, is 192° east of north true. The mean great circle distance is 16,086 kilometres (almost 10,000 miles)

Mintlaw's receive and transmit aerial system was a terminated rhombic at a feed height 80 feet above ground. This gives an aerial gain of around 12dBi over an octave (appx 8–16Mhz) and high angle, but still useful radiation characteristics at lower frequencies. The wave angle at the higher frequencies was a little high as it had been designed primarily for the 9–12Mhz region (night time F layer operation). Output power at the open wire feed was just over 1Kw in Scotland and probably around 50W at Patriot.

Patriot Hills high frequency UK directional aerial was an unterminated 'Vee' beam around 100m in length with an apex angle of 50° at a height of only 9 metres over what was thought would have been clean pure blue ice, but in fact turned out to be rather lossy and contaminated with rock and other debris. The estimated gain for the Vee is 10dBi but probably realised a few dBs less than this.

Mintlaw's radio aerials are mounted over damp boggy ground with no local obstructions. The site is classed as a good operational location for long range, low angle, high frequency applications in both the northerly and southerly directions.

Site elevations Mintlaw – 32 metres and Patriot 1000 metres above sea level.

The UK to Antarctica schedules rarely operated during UK daylight hours and then at weekends only. Signals via the F2 layer using multihop mode tended to produce signals on the whole that were weak but readable. For daytime schedules 23 Mhz produced the best results, which followed computer predictions. When schedules did occur during UK daylight they were around 80–85% successful, even during the geomagnetic disturbed periods. Over the past twenty years of Polar expeditions north/south paths have been found to be not being so critically affected by geomagnetic disturbances.

Because of the vast differences in power, the Scottish station had difficulties in receiving Patriot Hills signal. In all cases a 10–12dB increase in Patriot's power (not possible due to logistics) would have made a terrific difference. Patriot Hills' transceiver was powered by 12 V car batteries recharged with a solar cell bank.

The electromagnetic noise level at Mintlaw is normally very low with brief increases for rain and snow static and arcing from 33 Kv power line insulators during wet weather. Transmitting and receiving equipment consisted of the state of the art Kenwood TS850 SAT transceiver with preselection, a receiver that has one of the best sensitivies, selectivity and third order intercept figures. It also has the facility of adjustable crystal filters at two IFs.

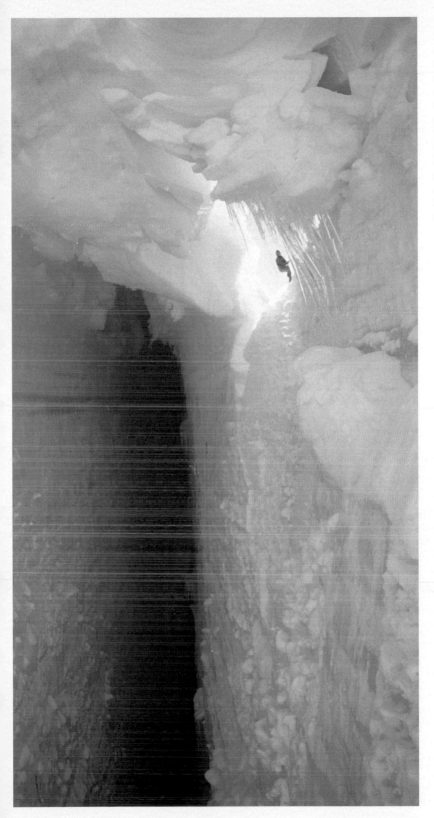

17 Crevasses often look harmless enough from a birds-eye view but a single step on a weak trap-door of snow can quickly lead to a long drop. This crevasse, with one climber just visible at its upper lip, was photo-graphed by a British Antarctic Survey member some way down its interior

19 Looking back towards Mount Deakin.
The apparently erratic course of the
author's track is caused by crevasse avoidance

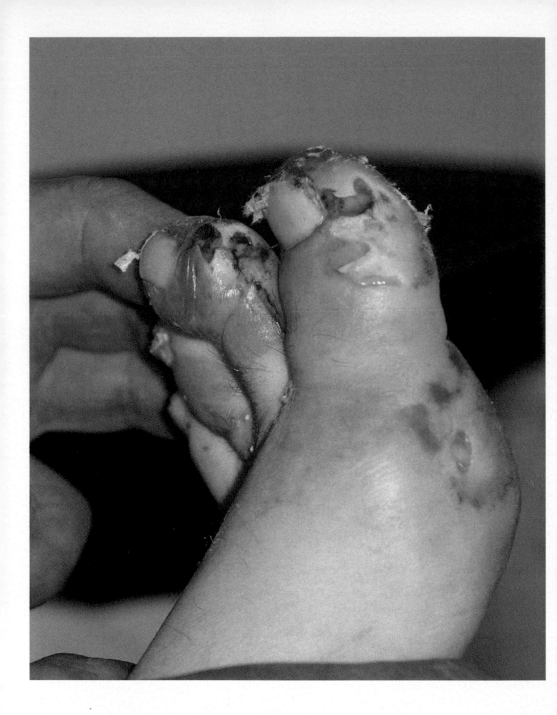

20 The author's left
foot with frost
damage soon after
the South Pole was
passed

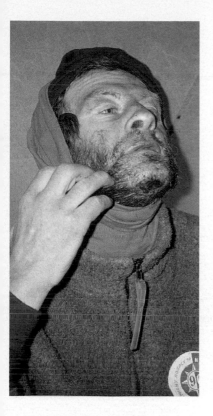

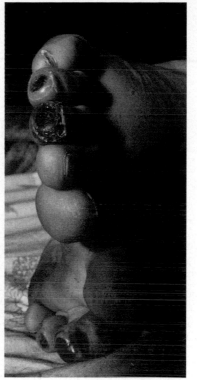

21a This photograph of the author's chin was taken in 1990 in the Siberian Arctic. Exactly the same wound re-opened on this expedition

21b One of the author's Transglobe team (Beverly Hoover) with toe-end frost damage; fairly common on manhaul journeys in extreme temperatures Thankfully this exact problem wasn't encountered this time around

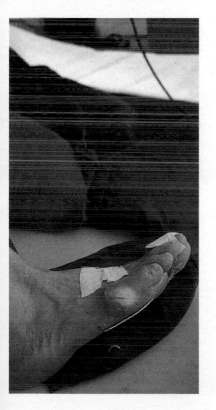

21c The author's right foot becomes infected in the bone during the third week

21d Dr. Mike Stroud inspects a frost-damaged finger

22a Hundreds of miles behind . . . hundreds of miles to go

22b Abreast the Cloudmaker and fiddling with a jammed trouser zip. This can be uncomfortable and embarrassing

23 A collapsed and partially snowed-in crevasse on the middle Beardmore glacier

24a The author's face, and especially eyelids remained swollen with liquid until long after passing the pole

24b Blue ice slopes on the Beardmore Glacier. These proved difficult to negotiate without crampons and with only one ski-stick

25 Approaching Mount Kyffin

26a Camping in the rock-fall zone through necessity

26b Dr Mike Stroud among the pressure waves and craters of a Beardmore Glacier crevasse field

27 A wealth of beauty but also danger can be detected in an icescape by the practised eye.

28a The common Krill. The basis of the Southern Ocean food chain and susceptible to slight climatic changes, such as those created by the ozone hole

28b Bull elephant seals fighting

28c Chinstrap penguin with chick

28d Leopard seal

28e Baby seal

28f Baby Crabeater seal

28g Elephant seal

28h Seals in an ice-pool

28i Albatross, monarch of the Southern Ocean skies

29a No shortage of penguins

29b Interloper

29c Decorative penguins

29d Happy penguin

29e Dirty little penguin

29f The original cuddly penguin

29g The morning gossip

29h Pavarotti penguins at evensong

30a The Nottingham KGB removed muscle samples from thighs without anaesthetics. Here Dr Mike Stroud wishes he were back in Antarctica

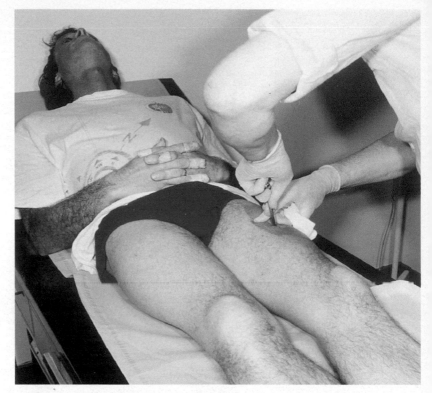

30b The results of 50 days' starvation in the Arctic in 1990. On this expedition, the team were even more emaciated and weaker due to the greater weights towed, distance covered and the longer period of starvation

30c Underwater tests by Dr Mike Stroud's staff at the Army Personnel Research Establishment

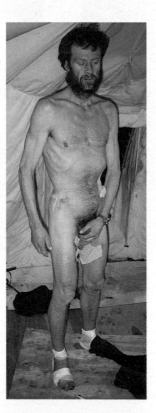

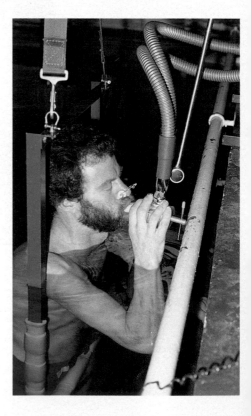

31 The author a week after returning
to London from Antarctica

32 The Prime Minister with
Laurence Howell and the author
on the expedition's return

The majority of the Mintlaw to Patriot Hills schedules started at 1900Z using either 16.3Mhz, 14.8Mhz or 12.2Mhz frequencies. By this time of the day and season the optimum working frequencies (OWFs) were dropping very fast and often contact was established at the higher frequency dropping down to the lower frequencies within 1 or 1.5 hours. Signals were never very strong, apart from one occasion.

In Mintlaw the signals averaged about 6dB above noise floor, which would have been acceptable for Morse code but proved difficult for intelligible voice communications, especially when transferred onto the public telephone switched network (PTSN).

Patriot Hills on the whole could hear Mintlaw nearly all the time, even on disturbed days when Mintlaw couldn't detect even a carrier. By the time the main schedule of the evening came at around 2210Z the Mintlaw ionosphere had settled into its 'night time mode' where contact with Patriots Hills was possible over the range 8–11.5 Mhz with perhaps a 3–6dB peak for the OWF.

Reception of 'Northern' Antarctic bases over the period 2000–0200Z was possible at Mintlaw on frequencies between 4 and 12Mhz. Signals were always weakest at the lowest frequency.

The one day Patriot was strong was probably caused by a patch of E type ionisation to Patriot's east, allowing the radio signal to be delivered at some strength into the lower night time F layer to the north. Signals for this one occasion using Patriot's omni-directional array were some 20dBs up on the Normal Vee. This lasted for around 15 minutes.

There was a marked change in received signals strengths as the signal progressed southwards towards and across the Pole. British Antarctic Survey (BAS) stations and others to the north of 72° South were always audible at Mintlaw during operational periods, often at great strength. Mintlaw radio was able to contact these (stations at 67, 65 and 72° South) on any day in the evening, even under the most disturbed radio condition. The maximum attenuation obtained on the worst day was a fade of 27dB (compared with the average) for the link between Faraday Base and Mintlaw. For every degree south of 70° South an additional loss of 2–3dB was noticed on the received signals, increasing on occasions to 5–6dB for during the most disturbed periods. It is not known whether it was due to just going over a critical 16000 Kms path distance (wave angle zero for both aerials), or because signals were being driven further into the Antarctic continent and into the Auroral Oval and were suffering from some Polar Cap absorption all the time. From what is known of propagation across the Antarctic continent the latter is the more likely; for instance South Pole station which is well equipped with 1–10Kw transmitters and extensive long range aerial systems; this station was always weak at Mintlaw, with only small peaks of 10dB for a few minutes when monitored continuously over a few evening periods.

It was found that the British Antarctic research base's (BAS) long range aerial efficiencies or local attenuation from topographic effects were very marked. If omni-directional or wide-band aerial units were in use with little or no low angle elements, signals received at Mintlaw were always some 10–20dB down (more than calculated) on stations employing directional 'Vee' or part (broken) rhombic arrays.

Farraday and Rothera bases (ZHF44 and ZHF45) were always strong at Mintlaw. Signy Island, South Georgia were always weaker, and Halley Bay's signals strengths very variable.

For the most part the ionospheric forecasting programmes for the UK to Antarctica (supplied by RACAL and BT) were reasonably good for Northern Antarctica and South Atlantic areas. Operational results showed that they should not or cannot be scaled for the interior of the continent south of 70°. During the Antarctic summer there is always a section of daylight ionosphere to pass through. High daytime D layer absorbtion can make life very difficult. For stations within or near the Auroral Oval the added problems of high absorption of signals passing through the D layer during disturbed periods.

Field party communications within Antarctica were conducted using 2 Watts Peak envelope power from a lightweight SMC Yeasu FT70G transceiver to a dipole – and were highly successful.

The UK to Antarctic communications were based on simplex working IFRB cleared frequencies, though it has been reported to the government department concerned that co-channel interference from South America on the 8,11 and 14.8 Mhz regions was common, military in nature and scheduled.

The rhombic employed by Mintlaw was definitely the best aerial that, within the limitations of the support structures, could have been used. A log periodic or similar array would have given a too wide beamwidth and would have picked up even more co-channel chatter from South America and Asia.

Patriot had links into Punta Arenas, in Southern Chile. There were periods in the expedition where communications were often better (before directional array was built by the expedition) via the UK. This was probably due to better and high gain arrays at both ends, frequency flexibility, operator experience and probably little to do with radio propagation.

Emergency and positional beacons

A SARSAT 406Mhz-unit using test protocol was used. This unit was manufactured by LOKATA – Now Kelvin Hughes – and had been used extensively on three previous expeditions. The unit was battery powered by a purpose designed lithium battery. The internal 121.5Mhz beacon was disconnected prior to the start of the journey.

The expedition had severe problems at times with the accuracy of the information from this system. Mostly and surprisingly was the problem of latitude errors. Some days the variation from actual (GPS confirmed) position was up to 100/120 nautical miles. Longitude variation was small, and prior to the start of the expedition was forecast to be more of a problem.

The SARSAT/COSPAS system operating in Antarctica seemed to have a number of difficulties: firstly, because the unit was operating in the Antarctic no local user terminal (LUT) can see the beacon via satellite in real time, be it 406MHZ or 121.5Mhz. The delay some days on a fix could be up to 6 hours, the signal and positional information being stored by the satellite and downloaded when it came into view of the LUT at Lasham UK. This delay was forecast by the rescue services.

The expedition beacon was identified and flagged as a test and development unit, therefore the computer at Lasham ignored it completely. A software mod was done to flag it to screen at Plymouth but still a manual search had to be completed for each path by the rescue services.

Inaccuracy in fixes seemed to be caused by the satellite sometimes remembering where the last fix was and 'merging' the results – this is considered not to be a very good idea.

All in all the inaccuracy in positional information meant that

265

the expedition could not rely on this data though the status code selected by the field party to indicate their well being, was always received correctly. Positional accuracy can get more difficult for VHF/UHF line of site radio at the Poles with high inclination of satellite passes and poor geometry etc. The inaccuracies seemed due to changes in the phase of the signal being received by the satellite, distorted perhaps by heavy particle precipitation in the D and E layers due to disturbed periods. It was when the Earth's geomagnetic was storm/substorm that the problems occurred.

On previous expeditions in the Arctic operating from Ward Hunt Island scintillation and phase changes on FM/SSB signals when satellite signals pass through the Auroral Oval was very evident. Perhaps it was this that was causing the problem. Until a LUT is installed on the Antarctic continent, *the expedition's communications personnel have no trust in the positional accuracy in the SARSAT/COSPAS system.*

Global Satellite Positioning System for Field Party

A handheld Global satellite positioning receiver (GPS) manufactured by Magellan, a 5000 series unit, worked very well, with only one bad fix to our knowledge in the mountains on the Beardmore Glacier, and even this could have been a data fix transfer problem of someone reading the wrong figures over the radio. External lithium batteries were used for this unit based on a bank of 6 diode isolated D cells with polarised plugs and sockets.

INMARSAT

An experimental INMARSAT suitcase satellite unit (MTI) was tried from Patriot Hills 80S 81W. The base radio operator there should be congratulated in setting up a suitcase unit from a very small tent. With the satellite over the Brazilian equator the figures showed the Atlantic West satellite only 0.35 degrees above the horizon. As the satellite orbit progressed both south and north of the equator during a twenty-four hour period it was found that calls could be made for 4 hours per day, if a channel was available.

Signal strengths were very variable from the satellite due to the amount of atmosphere the 1.2Ghz had to go through. Snow storms, clouds, and mist all added attenuation.

When North America woke up commercially in the afternoon, it was found even more difficult to get a telephone channel as the sensitivity of the satellite seemed to be reduced by 3dB.

INMARSAT gave the expedition a calculated period when the Satellite was most visible in the 24-hour period. It was very surprising to them that the forecasted peak of signal (maximum visibility) was some 3–4 hours earlier than actually occurred at Patriot. IDB sponsored not only the satellite equipment and transport, but also the space segment costs.

Laurence Howell, IEng. MIEIE.

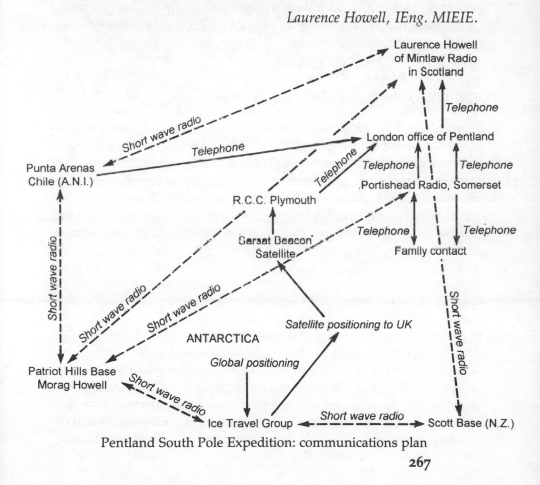

Pentland South Pole Expedition: communications plan

Morag Howell (36) was born in the Orkneys and educated at Fraserburgh Academy. She became the first woman to study electrical and electronic engineering at her college gaining an ONC, HNC and Marine Radio Operator's Certificate. She joined her husband Laurence on the 1988 Ellesmere Island-based North Pole expedition and manned the forward communications base on Ward Hunt Island for the 1989 expedition. In 1990, following her work with the first ever western expedition to set out from Northern Siberia, she was awarded the USSR's Honours Medal. She organised and planned, with her husband, the communications and Base set-up in Antarctica (Patriot Hills) and Chile (Punta Arenas). Morag cited as sole radio link for the American Woman's South Pole Expedition as well as for ourselves. Her job was extremely difficult and was carried out with great expertise for three bitterly cold months from a small tent and often in ninety-mile an hour blizzards. She said afterwards 'In Antarctica, a base is simply where one person is. Here there was me and nothing else for 2,000 miles.'

Laurence Howell (36), educated at Woodcote and Purley High School for Boys in Surrey. He joined British Telecom Satellite services whilst gaining technical qualifications at Croydon and Banff and Buchan colleges of technology. In 1978 he was seconded to the British Antarctic Survey (BAS) for a 33-month tour of duty as their radio operator. Whilst at Adelaide Island he made contact with Virginia Fiennes of the Transglobe Expedition Borga Base. In 1981/82 he worked with her at Alert N.W.1 and, alone, as radio operator on Ellesmere Island. Also in 1982 he returned to the Antarctic on emergency secondment to BAS following three fatalities and to survey war damage on South Georgia.

He joined my North Pole unsupported expeditions as Base commander in the Arctic in 1986 and was joined by Morag for the 1988 and 1989 expeditions. On the 1990 expedition he was based at a KGB camp on Sredniy Island in Northern Siberia. Laurence's civilian job, often on North Sea platforms, is senior communications engineer for Phillips Petroleum. With Morag he planned and organised all aspects of the Pentland South Pole expedition 1992/1993 communications. Using a commercial short wave radio station on his Scottish farm, he acted as UK Base communications controller throughout the Antarctic crossing journey.

268

The Pentland South Pole Expedition 1992–1993

The Team

Patron:	His Royal Highness The Prince of Wales
Organisers:	Charles Burton and Oliver Shepard
Polar Advisers:	Sir Vivian Fuchs and Dr Charles Swithinbank
Leader:	Sir Ranulph Fiennes
Science Leader & Team Member:	Dr Michael Stroud
Base Leader (Patriot Hills):	Morag Howell
Communications (UK):	Laurence Howell
Liaison (New Zealand):	John Parsloe
Liaison (UK):	Anton Bowring
Charity:	The Multiple Sclerosis Society
Financial Sponsor:	The Pentland Group

The Sponsors

Corporate: ABC Publicity & Communications,
(Dominic Carmel Boland)
Adventure Network International,
(Annie Kershaw, Mike MacDowell)
Aldershot News
Air New Zealand (B. Larsen)
Army Personnel Research Establishment
(Dr J. R. Allan, Dr W. R. Withey and Staff)
Berghaus International (Adrian Geere)
Be Well Nutrition (Dr Brian Welsby)
Bi-Polar Services (John Parsloe)
Biss Lancaster (for Dixons PR) (Pippa Sands)
Blacks Camping & Leisure (Alan Day)
British Antarctic Survey
(David Drewry, John Parran, Ann Roberts,

Susan Robertson, Bernard Moran, Ken Roberts,
Peter Bucktrout)
Canoxy (UK)
Cape Scaffolding Ltd
Cobles Company (John Parkinson)
Cosmetics-to-Go
Convatec Limited (Alan Hunter)
Coverplus (Peter Merron)
C.S.A. Ltd
Damart Thermawear (Martin Smith)
Dawson Consumer Products
(Duncan Burman, Graham Stuart)
Director General of Army Manning & Recruitment
(Major General J.F.J. Johnston)
D.O.T. Lasham
D.T.I. (Michael Kenyon)
Dunn Nutrition Unit, Cambridge University,
(Dr R. Whitehead, Dr Andy Coward)
E.A.E. Limited (Vic Towler)
Explorers Club of New York (Eileen Harsch)
F.K.I Communications Limited (Graham Plank)
George Fisher Limited (Michael Standring)
Gaybo Limited (Graham Goldsmith)
I.D.B. Mobile (Peter Coffman)
Karrimor International
(Michael Parsons, Angela Schofield)
KLM Royal Dutch Airlines
(J. Smit, Richard Oliver)
The Lady Magazine
LOKATA Limited (Michael White)
London University (Professor J.C. Waterlow)
Lyon Equipment (Ben Lyon)
Magellan Systems
Marlow Ropes (David Potter)
Mars Confectionery (Julie Will)
Microwave Modules Ltd
Mountain Equipment Ltd
(Peter Hutchinson, Jane Bennett)
Nottingham University
(Professor P. H. Fentem)

Occidental International Oil (Mike Fitzgerald, Clyde
   Sorrell, Jan Milne, Karen Waygood and others)
Olympic International (Brian Pursglove)
Olympus Optical (UK) (Ian Dickens)
Pentland Group (Steven and Andy Rubin, Richard
   Stephens, and many others)
Phillips Petroleum
Polar Desk (F.C.O.) (Dr Michael Richardson)
Portishead Radio (BT)
Positioning Resources (George Ritchie)
Port Stanley Head Postmaster, Falkland Islands
Quark (Mike MacDowell)
Queen's Medical Centre, Nottingham University
(Dr Ian MacDonald, Dr Greenhaff)
R.S.G.B. (Marcia Brimson)
Racal (Clive Moody)
Radiation Systems Int. (Darren Grimshaw)
Radio Society of Great Britain
Raychem (Ray Sharp)
R.C.C. Plymouth (Squadron Leader Bob Connolly)
Robert Fleming Insurance
(H. Clive Bowring, Bevil Granville)
Rolex Watch Co. (John Hunt, Michael Cronin)
Rothmans (UK) Limited (Daniel Oxberry)
Rotunda plc (A. L. Watson)
Royal Geographical Society
(Dr John Hemming, Nigel & Shane Winser,
Alison Glazebrook, Nicky Sherriff and Joanna)
The Royal Scots Dragoon Guards (Carabiniers &
   Greys)
(Colonel Melville Jameson, Corporal Campbell of the
   Pipes and Drums)
Royal New Zealand Air Force; Defence
   Environmental Medicine Unit (Squadron Leader S.
   J. Legg)
Scott Polar Research Institute (Dr John Heap)
Seaquest Cruises (Andrea Corman)
Silva (UK) (Tony Wale)
S.M.C. Communications (B. D. Gardner)
Snowsled Limited (Geoff Somers, Roger Dayne)

South Midland Communications
Spoggles Limited
Spring O'Brien & Co. Limited
(Chris Spring, David Kleinman)
Sun Microsystems (Don Taylor)
Times Newspapers Ltd
Total Oil (UK) (Nigel Abbott)
Trimble Navigation Ltd
Triwall Europe (David Fagg)
University of Auckland (Professor Paul Hill)
Upski Limited (John White)
WEXAS International (Simon Beeching)

Individual:

Clay Badger
Ian Crockford
Peter Daley
Maurice Daniels
Alan Day
Richard Diamond
Stephen Down
David Drewry
Adrian Elliot
Steve Elmore
The people of Exford
   Village on Exmoor
Adrian J. Fox
Julian Green
David Harrison
Peter Harrison
Paul Keighley
Annie Kershaw and the
   Punta Arenas and
   Patriot Hills staff of
   ANI
François Lochon

Peter and Elizabeth
   Martin
Shirley Metz
Richard Mumford
Charlie Newton
Mr P. B. Nicol and Mrs
   T. A. M. Nicol
Frances Pajovic
Warren Randell
Colin Raynor
Stephen Rubin
Sue and John Scott
Christopher Sinclair-
   Stevenson
Mike Smith
Alejo Contreras Staeding
Richard Stephens
Elspeth and Henry
   Straker
Don Taylor
Jeff Trolley
Ed Victor
John Walford

Appendix II

Topography and History of the Antarctic

The Formation of Antarctica

In 1969, scientists discovered the bones of the dog-like Lystrosaurus reptile in Antarctica. Such bones were also found in Africa and India. At the time the animal existed, it is reasonable to suppose that all three continents were temperate in climate and were attached to one another.

At some point more than 200,000,000 years ago, the land known by modern scientists as Gondwanaland split up into seven continents that drifted apart. One was Antarctica. Even 40,000,000 years ago there were trees in most of Antarctica.

20,000,000 years ago extensive ice was present in Antarctica and, by 12,000,000 years ago, the great ice sheet had begun to form, coinciding with a general cooling of the Southern Ocean. At that point West Antarctica was merely an icy archipelago of islands which was not overlaid until 4,000,000 years ago by its own ice sheet. Only 3,000,000 years ago did the polar regions resemble their current situation with ice at both Poles.

Around 50,000,000 years ago an effective ocean opened up between Antarctica and Australia. Likewise between Antarctica and South America some 25,000,000 years ago. This allowed temperatures to decrease and moisture to increase, an ideal condition for the evolution of great glaciers. Once 0°C was reached at sea-level, the West Antarctic ice-sheet began its build-up and by 3,000,000 years ago Antarctica was the highest continent in the world.

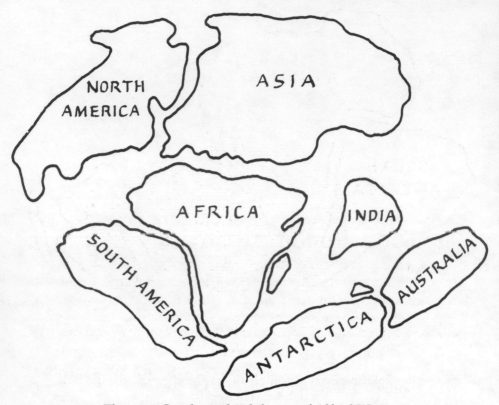

1. The 1912 Gondwanaland theory of Alfred Wegener

The ice-sheet with its hundreds of outlet glaciers retreats or advances in response at least partly to the amount of solar radiation received. This fluctuates because of irregularities in the Earth's solar orbit. Sometimes ice has covered far greater areas than it does now. During maximum glacial periods (such as that between 120,000 and 6,000 years ago) the increased ice build-up lowered sea levels everywhere by as much as 300 feet.

Likewise, 120,000 years ago, glacial retreats had probably removed the *entire* West Antarctic ice sheet and the oceans of the world covered much of today's inhabited terrain.

The reason the polar regions are so cold is because they receive less solar radiation due to the comparatively low angle of the sun in relation to the ground surface (the Poles receive 40 per cent less than the equator on average). Also they reflect more of the

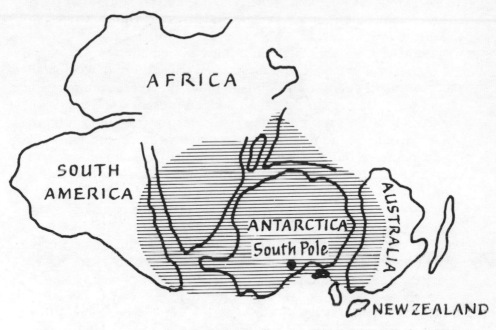

2. Probable formation of Gondwanaland 250 million years ago, from Dr Brian John

After splitting from the single mass, Gondwanaland, the two continents floated apart

received radiation and thus lose much of their potential for heating. Thirdly, the clarity of the polar atmosphere, due to lack of dust and water vapour, means that only a small amount of the long-wave radiation from the earth surface is trapped in the atmosphere: radiation which, elsewhere in the world, serves to heat the atmosphere.

Ice ages correspond with glacial advances and history records their effect on mankind. In the mid-eighteenth and nineteenth centuries many glaciers in Europe advanced into inhabited valleys. In the sixteenth and seventeenth centuries Alpine and Norwegian farmers suffered bitter winters and cold, torrential summers. Glaciers covered farmland. Famine killed 137,000 people in the last big Norwegian glacier advance and 2,000,000 Swedes emigrated in the late nineteenth century for the same reason.

277

The Arctic pack-ice sometimes extended so far south that polar bears swam ashore in the Faroes, and Eskimos (Inuit) arrived in Scotland in their kayaks.

Because ice ages fluctuate in a fairly systematic way, it seems safe to expect the next one in or after 4000 AD but 'accidental' surges can happen at any time. Should the West Antarctic ice sheet surge (it appears unstable to some present-day scientists), or should the East Antarctic sheet slide northwards, the Southern Ocean would be the more thickly covered with ice, the southern hemisphere would cool and all the world's coastal cities would be submerged. This is but one of many 'catastrophe scenarios' which can be produced by scientific hypothesis.

Ice-sheets are glaciers. The Antarctic ice-sheet is a single vast glacier bigger than the United States and containing 75 per cent of the world's fresh water. To think of this ice-sheet as static or immovable is a fallacy. Only 10,000 years ago an even bigger glacier, the Laurentide, covered North America and Canada: more than 5,000,000 square kilometres of ice.

Most glaciers are born in mountains where conditions often allow snow to collect and survive the summer melt. More snow then accumulates and a snow-patch grows into a baby glacier. In polar areas, where summer temperatures seldom rise above freezing, even small snowfalls may suffice for the birth of a glacier.

Trans-Antarctic mountains separate the two great glaciers or ice-sheets of Antarctica and the glaciers which drain a part of the far larger eastern sheet down to the western sheet include the Beardmore, second largest in the world and surpassed only by the Lambert Glacier in East Antarctica.

Fresh-water lakes of melt water often exist *beneath* glaciers and a number have been plotted beneath the East Antarctic sheet. Such bodies of water can burst out of their unseen reservoirs and, as in Iceland, cause damage. One such surge flowed at 50,000 cubic metres per second, flooded hundreds of square miles and transported huge ice blocks far from the glacier edge.

The Southern Ocean

At the Antarctic Convergence cold Antarctic water meets warmer waters and, at this well defined circumpolar boundary, both sea and air temperatures become markedly warmer. The make up of sea birds and sea creatures also changes at this point, an invisible line which undulates between latitudes 50° and 60°.

The Convergence is a turbulent area where the colder southern water sinks below the warmer waters of the Atlantic, Indian and Pacific Oceans.

The *surface* waters of the Southern Ocean which are close to the edge of Antarctica are driven by the East Wind Drift, and those further north by the West Wind Drift.

Superimposed over these two contra-rotating currents are many other localised drifts and the whole complex current/temperature structure allows an ideal breeding ground for the bottom end of the food chain of all Antarctic life.

Young krill hatch in the East Wind Drift but the growing fish tend to drift northwards with the West Wind Drift. Dense concentrations of krill relate closely to the zones of mixing between the waters of the different drifts.

Energy input to the sea by the sun, often affected by the infiltration of floating ice (and, unfortunately, by recently increased ultra-violet light levels due to the ozone hole), is converted to 'edible' biological material by minute plant cells. These phytoplankton provide food for zooplankton such as krill and the krill provide fodder for all the predators of sea and air. Phytoplankton productivity is limited in winter by the short daylight hours and the cover of sea ice. As temperatures increase in spring and summer, algae released from the base of the melting ice form blooms, which follows the path of the receding ice-front. Annual production of this plant matter south of the Convergence totals 610,000,000 tons and this is the basic food of the entire food web.

If Russian, Japanese and other fishing fleets are allowed to overfish krill swarms, this will seriously affect all the food web of creatures in the Southern Ocean. However, some scientists believe several million tonnes of krill could be fished yearly without affecting the general ecosystem. Currently 70,000,000 tonnes are taken annually by man. In South Georgia alone, birds and seals catch 7,000,000 tonnes annually. The 30,000,000 seals of Antarctica eat up to 130,000,000 tonnes of krill annually and research into the whole matter of what limits should be placed on man by man is of immediate importance.

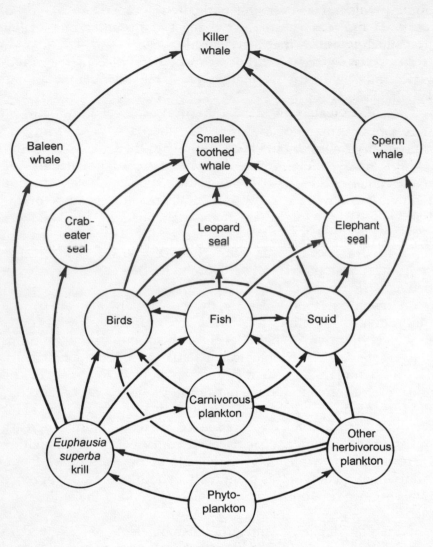

Antarctic food chain

The international BIOMASS programme scientists are successfully collecting the necessary data to establish that krill form the
pivotal role within the Southern Ocean ecosystem and that
overfishing must lead to the collapse of the upper levels of the
entire community.

Krill, which can live to five years or more, are the staple food
of most whales. Baleen whales locate krill swarms by acoustics.

Right whales skim the surface like dredgers with their mouths open. Humpback whales swim around krill swarms like cowboys rounding up cattle, then they dive deep and come up vertically with open mouths to engulf the concentrated krill.

Southern Ocean Whales (Adapted from David Walton)

Baleen Whales
Filter feeding baleen whales have no teeth but their mouths contain fibrous plates of baleen (whalebone) which act as giant sieves to strain plankton from sea water.

Species	Comments	»Length (metres)	»Numbers (1992)
Blue whale	Grey/blue. Flat broad head. Eat krill	30	12,000
Southern Right	Bulky and calloused-skinned. Eat small plankton	17	4,000
Fin	Dark topside. White underside. Eat krill	22	100,000
Minke	Smallest of species. Eat krill	8	400,000
Humpback	Notably long flippers. Calloused skin. Eat krill	14	5,000
Sei	Dark all over. Eat fish	18	Very few in Southern Ocean

Toothed Whales
These whales have stumpy teeth which enable them to catch large prey

Killer/Orca	Black and white. High dorsal fin. Eat anything	8	Several thousand
Sperm	Massive heads. Eat squid/fish	20	1000,000
Southern Bottlenose	Pale in colour. Beaked head. Eat squid	7	Thousands; not under threat
Long-finned Pilot	Black. Bulbous heads. Eat squid	6	Not under threat

Species	Comments	»Length (metres)	»Numbers (1992)
Southern Right Whale and Dolphin	Black tops. White undersides. Eat squid and fish	2.5	Rare in southern hemisphere
Amoux's Bottlenose	Brown with beaked heads	10	Not known
Hourglass Dolphins and Spectacled Porpoises	Black and white with dorsal fins	2.5	Not known

All the above breathe air. They cannot therefore survive in ice-covered water. They keep to the edge of the pack-ice which is a rich feeding area.

Whales were hunted by Stone Age man and harpoon heads dating to 3000 BC have been found. The medieval Basques used to cut up stranded whales in the Gulf of Gascony, melt the blubber and eat the flesh. They would also drive them on to the beach from fishing boats, or even kill them at sea, a technique they had perfected by AD 1200 and continued to follow for 700 years.

A description of a Basque whale killing runs: 'The whale, mortally wounded, would begin its terrible and pathetic death agony, thrashing the water with its tail in fear and pain, snapping its jaws and wallowing in a smother of foam, crimsoned with blood.' By 1550 there was hardly a whale left in the central reaches of the Atlantic.

In the early seventeenth century a new species of whale (the Greenland right whale) was discovered on the rim of the Arctic. They were slow swimmers, poor fighters, stayed afloat when killed, and their oil was plentiful. A single sub-Arctic whaling station could process 600 right whales in a season and, when the survivors retreated into the pack ice, whale-catcher boats soon tracked them down. By 1850 they were all but extinct.

At this point Wilkes, Ross and D'Urville returned from their Antarctic expeditions with reports of 'vast quantities of whales by the edge of the pack', and the southern killing began.

Most Northern whales, the rights, greys, bottle-nosed and beluga are slow moving, non-aggressive creatures. This was also true of the first southern species to be hunted, the Southern right. They were sixty feet long, sixty tons in weight and were slaughtered with ease. The sperm, blue, fin, humpback and killers for a while managed to put up a resistance of sorts but, in the long run, their fate was also assured.

Spermwhales live on squid and are known to dive down to 3,300 feet, taking over an hour and suffering wounds from the suckers of squid with tentacles up to thirty feet long. Once harpooned, sperms could prove difficult to 'catch'. In May 1887, for example, one of the *Bounty*'s longboats was towed off at eighteen knots by a harpooned bull sperm. Five other longboats later fixed separate harpoons to the fighting bull with no better result. Eight hours later a line was transferred to the *Bounty* herself but, *a day and a night after the initial harpooning*, the whale had towed the 350 ton brig, six longboats and 6,000 fathoms of rope for over forty-five miles.

Finwhales, at fifty tonnes, could keep pace with a naval frigate steaming at twenty-five knots. Blue or Sibbald rorqual whales grow up to 110 feet long and 150 tonnes in weight. They can swim for hour after hour at twenty knots, with short bursts of forty knots, but fiendish new Svend Foyn harpoons and ever faster steam vessels soon doomed even the greatest of the rorquals.

Many other lesser known whales went the same way, some species being driven close to extinction. In 1937 an International Agreement for the Regulation of Whaling was signed by nine nations. It should, in theory, have helped. In practice 1938 brought the greatest ever number of kills: 46,039 whales and 500,000 tons of oil.

By 1965, despite up-to-date tracking equipment, including helicopters, the South Georgia whaling fleets saw only four blue whales the whole season. Against 250,000 blues in 1900, there are now thought to be less than 500 in the world.

In 1972 France proposed that Antarctic waters should be declared a whale sanctuary but Japan, Norway, Iceland and a few other pro-whaling countries continue to seek to slaughter the great mammals of the southern seas. The 1990s finally saw fairly strict whaling controls in place.

South Ocean Seals (Adapted from John Smellie)

Species	Comments	»Length (metres)	»Numbers (1992)
Ross	Small bulky bodies. Eat fish and squid	2.2	650,000
Leopard	Lithe bodies with long 'killer' heads. Eat penguins, seals, krill. They co-operate in 'packs' to attack large prey	3.6	222,000
Southern Elephant	Bulls huge with 'proboscis'. Cows fat and dumpy. Can dive to 4,500 feet	4.5	700,000
Crabeater	Slim bodies. Eat krill	2.6	40 million
Weddell	Dark, heavy bodies	3.2	732,000
Antarctic Fur	Hind flippers very mobile. Eat fish/krill	2	1.5 million

Seals have the obvious advantage over whales that their appealing faces more easily stir human compassion. But the fate of seal species over the centuries roughly parallels that of whales in both hemispheres and they were, of course, far easier to kill in great numbers because of their habit, year after year, of returning to the same breeding ground. The sealers would be waiting with their clubs.

Seals were killed for their fur or their blubber. A British sealer captain wrote: 'It is impossible to push through the creatures unless with a weapon to clear a path.' The sealers used heavy spiked clubs and short stabbing knives. The cow-seals would 'simply watch the slaughter with incurious passivity, lying and even mating among the carnage until it was their turn to be clubbed, stabbed and flayed to death. An expert could kill, and skin fifty seals an hour standing knee-deep in blubber and blood. They found it more useful to keep the bull seals alive to stop their harems wandering off the rocks. If they became a nuisance they were blinded in one eye. It was "laughable to see these old goats, planted at intervals along the beach, keeping their remaining peeper fixed on their seraglio while we went about our business on their blind side."'

Estimates of the numbers killed reach 5,500,000. 'The harvest of the seas' an observer wrote in 1829, 'has been so effectively reaped, that not a single seal was seen although it is only a few years since countless multitudes covered these same beaches.'

Once the fur seals were gone, the hunters switched to the blubber-bearing elephant seals which weigh up to three tons.

In 1972 the Convention for the Conservation of Antarctic Seals afforded protection for all southern seals and put a stop to commercial sealing off Antarctica.

The current intention of the relevant international conservation bodies is that *all* fishing and hunting will be controlled to sustainable levels and that the Southern Ocean will never again be so thoughtlessly plundered by man.

Although penguins behave like whales and seals in many ways and are often dependent on the same food, they have never been endangered by man to the same extent as whales and seals although, early this century, hundreds of thousands were killed for their oil. There are sixteen species of penguin in the Southern Ocean but there were once many more. Penguin fossils as old as 40,000,000 years have been found, including some of a species almost as tall as man. They appear to have evolved from birds which could both swim and fly, but all species have since lost the ability to fly. As swimmers and divers they are unparalleled. Emperor penguins can dive to depths of 1,000 feet and stay below for up to eighteen minutes.

Sir Vivian Fuchs wrote:

> The incubation of the Emperor penguin's egg must be done in the depths of winter. This is the job of the male; there is no nest and the single egg is balanced across the top of his feet and covered with a fold of warm abdominal skin.
>
> The incubating male can withstand −54°F being insulated with double layered and high density feathers. The incubating birds go into a dense huddle (10 birds to each square metre), sometimes of as many as 5000 birds, in which there is a slow circulation with birds to the windward moving along the flank of the huddle and then, when they reach the lee-side, back into the centre, until the movement of the whole mass again exposes them at the rear.

Southern Ocean Penguins
(All species feed mainly on fish, squid and krill)

Species	Comments
Gentoo	Breed on sub-Antarctic islands. Brown skuas kill chicks.
Adélie	Breed mainly on Antarctic continent. Brown skuas kill chicks.
Chinstrap	Breed mainly on the Antarctic peninsula. The most abundant penguin species (8 million). Brown skuas kill chicks.
Emperor	The largest penguin. Starts to breed in winter on edge of Antarctic continent.
King	The next largest penguin. Takes twelve to fourteen months to rear chicks.
Crested	The five species of crested penguins include the *Fjordland*, *Snares Island* and *Erect* species which are restricted to New Zealand waters. They are unique in that they lay 2 eggs of different sizes, the smaller of which rarely, if ever, hatches. The *Macaroni* crested penguin breeds only after reaching five to seven years of age.
Humbold	The only threatened species. Main distribution is off South American coast.
Macaroni and Rockhopper	Breeds on sub-Antarctic islands.

By the time the chick hatches, the males have fasted for up to 115 days and lost up to 45 per cent of their body weight. They have a life expectancy of twenty years.

Antarctica is best known for its penguins, seals and whales. But it is rich also in sea birds. A broad picture of these is given here.

Species	Number of Species	Distribution	Breeding Population (in millions of pairs)
Albatross	6	Sub-Antarctic	0.1
Shags	2	Sub-Antarctic Peninsula	0.1
Petrels	19	Throughout	100
Storm Petrels	3	Throughout	10
Diving Petrels	2	Sub-Antarctic	10
Gulls, skuas	3	Throughout	0.1
Terns	2	Sub-Antarctic	0.1
Penguins	7	Throughout	10

Although huskies are not a Southern Ocean animal, man has worked with generations of Antarctic-born dogs for up to eighty years. The Antarctic Treaty decreed that all dogs should be removed from the continent since seals were being killed for their food and because they might impart disease to endemic animals.

By 1993 a few dogs remained at the Australian Mawson base and the British Rothera base. A 1992 report from Rothera simply stated 'Being involved with the dogs has undoubtedly contributed greatly to maintaining people's "positive" health, interest and high morale during the long winter period. It is strongly felt that all the dogs should be allowed to live out their natural lives here.'

Whether or not the remaining dogs are removed or allowed to die out *in situ*, there will be none left on the continent by the year 2000.

No comments on the Southern Ocean would be complete without a mention of icebergs. The largest ever recorded was over 160 kilometres long. All icebergs fragment or calve from glaciers or ice shelves and some float as far north as 26 degrees south. Antarctica is at all times sending a barrage of icebergs north into the southern shipping lanes.

Soviet sailors in 1965 measured a berg at 87 miles long and 2700 square miles in area. One great berg 25 miles by 45 miles in size dislodged a second chunk 13 miles by 36 miles, and the larger of the two alone contained sufficient drinking water for all California's needs for many years. The cost of towing such bergs to Los Angeles, or indeed to water-hungry Arab countries, has to date prevented any commerce in 'iceberg water' starting up.

Brief History of Antarctic Exploration

AD 650

According to the legends of Polynesian Rarotonga, their chief Ui-te-Rangiora set out in the war canoe *Te-Iui-O-Atea* and headed south until the ocean was covered with 'white powder and great white rocks rose high into the sky'.

The ancient Greeks named the constellation of stars above the North Pole *arctos* (bear). Later they dubbed the South Pole region as 'opposite the bear' or *anti-arctos*. Aristotle deduced that Earth was a sphere and that the northern landmass of Eurasia *must* be balanced by some then-unknown southern continent, *Antarktikos*. For over a thousand years religions branded as heresy such geographical theories not based on theology. It took travellers such as Marco Polo, Columbus and Magellan to reintroduce common sense to cartography.

By the sixteenth century, when America was first charted, mapmakers assumed a great and rich country to the south of Africa. For 200 years sailors discovered, and annexed for their countries, a number of southern islands which they thought were different parts of the unknown southern continent (Solomon Islands 1568, Falkland Islands 1592, Espiritu Santo 1606, and Australia 1616).

1578

Francis Drake, sixty years after Magellan's circumnavigation, set out 'to enter the South Sea and to explore and claim suzerainty over all lands not already in the hands of a Christian Prince'. Drake, in the *Golden Hind*, discovered Cape Horn, the first recorded incursion into the southern seas.

288

1675

A London merchant, Antonio de la Roché, attempted to round Cape Horn and sighted an Antarctic island to the south of latitude 54°.

1699

The astronomer Edmond Halley was sent south by the Admiralty to seek for 'South unknown lands' and conduct a survey of magnetic variation. He penetrated almost as far as South Georgia.

1722

The colourful Frenchman, Yves Joseph de Kerguelen-Tremarec, in the *Fortune*, discovered the Kerguelen Islands south of 49°. He returned with tales of a paradise and was sent out a second time. Co-travellers on the latter journey put the lie to his story-telling and he was imprisoned.

The Dutchman Jacob Roggeveen managed to reach almost to 65° and reported the presence at that record southing of many birds, indicating nearby land.

1738/1739

The French captain Jean-François-Charles Bouvet de Lozier, in the *Aigle*, sighted Bouvet Island south of 54°, but did not circumnavigate it and assumed it to be part of the 'Unknown Continent'.

1770

The English Captain James Cook, in the *Resolution*, circumnavigated the globe, partly to counter French ambitions in the southern seas and partly to observe a transit of the sun by Venus. Cook exploded all notions as to a southern paradise; whatever land there was would be too cold and bleak.

1773/1775

Cook, in the *Resolution* (and *Adventure*), sailed south of the Antarctic Circle, the first to do so, and, in 1774, he reached 71° south, a record that stood for fifty years. He had reached to within a day's sailing of the mist-shrouded Antarctic coastline, without knowing it.

He went on to sail around the Antarctic continent, and his death was the end of an era. His reports of whales and fur seals in the southern islands were to attract a new brand of 'explorer', the seal-hunter and the whaler.

Cook crossed 15,000,000 square miles of uncharted oceans and left no place where the 'unknown continent' could hide except in the extreme southern latitudes that he had 'ringed'. His sailors were men of iron. The sailor, Alan Villiers, wrote: 'To touch the rigging was to risk frost-burn which sears like flame and to fight the iron-hard sails aloft meant bloodied hands, minced fingers and nails torn out by the roots. For this work could not be done in gloves, a sailor must have his "feel" to work.'

Cook summarised his theory with the words: 'I firmly believe there *is* a tract of land near the Pole which is the source of all the ice spread over this vast Southern Ocean.'

A great many sealers and whalers may well have landed on various Antarctic islands, perhaps even on the peninsula of the continent. But they tended to keep data of their voyages secret to prevent other hunters finding *their* slaughter grounds.

An unsolvable mystery exists to this day as to exactly who first sighted mainland Antarctica. There are three main claimants:

1819/1820

An English merchant ship, *Williams*, skippered by William Smith, discovered the South Shetland Islands. A Royal Navy officer, Edward Bransfield, then took the *Williams* south again and, if he is to be believed, sighted the north tip of Graham Land and went ashore on 30 January 1820: the first landing on the mainland. Because the Admiralty later lost the *Williams* log, the claim remains disputed.

A Russian naval officer, Captain Thaddeus Bellingshausen, in the *Vostok*, only three days earlier and 1,500 miles around the coastline, reported sighting the Antarctic ice-cap but, unlike Bransfield, did not recognise this as the mainland. Some historians now believe that Bellingshausen saw only islands, others give him the benefit of the doubt.

An American businessman named Nathanial Palmer, in the *Hero*, arrived on the scene ten months later and claimed to have sighted the mainland. Most non-American historians are convinced Palmer in fact sighted Deception Island, not a part of the mainland.

1820

An ambitious British sealing voyage under Robert Fildes (the *Cora*). No details available.

1821

The American Captain John Davis, in the *Cecilia*, announced the first landing on the mainland. Another oft-disputed claim.

1821/1822

The British/American expedition in the *Dove*, (and *Eliza*), skippered by Captain Powell, discovered the South Orkney Islands. All these early explorers had to sail 10,000 miles before they could even approach the 'unknown continent'. They usually arrived with damaged ships and sick crews. On stormy days, great rollers surged relentlessly across the vast expanse of the Southern Ocean, three quarters of a mile from crest to crest and sixty feet in height. Fog, icebergs and hundred-knot winds did not help.

Dias, Magellan, Columbus and other great explorers of previous centuries and more northerly latitudes all *rediscovered* lands already peopled and previously visited by Vikings or Romans. Not so the nineteenth-century Antarctic searchers. No human had preceded them since the dawn of time.

1823

The Scots sealer James Weddell, in the *Jane*, penetrated the Weddell Sea to 74°15'. Even modern icebreakers have often failed to reach such a southing. Weddell brought back the first species of an inshore seal which is named after him.

1828

Henry Foster (HMS *Chanticleer*) was sent by the British Admiralty to study gravity and magnetism at the South Shetland Islands.

1831

The British sealer, James Biscoe, in the *Tula*, circumnavigated Antarctica at an unprecedentedly southerly latitude. He discovered Enderby Land, Adelaide and Biscoe Islands.

1833–1839

British sealing voyages: Peter Kemp (the *Magnet*) and John Bellamy (the *Eliza Scott* and the *Sabrina*).

1837

The Frenchman, Commander Dumont d'Urville, in the *Astrolabe* (and *Zelée*), discovered Adélie Land and Wilkes Coast.

1839

The first-recorded woman to cross the Antarctic Circle was lost on board the *Sabrina*, owned by the Enderby brothers who were British oil merchants. Her name and nationality is not known. (The Enderbys paid for many British polar ventures including the voyages of Weddell and Biscoe.)

1840

The American naval officer, Lieutenant Charles Wilkes, in the *Vincennes*, discovered Wilkes Land and charted 1,500 miles of Antarctic coastline. He established that Antarctica was a continental landmass; not just floating ice.

1841/1843

The British naval officer, Lieutenant James Clark Ross, first to reach the North Magnetic Pole, set out in 1839 to reach the South Magnetic Pole in *Erebus* and *Terror*. When, in 1840, he learnt that d'Urville and Wilkes had already visited his intended area of survey, he switched to the previously unexplored area to the east of the meridian 170° east. He penetrated the pack ice and followed the coastline of South Victoria Land (which he named after his Queen) for 600 miles. He discovered and surveyed new mountain ranges, volcanoes and the remarkable Ross Ice-Shelf. His explorations opened the way for subsequent attempts on the South Pole itself.

1844/1845

British magnetic observation voyage under Thomas Moore (the *Pagoda*).

1872/1876

The British naval officers Wyville and Thompson (the *Challenger*) took the first steam vessel south of the Antarctic Circle on a voyage of oceanographic ice research.

1873/1874

The German sealer Dallman, in the *Grönlund*, first charted Bismarck Strait.

1882

The first IGY (International Geophysical Year). In the early nineteenth century Alexander von Humboldt persuaded the British and the Russians to set up a worldwide network of geomagnetic monitoring stations. Scientists Gauss, Maury and Weyprecht inspired further international cooperation starting with IGY 1882. 1932/1933 was the next IGY followed by 1957.

1892

The Norwegian captain Carl Larsen discovered the Larsen Ice-Shelf.

1892/1893

The Scotsmen William Bruce and W. Burn Murdoch in the *Balaena* (and *Active*) discovered Active Sound.

1894/1895

The Norwegian whaling captain Henrik Bull (the *Antarctic*) introduced the deadly Svend Foyn harpoon which tolled the knell for a million Antarctic whales. Carl Borchgrevink was the resident scientist. Four of the ship's complement landed near Cape Adare for four hours: the first landing except on the far more northerly Antarctic Peninsula.

1895/1899

The 1895 International Geophysical Congress declared: 'The greatest piece of exploration still to be undertaken is that of Antarctica.' It urged all its members to send scientific teams south.

First to respond were the Belgians. Their naval officer Adrien de Gerlache de Gomery, in the *Belgica*, led a scientific mission which discovered and mapped Gerlache Strait. The *Belgica* was the first ship to overwinter in the pack ice and the crew included two famous explorers, Roald Amundsen and Dr Frederick Cook (who was later the first claimant to reaching the North Pole).

1898–1900

The British-sponsored Norwegian Carl Borchgrevink, in the *Southern Cross*, surveyed the coast of Victoria Land and was first to overwinter on the mainland. He pioneered husky-drawn sledge travel in Antarctica. From his experiences, the South Pole travellers of the next decade learnt a great deal. He introduced what came to be known as the 'Heroic Era' of Antarctic history.

1901–1903

The Greman Erich von Drygalski, in the *Gauss*, discovered Kaiser Wilhelm II Land. The second vessel to overwinter in the pack-ice. Drygalski once used penguins to stoke the ship's furnace when it ran out of fuel.

1901–1904

The Swede Otto Nordenskjöld, in the *Antarctic* (see 1894), mapped parts of the peninsula and spent *two* winters on Snow Hill Island.

1901–1904

The British naval captain Robert Falcon Scott (the *Discovery*) led the British National Antarctic Expedition. He and his colleague Ernest Shackleton used a tethered balloon to take aerial photographs. This expedition made many scientific discoveries, travelled hundreds of miles inland for the first time, and opened the way for the conquest of the South Pole. Experiments for travel were conducted using manhaul, pony, dog and motor sledge techniques.

1902–1904

The Scotsman, William Bruce, in the *Scotia*, conducted an oceanographic study of the Weddell Sea and discovered the Caird Coast.

1904–1905

The Norwegian Captain Carl Larsen (the *Fortuna*) established the first whaling station on South Georgia.

1907–1909

The British merchant seaman, Ernest Shackleton (the *Nimrod*) pioneered the Beardmore Glacier route to within ninety-seven miles of the Pole. His colleague, Douglas Mawson (an Australian

Yorkshireman), led a team to the South Magnetic Pole. Shackleton and his teams manhauled but they also experimented with ponies, dogs and the first 'tracked' vehicle to be used in Antarctica.

1908–1910

The Frenchman, Doctor J. B. Charcot (the *Pourquoi Pas?*) completed much scientific research and discovered the Fallières Coast.

1910–1913

The German army officer, Wilhelm Filchner, in the *Deutschland*, charted the edge of the Weddell Sea's ice-shelf. He discovered the Filchner Ice-Shelf and the Luitpold Coast.

1910

The Scotsman, William Bruce, proposed but did not organise a crossing of the Antarctic continent. Filchner researched the idea further but did not attempt to undertake the journey. Filchner's summary of his Antarctic experience was to advise the Kaiser: 'The Scandinavians, British, Russians and Canadians should explore this region: they are specialists in the Arctic and thus also in the Antarctic.'

1910–1912

The Norwegian explorer, Roald Amundsen, in the *Fram*, anchored in the Bay of Whales with the specific purpose of beating Scott to the South Pole. This he did, via the Axel Heiberg Glacier, on 14 December 1911.

1910–1913

Robert Scott, in the *Terra Nova*, landed at Ross Island to conduct scientific research and to explore inland. He and four of his colleagues died on their return journey from the South Pole which they reached on 17 January 1912.

296

1911–1914

The Australian, Douglas Mawson, (the *Aurora*) set out to survey a large area of the Antarctic coastline and interior. The story of his personal experiences remains one of the greatest survival tales ever written.

1914–1917

Sir Ernest Henry Shackleton (the *Endurance* and the *Aurora*) attempted the first crossing of Antarctica. Before reaching his intended start-point, the *Endurance* was crushed in pack ice. The story of how he led his men to survival includes an 800-mile open boat journey in the Southern Ocean. His skipper, Frank Worsley, wrote, 'Of all his achievements, great as they were, Shackleton's one failure was the most glorious'. (Sir Vivian Fuchs estimates that, even had Shackleton made his landfall in 1915 as planned, he would not have survived the 1,000-mile overland journey to his depot at Beardmore Glacier. 'His chances of success would have been very small indeed . . . the loss of *Endurance* may have saved a worse disaster.')

1921–1922

Sir Ernest Shackleton and Frank Wild (the *Quest*) proposed to circumnavigate Antarctica. Shackleton died on board, of a massive heart attack.

1925–1939

Neil Mackintosh (British), with the Discovery Investigations Expeditions, conducted a series of marine investigations in Antarctic waters (*Discovery*, *William Scoresby*, *Discovery II*).

1927

A Norwegian expedition managed to land on the world's most isolated island, 1,000 miles from anywhere, Bouvet Island.

1928–1929

The Australian aviator, Hubert Wilkins, with American pilot, Carl Eielson, pioneered air reconnaissance in Antarctica.

1928–1930

The American naval officer Richard E. Byrd (*City of New York*) took a biplane as part of a well-equipped expedition to Antarctica. In November 1929 he and his crew flew over the South Pole. Major discoveries were made from the air.

1929–1931

Sir Douglas Mawson (see 1911), in the *Discovery*, discovered and charted hundreds of miles of coastline and fixed the boundaries of the Australian Antarctic territory.

1929–1930

The Norwegian, Lars Christensen, (the *Norvegia*) with air reconnaissance made extensive discoveries in Queen Maud Land.

1933–1935

Richard E. Byrd established Little America II base and conducted extensive scientific research.

1934–1937

The Australian, John Rymill, (*Penola*) led the British Graham Land Expedition to survey the peninsula coast and islands.

1935–1936

The American pilot, Lincoln Ellsworth, flew a Northrop monoplane from the peninsula to the Bay of Whales.

1935–1937

The Norwegian, Mrs Mikkelson, (the *Thorshavn*) became the first woman to set foot on the continent. By 1993 there were still nations not allowing women to participate in their polar programmes within Antarctica. The Norwegians, Russians and Americans have long involved women in all their stations.

1938–1939

The German explorer/airman Alfred Ritscher (the *Schwabenland*) carried two ten-ton Wal seaplanes on board. Initially their activities were kept quiet. In March 1939 Ritscher announced having discovered and surveyed 135,000 square miles of Antarctica. Swastika markers were air-dropped onto a series of points delineating territory which might, after the war, be claimed by Germany. No such claims were in fact ever advanced.

1939–1941

Richard E. Byrd led a further extensive air-mapping and scientific expedition.

1943–1945

John Marr and Andrew Taylor (the *Fitzroy*, the *William Scoresby*, the *Eagle*) led British Government expeditions (Operation Tabarin) to establish science bases.

1946–1947

Admiral Byrd and Admiral Couzen led USN Operation High Jump, an enormous undertaking with political overtones. Thirteen ships, including icebreakers and submarines, carried 4,700 men and twenty-three aircraft and helicopters to Antarctica. This effort concluded when 3,900,000 square miles had been overflown and sixty per cent of the continent's coastline photographed.

1946–1947

Edward Bingham and Kenneth Pierce-Butler (the *Fitzroy*, the *Trepassey*, the *John Biscoe* and the *William Scoresby*) established the Falkland Islands Dependencies Survey (forerunner to the British Antarctic Survey).

1947

Both Argentina and Chile established manned weather stations in Antarctica.

1948–1953

French scientists established a research station in Adélie Land.

1948–1960

Dr Vivian Fuchs (the *Shackleton* and the *John Biscoe*) led Falkland Islands Dependencies Survey expeditions.

1949–1952

Norwegian John Giaever (the *Norsel*) led a multi-disciplined scientific expedition of Norwegian, British and Swedish researchers to Queen Maud Land. This was the first fully international expedition.

1956–1957

Private expeditions could no longer expect to make great discoveries in Antarctica. In October 1956, US naval Captain George Dufek landed an aircraft at the South Pole (the first man to stand there since Scott's team) and, as part of the 1957 IGY (International Geophysical Year), the Americans built a science station at the South Pole. They named it Amundsen-Scott Base.

As their part of the IGY, New Zealand, Australia, South Africa and Britain funded the Commonwealth Trans-Antarctic Expedition which was initiated and led by Dr Vivian Fuchs (the *Theron* and the *Magga Dan*). The plan was to conduct seismic soundings and a gravity traverse by snow vehicles across the breadth of the continent to discover the depth of the ice-sheet and the form of the rock surface beneath. Dr Fuchs approached Sir Edmund Hillary who agreed to lay a cache-line between Ross Island and the Pole. The two men, after many difficulties, managed to cross from opposing sides of the continent and met at the Pole on 19 January 1958. They then completed Fuchs's continental crossing just before the polar winter closed in, by reaching MacMurdo (2,158 miles from Fuchs's start-point) on 2 March 1958.

The Russian contribution to IGY 1957 was to establish science stations close to the the South Geomagnetic Pole and the Pole of Inaccessibility.

After the 1957 IGY

Innumerable localised expeditions by government scientists of many nations have taken place, some highly ambitious, since 1957 and on an annual basis. Many have been fine examples of co-operation between two or more countries. In addition, a handful of *private* expeditions have managed to raise the considerable sums needed to visit and operate in Antarctica. These include:

1979–1982

(Quoted from *The Explorations of Antarctica: the Last Unspoiled Continent* by Professor G. E. Fogg and David Smith)

> The staggering achievement of linking up trans-polar expeditions, north and south, into a journey encircling the earth was proposed by Charles de Brosses, an eighteenth-century French geographer, but it had to wait until the idea was revived by Lady Twisleton-Wykeham-Fiennes and until her husband, the authorities having ridiculed it, decided to prove it could be done. To minimize political complications, the great circle through Greenwich was chosen, which meant starting the Antarctic leg near Sanae, the South African base, and taking an unexplored route to the Pole. A

301

forward base was established in the Borga Massif, 240 kilometres south of Sanae, in which the party with Lady Fiennes as radio operator overwintered.

The crossing was accomplished without serious accident; the Pole was reached on December 15, 1980 and Ross Island was reached 67 days after the start of the journey. This had been done against the advice of many experts by men without previous Antarctic experience. That it was successful was due to the perfection of techniques of travel and survival in polar regions which were available in 1980, careful planning, and the highly developed instinct for survival and determination to succeed of the people concerned. The subsequent Arctic crossing was even more testing and one can only admire the hardiness of those involved, who brought the whole preposterous venture to a successful conclusion and became the first men to have stood at both Poles.

Expeditions such as this contributed valuable scientific information about the Antarctic continent but most of our knowledge has come from more humdrum systematic work which began in IGY 1957.

1985–1986

Robert Swan, Roger Mear and Gareth Wood manhauled to the South Pole from Ross Island, covering a distance of 828.3 miles without aerial resupply. Their ship (the *Southern Quest*) sank off Ross Island.

1986–1987

Norway's Monica Kristensen (the *Aurora*) led an air-supplied attempt with dog teams to reach the South Pole by Amundsen's route *and* return to the Bay of Whales. Severe snow conditions forced the teams to turn back only 273.4 miles short of the Pole.

1989–1990

A little-known journey by four Norwegian skiers using dog teams and air support crossed Antarctica. Two of this team were airlifted out at the Pole.

1989–1990

A six-man international team led by Will Steger (USA) and Jean-Louis Étienne (France) used dog teams, air and (USSR) tractor resupply to cross the longest span of Antarctica (4,007.8 miles), via the South Pole.

1989–1990

The South Tyrolean, Reinhold Messner, and the German, Arved Fuchs, crossed the Antarctic continent by manhaul and resupplied by air.

1992–1993

The Norwegian, Erling Kagge, manhauled solo and unsupported to the South Pole.

1992–1993

The American Ann Bancroft led the American Women's Expedition which manhauled (womanhauled) with air resupply to the South Pole.

1992–1993

The Pentland South Pole Expedition achieved the first unsupported crossing of the Antarctic continent.

The Antarctic Treaty

To date the continent of Antarctica remains about the only territory which has not been fought over. This happy status is due mostly to the continent's remoteness, but as technology has increasingly trivialised the word 'remote', so it has become more important for all interested countries to reach a formal agreement as to what is and is not mutually acceptable behaviour 'down south'.

The Nazi Third Reich dropped hundreds of markers emblazoned with swastikas onto 'their' part of the continent in 1939.

Post-war Germany has never pressed these claims but, in 1944, Chile and Argentina made claims to areas which had already been claimed by the United Kingdom. All three countries hastened to 'establish a presence' on the peninsula and on nearby sub-Antarctic islands by building and manning bases. By 1945 the British had three operating military bases in place and, in 1952, Argentinian soldiers fired shots over the heads of a British landing party.

In 1946 the US sent a huge military task force, Operation High Jump, to establish a basis for future claims, and Australia established Mawson, the first ever permanent base in East Antarctica, to maintain their interests on the continent.

Mounting international tensions were saved only by a fortunate increase in the interest of the world scientific community (sixty-seven countries) and the advent of the 1957 International Geographical Year (IGY). This in turn led to the Antarctic Treaty of 1961.

The Treaty did not eliminate all territorial jockeying for position. The US and USSR both continued to position bases where science had little to do with site-selection. Some countries introduced post offices, or schools, to solidify their presence and Argentina went so far as to fly a pregnant woman to its Esperanza base, in 1978, so that she could give birth to the first native of Antarctica. Nonetheless, since the Treaty, no new specific territorial claims have been made.

The 1982 Falklands conflict was confined to British and Argentinian troops. The Argentinian claim on 'their' areas of Antarctica, including the Falklands, remains unchanged at the time of writing.

The original 1961 Treaty was, over the succeeding thirty years, augmented at bi-annual meetings to discuss all aspects, especially conservation. The *Convention for the Conservation of Antarctic Marine Living Resources* (CCAMLR) was adopted in 1980 to monitor international fishing activities.

In 1991 the *Protocol on Environmental Protection* was agreed, which incorporates a sixty-year moratorium on mining, increased protection for marine and terrestrial ecosystems and more stringent rules on waste disposal. There is reason to believe that the protest activities of Greenpeace in the late 1980s were instrumental in accelerating, if not prompting, official governmental adoption of the Protocol.

Although no minerals have to date been found that would merit economic exploitation, the 1991 Protocol's mining moratorium was the result of a struggle between countries wishing to leave mining options open but controlled and countries, especially France and Australia, who felt – such was the environmental threat – that all mining should be banned altogether. They further advocated, and indeed still do, that only the setting up of all Antarctica as a 'World Park' will achieve an adequate level of protection for its environment. In theory I agree with this. In practice a *slow* approach to adequate controls might be a more realistic route to the same long-term goal, bearing in mind the often contradictory political strains that must be taken into account.

Antarctica affords unique opportunities as a 'clean' baseline against which to assess the impact of pollutants on global ecosystems (in the atmosphere, on land and at sea) elsewhere in the world. It is the only continent without a native population, free from war and lacking in manufacturing and mining industries. It has no national government and its temporary inhabitants are concerned only with research. The Treaty is the best hope of mankind to maintain and enhance this happy state of affairs.

The articles of the Antarctic Treaty stipulate as follows:

1. No military use will be made of Antarctica, although military personnel and equipment may be used there for any peaceful purpose.
2. There will be complete freedom of scientific investigation.
3. Treaty Nations will exchange plans for scientific programmes, scientific data will be freely available and scientists will be exchanged between expeditions when practicable.
4. No activities during the Treaty will in any way affect claims to sovereignty made by any nation. In effect, territorial claims are frozen.
5. Nuclear explosions and nuclear waste disposal are banned from Antarctica.
6. The Treaty applies to all land- and ice-shelves south of 60°S, but not to the seas.

305

7. All Antarctic stations, and all ships and aircraft supplying Antarctica, shall be open to inspection by observers from any Treaty nation.
8. Observers and exchange scientists shall be under the jurisdiction only of their own country, regardless of which national stations they may visit.
9. Treaty Nations will meet at intervals to consider ways of furthering the principles and objectives of the Treaty. Attendance at these meetings will be limited to countries showing substantial scientific research activity in Antarctica. Unanimous approval will be necessary for any new measures to become effective.
10. All Treaty Nations will try to ensure that no one engages in any activity in Antarctica contrary to the Treaty.
11. Any dispute between Treaty Nations shall be settled by the International Court of Justice.
12. The Treaty may be modified at any time by unanimous agreement. After thirty years any Consultative Party may call for a conference to review the operation of the Treaty. The Treaty may be modified at this conference by a majority decision.
13. The Treaty must be legally ratified by any nation wishing to join. Any member of the United Nations may join as well as any other country invited to do so by the Treaty Nations. All notices of accession and ratification are deposited with the Archives of the United States of America.
14. The Treaty, translated into English, French, Russian and Spanish was signed on 1st December 1959.

The following countries are adherent to the Treaty, are active in research and are entitled to vote at Treaty meetings: UK, USA, South Africa, Belgium, Japan, Norway, France, New Zealand, Australia, Argentina, Russia, Chile, Poland, India, Brazil, Germany, Uruguay, Italy, Peru, Spain, China, Sweden, Finland, South Korea, Netherlands, Ecuador.

Research in Antarctica

Antarctica houses no factories and the only humans that live there are scientists of different nations working in harmony for the knowledge and the good of all humanity.

Many alarming news stories over the past decade have been caused by over-simplification of discoveries emanating from Antarctica.

Because the Antarctic ecosystems are complex, like all others, it has proved difficult to unravel their interconnecting links and the checks and balances which ensure their continuity. No Antarctic ecosystem has yet been successfully modelled by international science.

In some respects the frozen continent might seem a barren place for scientists. For botanists, for instance, only lichens and algae survive. The largest permanent inland inhabitant of the continent is a wingless midge. Of all Antarctic birds only the Emperor penguin remains through the long dark winter.

Not far from Ross Island, however, scientists can work in unique 'dry valleys', which cover 4,000 square miles of ice-free terrain where the air is so dry that skin and shoes crack and fissure. Holes drilled here have produced frozen ground cores with micro-organisms up to one million years old. When revived in laboratories some of these life forms began to grow again. 200,000-year-old dry valley rocks, when broken open by geologists, have revealed microbes that thrive just below the rock surface where sunlight and moisture can reach them. Glaciologists, from studies of deep cores drilled from the ice-sheet, have obtained remarkable data on ice accumulation, past climates and atmospheric conditions.

They have learned, for example, that in the past 10,000 years the incidence of both lead and mercury has doubled. Information about past temperature levels is obtained through variations recorded in the hydrogen and oxygen isotope ratios in ice layers.

Debris trapped in the ice reveals how weather has changed in the past and this helps predict future likely weather patterns.

Over the millennia the ice has built up a frozen record of matter, including pollen, dust, volcanic ash and meteorites, all of which provide clues about past conditions at given periods of time.

American scientists in 1968 drilled to the bottom of the ice-sheet at 7,100 feet, and this gave evidence that a slushy layer existed, a sub-ice 'lake' formed by heat flowing up from the earth below. This could form a lubricating cushion over which the upper layers of the ice-sheet might at some period surge out-wards and downwards into the ocean.

Soviets have drilled down to 1,466 feet and retrieved bottom sediment from the sea beneath an ice-shelf. Americans, in similar studies beneath the Ross Ice-Shelf, have discovered new forms of deep sea life that have been without sunlight or air for millions of years.

In addition to drilling, extensive radar-sounding surveys have criss-crossed the continent; the Americans and British by air, the Soviets, French and Australians by tracked vehicles. This has produced detailed maps of Antarctica's rocky profile, sometimes over a mile beneath the ice sheet.

In 1976 the US Siple Station was set up to help study the aurora using a very high frequency scale; the ionosphere is studied by using Very Low Frequency (VLF) transmitters and receivers at opposite ends of the globe. Lightning flashes and other phenom-ena create radio noises called 'whistlers' which bounce back and forth along the magnetic lines of force between the Earth's Poles.

Scientists (including my wife, in a tiny way, who set up and manned a VLF receiver at Borga in Queen Maud Land in 1979–80), have gradually compiled a data bank about the atmos-phere and the earth's magnetic field through studying the behav-iour of whistlers.

The majority of cosmic rays never reach earth and are difficult to monitor because the earth's magnetic field reflects most of them back into space. Not so at the Poles where the magnetic field curves inwards and allows the rays to be studied.

The value of Antarctic science to mankind has been highlighted by the 'ozone hole' discovery.

British scientists had been measuring ozone levels in Antarctica for over thirty years with a simple instrument which compares the intensities of two wavelengths of ultra-violet (UV) light from the sun. One of the these is strongly absorbed by ozone high in the atmosphere and the other only weakly absorbed. The meas-ured ratio of the two intensities indicates the level of ozone present in the atmosphere.

In 1985 three British scientists (Joe Farman, Brian Gardiner and Jonathan Shanklin) demonstrated that the atmosphere above Antarctica was losing ozone annually and that an ozone hole in the atmosphere was present above the continent during the early spring (September until November) every year.

In May 1988, two hundred researchers from nine countries reached a scientifically-based consensus that the ozone layer over Antarctica *was* thinning and that chlorofluorocarbons (CFCs) were, with nitrogen oxides and other chemicals, largely responsible.

Most CFCs are released in the northern hemisphere. They then spread throughout the world and diffuse into the stratosphere where they are broken down to produce chlorine. Winter conditions at the Poles alter the chemical balance between the chlorine and other gases. Then the summer sun returns and the chlorine participates in chemical reactions which destroy ozone and create an ozone hole the size of the United States and reaching as far north as New Zealand.

Ultra-violet light in dangerous levels then reaches the Earth unfiltered. This causes skin cancers, weakens immune systems, kills crops and sensitive ocean creatures, and plays a role in allowing the Earth's atmosphere to warm up: the so-called *greenhouse effect*.

International concern in 1987 resulted in the Montreal Protocol, strengthened in 1990, which agreed to a reduction of CFC production in aerosols and other goods. For some CFCs a reduction of 85 per cent is needed merely to maintain an ozone status quo since they remain in the atmosphere for over a hundred years after release. Likewise carbon dioxide emissions from cars and other human activities are long-lived gases which adversely affect the climate and will long remain a key example of our continuous abuse of Mother Earth.

Only science can produce proven data which, unlike mere theories of impending doom, will convince humanity to take more care of the fragile environment. Antarctica is proving to be the best place for monitoring the health of the planet.

There is a growing realisation that climatic change is but one aspect of environmental change along with chemical pollution, ozone depletion, desertification, loss of biological diversity and acid rain. Everything is interlinked. For instance the impact of the greenhouse effect on ecosystems depends upon how the warming is distributed in space and across the year *and* on its

309

effect on the southern pressure systems and winds. There are many imponderables.

What is *certain* is that our atmosphere acts as a blanket which keeps the Earth's surface warmer than it would be if there was no atmosphere containing radiative absorbing gases. The effectiveness of the blanket is proportionate to the concentration in the atmosphere of those gases, the 'greenhouse gases'.

What is equally certain is that human activities are increasing the concentration of greenhouse gases in the atmosphere at an alarming rate.

If the gases cause a general warming and if that causes the areas of Southern Ocean pack ice to reduce, the sea ice algae so vital to all the food chain will diminish accordingly. Seals, penguins and other pack ice-dependent creatures could then be seriously affected.

Satellite monitoring shows that Antarctica has of late shed 11,000 square miles of ice and some scientists take this as an indication that increased carbon dioxide levels in the air are warming average temperatures. They further postulate that such warming and melting will change the saltiness and temperature of the teeming, fertile Antarctic Convergence, cause sea levels to rise and spark worldwide weather changes.

Should even a small proportion of the ice-sheet melt, world sea levels would rise catastrophically from a human point of view, but some current estimates indicate Antarctica's ice volume to be on the increase and predict that minimal global warming could in fact produce *greater* precipitation and more, not less, ice.

Only a very few of the changes currently monitored and proven can be pinned down as *known effects of known causes*. Ecosystems change constantly, to dance to complex rhythms which humans in most cases do not yet comprehend. Antarctic ecosystems, like all others, shift at variable rates due to an undetermined range of factors in which climate shifts may or may not be implicated.

The scientific consensus by 1993 seems to indicate that some warming *is* occurring but its effect on the pack ice of the Southern Oceans is unclear.

Many years of international research in all disciplines must and will continue in Antarctica for the good of the planet and the education of its apparently suicidal denizens.

310

Some Relevant Data

The nautical mile is one sixtieth of a latitudinal degree or one minute of latitude. One nautical mile is equivalent to 1.185 km or 1.15 statute miles. (Unless stated otherwise mileages in this book are in statute miles. 1 statue mile = 0.87 nautical mile)

Beaufort Scale
Force 1 = 1 nautical mile per hour
Force 2 = 4 nautical miles per hour
Force 3 = 9 nautical miles per hour
Force 4 = 14 nautical miles per hour
Force 5 = 20 nautical miles per hour
Force 6 = 26 nautical miles per hour
Force 7 = 33 nautical miles per hour
Force 8 = 42 nautical miles per hour
Force 9 = 51 nautical miles per hour
Force 10 = 62 nautical miles per hour
Force 11 = 75 nautical miles per hour
Force 12 = 92 nautical miles per hour

Crevasse Danger Scale
The pressure of a horse's hoof = 15 lbs per square inch
The pressure of a dog's paw   = $3\frac{1}{2}$ lbs per square inch
The pressure of a man's boot = $2\frac{1}{4}$ lbs per square inch
The pressure of a man's ski   = $\frac{1}{2}$ lb per square inch

Outline	Water freezes at 32°F	= 0°C
Temperature	Average human body 98.4°F	= 37°C
Chart	82 degrees of frost 50°F	= −45.5°C
(The lowest absolute	72 degrees of frost 40°F	= −40° C
temperature	52 degrees of frost 20°F	= −29° C
recorded in	32 degrees of frost 0°F	= −18° C
Antarctica is −52°C)		

Wind Chill Factor

Air temp (°C)

	Zero	2.5	5	10	20
			Wind speed (mph/ms⁻¹)		
0	19	0	− 7	−12	−18
−5	16	− 6	−13	−19	−26
−10	13.4	−11	−19	−26	−33
−20	9	−21	−31	−40	−48
−30	4.5	−31	−43	−54	−63
−40	0	−41	−55	−68	−78

Basic conversions:

1 pound	= 0.45 kilograms
1 stone	= 6.350 kilograms
1 foot	= 0.3048 metres
1 yard	= 0.91 metres
1 mile	= 1.60934 kilometres
1 square foot	= 0.92903 square metres
1 square mile	= 2.59 square kilometres
1 pint	= 0.57 litres

Glossary

Beset   When a ship is set in the sea-ice and cannot move.

BIOMASS   Biological Investigations of the Marine Antarctic Systems and Stocks. A body of twelve countries pooled their research expertise over a ten-year period to make a joint study of the physical and biological processes in the Southern Ocean. BIOMASS was their programme.

Blizzard   A high wind which picks up snow from falling crystals and ground snow and creates weather conditions in which it is difficult to travel. An often misused term.

Brash Ice   Fragments of broken ice not more than two metres in width and floating on the sea.

Bergy Bits   Pieces of ice semi-submerged with less than five metres above the surface of the sea.

Fast Ice   Unbroken sea-ice attached to the coast.

First Year Ice   Floating sea-ice less than one year old.

Floe   Any piece of sea-ice that floats free.

Frost Smoke   Fog-like clouds caused by cold air contacting warm water between floes.

Growler   A small-scale bergy bit, just awash and often invisible from a ship's deck.

Hummocked Ice   Rough sea-ice caused by previous break-up. Over a period, melting and drifting smooths out and rounds off the hummocks.

Ice Edge   The boundary between sea-ice and open sea.

Ice Foot   Fringes of ice along the ice edge often structured by sea spray.

Ice Front   The ice cliff being the seaward face of an ice-shelf.

Ice Sheet   A continuous mass of ice/snow of a considerable thickness and of an area greater than 20,000 square miles.

Ice Sheet Margin   A zone of shattered ice where outlet glaciers accelerate as they discharge onto the shore or into the sea.

Ice-Shelf   A floating sheet of ice of considerable thickness. The seaward cliffs range from 6 feet to 200 feet high.

Ice Wall   An ice cliff forming the seaward margin of an inland ice sheet or ice piedmont.

Ice Piedmont   Ice covering a coastal strip of low land backed by mountains.

Katabatics   Powerful winds blowing downhill which have become denser through cooling.

Lead   Navigable passage through sea-ice.

Multi-year Ice   Floating floes older than three years.

Névé   Old snow which has been transformed by weathering processes into dense material.

Nunatak   The top of a buried rock feature piercing the surrounding snow. Often pyramid-shaped.

Pack Ice   An area of sea-ice not fast to land or other non-moving ice body.

Pressure Ice   Sea-ice that has been squeezed, and rafted up into 'pressure ridges', by surrounding floes.

Sastruga (plural Sastrugi)   Fluted ridge carved into hard ice of varying shapes by the prevailing wind (from a few inches to five feet high).

SCAR   The Scientific Committee on Antarctic Research formed in 1958 at the end of the 1957 IGY to promote and co-ordinate all scientific research in the Treaty area and the sub-Antarctic islands.

Shuga   Soggy, porridge-like mass of ice suspended in the water.

Twin Otter   The DHC Twin Otter aircraft is easily adaptable for landing on smooth snow or ice (or water) by affixing skis or pontoons. It has a relatively short take-off/landing ability and has become the main polar workhorse.

Water Sky   Dark sky patches caused by open water areas in pack ice being reflected on the base of clouds.

White-out   A condition of diffuse light when no shadows exist due to continuous cloud layer that appears to merge with the snow/ice surface. No surface irregularities (i.e. sastrugi) are visible although a dark object can be seen as in a mist.

Windcrust   Snow crystals compacted by wind (up to six inches thick) on the surface. No ski tracks or footprints can be left in such crusts.

Bibliography

The Ice Age; Brian S. Johnson. Collins, London, 1977

Antarctica: The Last Continent; Ian Cameron. Cassell, London, 1974

In the Footsteps of Scott; Roger Mear & Robert Swan. Jonathan Cape, London, 1987

Arctic & Antarctic; David Sugden. Blackwell, Oxford, 1982

The Crossing of Antarctica; Sir Vivian Fuchs and Sir Edmund Hillary. Macmillan Publishing, New York, 1958

Of Ice and Men; Sir Vivian Fuchs. Anthony Nelson 1982

A Time to Speak; Sir Vivian Fuchs. Anthony Nelson 1990

The White Desert; John Giaever. Chatto & Windus, London, 1954

Shackleton; Roland Huntford. Hodder & Stoughton, London, 1986 (Permission from AP Watt Ltd., London)

The Last Place on Earth; Roland Huntford. Weidenfeld & Nicolson, London, 1986 (Permission from AP Watt Ltd., London)

To the Ends of the Earth; Ranulph Fiennes. Hodder & Stoughton, London, 1983

The Great Antarctic Rescue; F. A. Worsley. Times Books, USA 1977

Captain Oates: Soldier & Explorer; S. Limb & P. Cordingley. Batsford Publishing, London, 1982

Diary of the Discovery Expedition 1901–1904; Edward Wilson. Blandford Press, Dorset, (ed. Ann Savours) 1966

Scott's Last Expedition: the Personal Journals of Capt. R. F. Scott CVO RN. John Murray Ltd, London, 1973

Amundsen; Bellamy Partridge. Robert Hale, London, 1953

Mawson's Will; Lennard Bickel. Stein & Day, USA 1977

Antarctica: Both Heaven & Hell; Reinhold Messner. Crowood Press, Crowood Lane, Ramsbury, Marlborough, Wiltshire, 1991

Crossing Antarctica; Will Steger & Jon Bowermaster. Bantam Press, London, 1991

The Last Wilderness; Paul Brown. Hutchinson, London, 1991

Antarctic Odyssey; Phillip Law. Heinemann, Australia, 1983

Animals of the Antarctic; Bernard Stonehouse. Peter Lowe 1972

The Faith of Edward Wilson; George Seaver. John Murray Ltd, London, 1948

The Pilgrim's Progress; John Bunyan. Oxford University Press, Oxford, 1902

Scott of the Antarctic; Elspeth Huxley. Weidenfeld & Nicolson Ltd., London, 1977

The Worst Journey in the World; Apsley Cherry-Garrard. Penguin Books, London, 1922

The Birthday Boys; Beryl Bainbridge. Gerald Duckworth, London, 1991

On the Ice in Antarctica; Theodore K. Mason. Dodd, Mead, USA. 1978

Zen and the Art of Climbing Mountains; Neville Shulman. Element Books, Shaftesbury, Dorset, 1992

Antarctica, Cambridge, Conservation & Population; Colin Bertram. G. C. L. Bertram 1987

Source Notes

p. 23   Oddly enough it was the sufferings . . . *Amunsden*, Bellamy Partridge (Robert Hale, 1953)

p. 24   Until now Scott . . . *The Last Place on Earth*, Roland Huntford (Weidenfeld & Nicolson, 1986)

p. 24   It was clear that Scott's quest . . . ibid.

p. 24   To a question . . . *Shackleton*, Roland Huntford (Hodder & Stoughton Ltd, 1986)

p. 24   At home, as Shackleton knew well . . . ibid.

p. 24   I felt that the underlying urge . . . *The Crossing of Antarctica*, Sir Vivian Fuchs & Sir Edmund Hillary (Macmillan Publishing, New York, 1958)

p. 25   The Pole will unshackle me . . . *In the Footsteps of Scott*, Roger Mear & Robert Swan (Jonathan Cape, 1987)

p. 25   His philosophy is that . . . ibid.

p. 25   Now here we are . . . *The Crossing of Antarctica*, Sir Vivian Fuchs & Sir Edmund Hillary (Macmillan Publishing, New York, 1958)

p. 25   We hope to show . . . ibid.

p. 26   For me travelling in the wilderness . . . *Antarctica: Both Heaven and Hell*, Reinhold Messner (Crowood Press, 1991)

p. 27   Excitement has disappeared . . . *Times Magazine*

p. 28   What persuaded these men . . . *Scott of the Antarctic*, Elspeth Huxley (Weidenfeld & Nicolson, 1977)

p. 32   The only blonde . . . *Spectator* 20 February, 1993

p. 39   The choice of an airfield . . . Document by Charles Swithinbank

p. 40   On behalf of . . . John Walford letter to author

p. 41   In Antarctica the senses . . . *Independent on Sunday Magazine*.

p. 46   These brutes grow . . . *The Great Antarctic Rescue*, F.A. Worsley (Times Books 1977)

p. 47   The great unceasing . . . ibid.

p. 47   In six hours the wind . . . *Antarctic Odyssey*, Phillip Law (Heinemann Australia, 1983)

p. 49   I have decided . . . *Amundsen*, Bellamy Partridge (Robert Hale, 1953)

p. 52   The starting was worse . . . *The Worst Journey in the World*, Apsley Cherry-Garrard (Penguin, 1922)

p. 53   With sledge loads . . . *Antarctica: Both Heaven and Hell*, Reinhold Messner (Crowood Press, 1991)

p. 54   Mountaineers are very special people . . . *Zen and the Art of Climbing Mountains*, Neville Shulman (Element Books, Shaftesbury, Dorset, 1992)

p. 55   I hope it won't be . . . *Amunsden*, Bellamy Partridge (Robert Hale, 1953)

p. 55   I leave in fine company . . . *In the Footsteps of Scott*, Roger Mear & Robert Swan (Jonathan Cape, 1987)

p. 63   The interior of a large crevasse . . . *The White Desert*, John Giaever, (Jonathan Cape, 1954). Fred Roots on a 1950 expedition.

p. 63   These crevasses are impressive . . . *Amundsen*, Bellamy Partridge (Robert Hale, 1953)

p. 64   Ninnis knew exactly . . . *Mawson's Will*, Lennard Bickel (Stein & Day, 1977)

p. 64   Mawson stopped his dogs . . . ibid.

p. 84   The Eskimo did not hurry . . . *The Last Place on Earth*, Roland Huntford (Weidenfeld & Nicolson, 1986)

p. 85   Establishing a steady rhythm . . . *Crossing Antarctica*, Will Steger & Jon Bowermaster (Bantam Press, 1991)

p. 91   Biggest and heaviest . . . *The Last Place on Earth*, Roland Huntford (Weidenfeld & Nicolson Ltd, London, 1986)

p. 91   He was bigger . . . *Mawson's Will*, Lennard Bickel (Stein & Day, 1977)

p. 94   These are frightening days . . . *Crossing Antarctica*, Will Steger & Jon Bowermaster (Bantam Press, 1991)

p. 94   If a man ventured . . . *The Worst Journey in the World*, Apsley Cherry-Garrard (Penguin, 1922)

p. 95   It demanded physical steel . . . *Mawson's Will*, Lennard Bickel (Stein & Day, 1977)

p. 99   During any climb . . . *Zen and the Art of Climbing Mountains*, Neville Shulman (Element Books, Shaftesbury, Dorset, 1992). Foreword by Chris Bonington.

p. 99   Jean-Louis sounded . . . *Crossing Antarctica*, Will Steger & Jon Bowermaster (Bantam Press, 1991)

p. 99   Over the years . . . ibid.

p. 102   The constant wind . . . ibid.

p. 103   We have forgotten . . . *The Worst Journey in the World*, Apsley Cherry-Garrard (Penguin, 1922)

p. 103   Survival in extreme conditions . . . *Shackleton*, Roland Huntford (Hodder & Stoughton Ltd, 1986)

p. 103   Their normal social relations . . . *The Worst Journey in the World*, Apsley Cherry-Garrard (Penguin, 1922)

p. 103   Johansen flared up . . . *The Last Place on Earth*, Roland Huntford (Weidenfeld & Nicolson, 1986)

p. 104   The particular risk . . . ibid.

p. 104   We sat in our sleeping bags . . . *In the Footsteps of Scott*, Roger Mear & Robert Swan (Jonathan Cape, 1987)

p. 105   Neither of them . . . *The Worst Journey in the World*, Apsley Cherry-Garrard (Penguin, 1922)

p. 105   Robert was surprisingly slow . . . *In the Footsteps of Scott*, Roger Mear & Robert Swan (Jonathan Cape, 1987)

p. 105   We started every stage . . . *Antarctica: Both Heaven and Hell*, Reinhold Messner (Crowood Press, 1991)

p. 107   All five individuals . . . *In the Footsteps of Scott*, Roger Mear & Robert Swan (Jonathan Cape, 1987)

p. 128   He was in agony . . . *Scott of the Antarctic*, Elspeth Huxley (Weidenfeld & Nicolson, 1977)

p. 129   What I have heard . . . *Crossing Antarctica*, Will Steger & Jon Bowermaster (Bantam Press, 1991)

p. 133   Sometimes it was difficult . . . *the Worst Journey in the World*, Apsley Cherry-Garrard (Penguin, 1922)

p. 133   My thoughts begin . . . *Crossing Antarctica*, Will Steger and John Bowermaster (Bantham Press, 1991)

p. 133 All Zen practice . . . *Zen and the Art of Climbing Mountains*, Neville Shulman (Element Books, Shaftesbury, Dorset, 1992)

p. 143 The general trend . . . *The Worst Journey in the World*, Apsley Cheery Garrard (Penguin, 1922)

p. 159 Since the base was set up . . . *The Last Wilderness*, Paul Brown (Hutchinson, 1991)

p. 161 A low temperature . . . *The Worst Journey in the World*, Apsley Cheery-Garrard (Penguin, 1922)

p. 161 It blew from Force Four . . . ibid.

p. 162 I wish to God . . . *The Last Place on Earth*, Roland Huntford (Weidenfeld & Nicolson, 1986)

p. 175 They relished the freedom . . . *Mawson's Will*, Lennard Bickel (Stein & Day, 1977)

p. 178 It was slightly . . . *The Crossing of Antarctica*, Sir Vivian Fuchs and Sir Edmund Hillary (Cassell, 1958)

p. 179 We were heading . . . *In the Footsteps of Scott*, Roger Mear and Robert Swan (Jonathan Cape, 1987)

p. 184 As we skimmed . . . *The Crossing of Antarctica*, Sir Vivian Fuchs & Sir Edmund Hillary (Macmillan Publishing, New York, 1958)

p. 184 One of the great difficulties . . . *The Worst Journey in the World*, Apsley Cherry-Garrard (Penguin, 1922)

p. 188 Only by wearing . . . *Mawson's Will*, Lennard Bickel (Stein & Day, 1977)

p. 188 Without crampons . . . *Shackleton*, Roland Huntford (Hodder & Stoughton Ltd, 1986)

p. 188 The descent of the Beardmore . . . *Antarctica: Both Heaven and Hell*, Reinhold Messner (Crowood Press, 1991)

p. 192 The winds were Gale Force Seven . . . *Shackleton*, Roland Huntford (Hodder & Stoughton Ltd, 1986)

p. 194 The blisters on my fingers . . . ibid.

p. 196 The hardest and most dangerous . . . *Antarctica: Both Heaven and Hell*, Reinhold Messner (Crowood Press, 1991)

p. 197 Blue ice showed . . . *Scott's Last Expedition: the Personal Journals of Capt. R. F. Scott* (John Murray, 1973)

p. 198 You look around . . . *Antarctica: Both Heaven and Hell*, Reinhold Messner (Crowood Press, 1991)

p. 199 The Keltie Glacier . . . *The Worst Journey in the World*, Apsley Cherry-Garrard (Penguin 1922)

p. 203 Please remember . . . *Capt. Oates: Soldier & Explorer*, S. Limb & P. Cordingley (Batsford, 1982)

p. 203 My diary functions . . . *Antarctica: Both Heaven and Hell*, Reinhold Messner (Crowood, Press, 1991)

p. 204 In what he tells us . . . *The Last Place on Earth*, Roland Huntford (Weidenfeld & Nicolson, 1986)

p. 205 We go two miles . . . *Antarctica: Both Heaven and Hell*, Reinhold Messner (Crowood Press, 1991)

p. 205 There were times . . . *Scott's Last Expedition: the Personal Journals of Capt. R. F. Scott* (John Murray, 1973)

p. 207 I cannot describe . . . *The Worst Journey in the World*, Apsley Cherry-Garrard (Penguin 1922)

p. 210 An awful place . . . *Shackleton*, Roland Huntford (Hodder & Stoughton Ltd, 1986)

p. 210   As I approached the col . . . *In the Footsteps of Scott*, Roger Mear & Robert Swan (Jonathan Cape, 1987)

p. 217   We got him on his feet . . . *Scott's Last Expedition: the Personal Journals of Capt. R. F. Scott* (John Murray, 1973)

p. 217   They were starving . . . *Shackleton*, Roland Huntford (Hodder & Stoughton Ltd, 1986)

p. 220   It was a horrid sight . . . *Scott of the Antarctic*, Elspeth Huxley (Weidenfeld & Nicolson, 1977)

p. 220   Perhaps it has . . . *The Worst Journey in the World*, Apsley Cherry-Garrard (Penguin, 1922)

p. 226   If you are a brave man . . . ibid.

p. 231   Nothing is so important . . . *Antarctic Odyssey*, Phillip Law (Heinemann Australia, 1983)

p. 231   Few leaders . . . *Shackleton*, Roland Huntford (Hodder & Stoughton Ltd, 1986)

p. 233   Amundsen had to tread warily . . . *The Last Place on Earth*, Roland Huntford (Weidenfeld & Nicolson, 1986)

p. 236   There are those . . . *The Worst Journey in the World*, Apsley Cherry-Garrard (Penguin, 1922)

p. 237   Shackleton's party . . . Letter in *Daily Telegraph*

p. 238   Citizens who were indirectly angry . . . *Antarctica: Both Heaven and Hell*, Reinhold Messner (Crowood Press, 1991)

p. 238   With a single news article . . . ibid.

p. 241   One continues . . . *Scott's Last Expedition: The Personal Journals of Capt. R. F. Scott* (John Murray 1973)

p. 241   Moisture is our mortal enemy . . . *Crossing Antarctica*, Will Steger & Jon Bowermaster (Bantam Press, 1991)

p. 243   As the wind . . . *Antartica: Both Heaven and Hell*, Reinhold Messner (Crowood Press, 1991)

p. 284   It is impossible . . . *Antarctica: the Last Continent*, Ian Cameron (Cassell, 1974)

p. 285   The Incubation . . . *The Crossing of Antarctica*, Sir Vivian Fuchs & Sir Edmund Hillary (Cassell, 1958)

Index

322

323

324

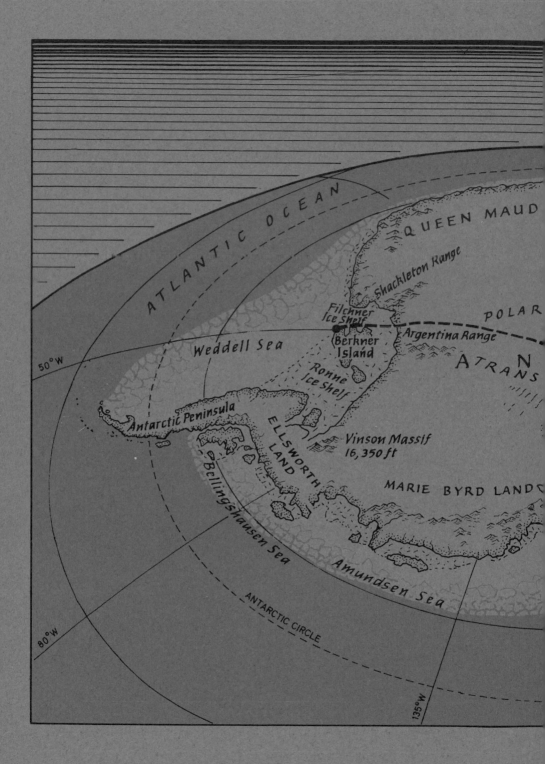

A T L A N T I C   O C E A N

QUEEN MAUD

Shackleton Range

Filchner
Ice Shelf

POLAR

50°W

Weddell Sea

Berkner
Island

Argentina Range

A   T R A N S

N

Ronne
Ice Shelf

Antarctic Peninsula

ELLSWORTH
LAND

Vinson Massif
16,350 ft

MARIE BYRD LAND

Bellingshausen Sea

Amundsen Sea

80°W

ANTARCTIC CIRCLE

135°W